Political Fellini

Political Fellini
Journey to the End of Italy

Andrea Minuz

Translated by Marcus Perryman

Published by
Berghahn Books
www.berghahnbooks.com

English-language edition
©2015, 2018 Berghahn Books
First paperback edition published in 2018.

Original Italian-language edition by Andrea Minuz,
Viaggio al termine dell'Italia: Fellini politico,
©2012 Rubbettino Editore

All rights reserved. Except for the quotation of short passages
for the purposes of criticism and review, no part of this book
may be reproduced in any form or by any means, electronic or
mechanical, including photocopying, recording, or any information
storage and retrieval system now known or to be invented,
without written permission of the publisher.

Library of Congress Cataloging-in-Publication Data

Minuz, Andrea.
 [Viaggio al termine dell'Italia. English]
 Political Fellini : journey to the end of Italy / Andrea Minuz ; translated by Marcus Perryman. — English-language edition.
   pages cm
 Includes bibliographical references and index.
 ISBN 978-1-78238-819-7 (hardback) — ISBN 978-1-78533-828-1 (papaperback)
 ISBN 978-1-78238-820-3 (ebook)
 1. Fellini, Federico—Political and social views. 2. Italy—In motion pictures. I. Title.
 PN1998.3.F45M5413 2015
 791.4302'33092—dc23

2015003135

British Library Cataloguing in Publication Data

A catalogue record for this book is available from the British Library

ISBN 978-1-78238-819-7 (hardback)
ISBN 978-1-78533-828-1 (paperback)
ISBN 978-1-78238-820-3 (ebook)

To Silvia, who detests Fellini, or so she says

There can be no appeals to genius as the sole origin of the energies of great art.
—Stephen Greenblatt

Good heavens, what sadness, what wretchedness, those conversations, those faces, all that falsehood! Is that what we're really like? Yes, God help us.
—Indro Montanelli, reviewing *La dolce vita*

All the characters in the film should look out from the poster, staring at the spectators as they pass by. These characters should be as if stunned into immobility, aghast, amiable, reluctant, shameless, a sort of indelible old, lavish photo reflected in a festive mirror, one Sunday.
—Federico Fellini, letter to Giuliano Geleng,
describing the poster he wanted to advertise *Amarcord*.

But can there be a separation between "elective spirits" and the "nation"?
—Antonio Gramsci

Contents

Preface to the English edition	viii
Acknowledgments	x
Essential Chronology by Fabio Benincasa	xi
Introduction. Political Fellini?	1
Chapter 1. Fellini and "Italian Ideology"	5
Chapter 2. Mythical Biography of a Nation	33
Chapter 3. *La Dolce Vita* and Its Relevance Today	58
Chapter 4. Fellini, Mussolini, and the Complex of Rome	78
Chapter 5. Fellini and Feminism	111
Chapter 6. A Public Dream: Italy and *Prova d'orchestra*	136
Chapter 7. You Don't Interrupt an Emotion	162
Appendix. The Divo and the Maestro: Fellini in the Andreotti Archives	183
Selected Bibliography	190
Index	194

Photo section follows Chapter 4

Preface to the English Edition
After *The Great Beauty*

When I handed over the final version of this book, Paolo Sorrentino's film *La grande bellezza* had not yet been screened. Since, in the book, I spoke at length about *La dolce vita*—a declared source and inspiration for Sorrentino's film—naturally I followed its progress with great interest.

To my mind, the success of *La grande bellezza*—winner of the Academy Award for best foreign picture in 2013—and the intense debate that accompanied the film in Italy confirm the essential hypothesis in the book. First, Fellini's extraordinary relevance today, his ability in *La dolce vita* to touch so deeply so many aspects of Italian life. And the political and not merely artistic importance of his films, particularly their close relationship with history, identity, and the Italian national character, all of which are dealt with in this book.

Researching the book, I knew about Sorrentino's project, which he had spoken about it in various interviews. However, when he talked about the film that was to become *La grande bellezza,* he referred mainly to the work of the photographer Umberto Pizzi. Pizzi has a great deal of experience as a photo reporter; he is what you could call a modern-day Rome-based paparazzo. In his shots, which he sells to gossipy newspapers, Pizzi tells a story in visual images that is the postmodern version of Rome's decadence, the politics, art, culture, and high society of the Eternal City. His work is an extraordinary anthropological study of the present day.

I was very curious to read about Sorrentino's fascination with Pizzi's photographs and his idea of using them for a sort of updated *La dolce vita*. After the release of *La grande bellezza,* probably wisely, Sorrentino played down the comparison with Fellini's masterpiece and distanced himself from Pizzi's photographs. Not only to defend his own artistic vision, as is only right and proper, but probably also to avoid legal wrangles with Umberto Pizzi. And in point of fact, in *La grande bellezza* the ferocious images of Pizzi become something else; they take on something of the glossy magazine. However, what remains is the idea of looking at the decadence of Rome as the archetype of all decadence and making Rome the stage for the whole of Italy.

After its presentation at the Cannes Film Festival, numerous comparisons were made between *La dolce vita* and *La grande bellezza*. But why all the discussions in Italy about Sorrentino's film?

When *La grande bellezza* was released for public screening, during the promotional tour and in numerous interviews Paolo Sorrentino admitted that he was completely taken back by the contrasting reactions of the critics. "When I made *Il Divo* [about the controversial figure of Giulio Andreotti] I thought there would be all hell to pay, but nothing happened. Then I made this film and suddenly there's all hell to pay." And yet, it is not at all surprising. In Italy, we are more at peace with the ghost of Andreotti than with the spirit of beauty. Beauty and an aesthetic conception of life are—for us—a "mission" and a national obsession. As the poet D'Annunzio warned, "the fate of Italy is inseparable from the fate of beauty, of which it is the mother."

It is a myth that comes and goes throughout the complex course of Italian history, each time reincarnating in new forms and taking on a huge variety of discourse. An idea that is far from ephemeral and decorative, actually a continuously evolving battle ground. As the important research of Stephen Gundle[1] has shown, in relation to the question of Italian beauty, all the stereotypes of national identity and ideological questions immediately come into play. This was also the case with the discussions prompted by *La grande bellezza*, a film that was seen to have a strong political dimension despite the fact that—unlike *Il Divo*—it does not address Italian politics.

Through its reference to Fellini and *La dolce vita*, Sorrentino's film reaches into the depths of the Italian unconscious, using the idea of beauty as a political subject, an allegory of the nation, and a cultural brand to be exported. An idea that is of fundamental importance, today, if we want to understand the cinema of Federico Fellini.

Rome, June 2014

Note

1. S. Gundle, *Bellissima: Feminine Beauty and the Idea of Italy* (New Haven and London: Yale University Press, 2007).

Acknowledgments

For their amenability and help in the research of this book, I would like to thank Luciana Devoti (head of the Andreotti Archive), Giuseppe Ricci (of the Federico Fellini Foundation), and Michela Zegna (of the Bologna Film Library). I would also like to thank the staff of the Luigi Chiarini Library of the National Film School in Rome and of the Archive and Library of the International Women's Home in Rome for their kind help.

This book would not have seen the light of day without the help of Thea Apollonio, Fabio Benincasa, Claudio Bisoni, Elena Dagrada, Fabrizio Natalini, Chiara Supplizi, and Christian Uva. To them, and to all those I have forgotten to mention who found themselves drawn into tedious conversations about Fellini, go my sincerest thanks.

Essential Chronology

By Fabio Benincasa

1920—January 20: Federico Fellini is born in Rimini, to Urbano, a sales representative, and Ida Barbiani, originally from the Esquilino district of Rome. **April–May:** Violent strikes and rallies lead to the resignation of the Nitti government. **June 9:** Giolitti becomes prime minister. **September 27:** An agreement between the CGIL Trade Union and industrialists ends the so-called "two-year red period."

1921—January 21: The Socialist Party splits, giving rise to the foundation in Livorno of the Communist Party of Italy, under Bordiga and Gramsci.

1922—October 28: Mussolini's March on Rome. The King asks him to form a government.

1924—April 6: New electoral law to ensure parliamentary majority: the National Fascist Party obtains a large majority. **June 10:** The anti-fascist Socialist parliamentarian, Giacomo Matteotti, is kidnapped and murdered. **October 6:** Beginning of regular radio broadcasts in Italy.

1925—January 3: In an address to Parliament, Mussolini takes responsibility for the murder of Matteotti. **December 24–31:** So-called "highly fascist laws" begin to usher in a dictatorship. Mussolini assumes the title "head of the government"; press restrictions are introduced.

1926—April 3: Abolition of the right to strike and trade unions placed under control. **November 5–25:** Dissolution of political parties, introduction of the death penalty, internal exile to the frontier, and special tribunals. **November 8:** Despite enjoying parliamentary immunity, Gramsci is arrested; Togliatti becomes Communist Party secretary.

1927—June 4: Gramsci sentenced to twenty years in prison. **November 17:** Incorporation of the EIAR: the State Radio Broadcaster, later RAI (radio and television).

1928—January 15: EIAR begins broadcasting.

1929—February 11: The Lateranensi Pacts settle the so-called "Roman question" with the mutual recognition of the Kingdom of Italy and Vatican City. **June:** Fellini obtains primary school diploma.

1930—March 20: Accused of Trotskyism, Bordiga is expelled from the PCI, the Italian Communist Party. **April 13:** Nuvolari wins the Mille Miglia, closing in on and finally overtaking Varzi at the end of the race by not switching on the headlights. **September:** Fellini is enrolled in the Ginnasio, Rimini.

1933—January 30: Hitler becomes Chancellor. **August 14:** The transatlantic ocean liner *Rex* wins the Blue Riband.

1936—May 9: Ethiopia is annexed by Italy, proclamation of the Italian Empire, fascism at the height of its popularity. **August:** Fellini, *avanguardista* (for the fourteen-to-seventeen age range) in the Gioventù Italiana del Littorio (the Italian Fascist Youth Movement), attends camp.

1937—April 27: Death of Gramsci. **April 28:** Mussolini opens Cinecittà.

1938—February: Fellini publishes his first humorous cartoons in *La Domenica*, the Sunday edition of *Corriere della Sera*. **March 1:** Death of Gabriele d'Annunzio. **May 3:** Hitler visits Rome. **July:** Fellini leaves school and decides to go to University in Rome.

1939—January 19: The Chamber of Deputies becomes the Chamber of Fascism and Corporations. **March:** Fellini moves to Rome, in Via Albalonga 13, with his mother and brothers. **March 7:** He begins working for *Marc'Aurelio* and meets, among others, Maccari, Steno, and Aldo Fabrizi, with whom he would work on a regular basis. **April 4:** Italy invades Albania. **September 1:** Germany invades Poland and World War II commences.

1940—January–February: Fellini works as a gagman for the radio and for the cinema with Mattoli and Macario (*Il pirata sono io* [The Pirate's Dream]). He joins the intellectuals in the Zavattini circle. **June 10:** Mussolini declares war on France and Great Britain, joining an alliance with Germany and Japan.

1942—Fellini writes the screenplay for *Avanti c'è posto* (Before the Postman) with Fabrizi. At the radio station, he meets Giulietta Masina. **June 4:** The clandestine Action Party is formed. **October:** Members of the dissolved Popular Party form the Christian Democrat Party. **November 5:** The Axis defeated at El Alamein.

1943—February 2: The six-month Battle of Stalingrad ends with the defeat of the German army. **May 16:** Release of *Ossessione* by Visconti. **June 24:** Release of *Campo de'Fiori* (The Peddler and the Lady), screenplay by Fellini. **July 25:** The Grand Council of Fascism votes against Mussolini, who is arrested and replaced by Badoglio. **September 8:** Italy signs a separate armistice with the Allies. The King flees Rome and the country is in chaos with the armed forces disbanding. Rome is occupied by German troops. **September 9:** Communists, Socialists, Christian Democrats, and other parties form the CLN, the Committee for National Liberation. **September 10:** Mussolini is rescued from prison by German commandos and taken to Germany. **September 13:** The Italian Social Republic is founded. **October 30:** Fellini marries Giulietta Masina.

1944—April: The so-called "turning point of Salerno": the PCI joins the anti-fascist movement of the other parties in a government of national unity headed by Badoglio. **June 4:** Liberation of Rome.

1945—April 28: Mussolini captured and shot in Dongo. End of the war in Italy. **August 6–9:** Atom bombs are dropped on Hiroshima and Nagasaki. End of World War II. **September 24:** Premiere of *Roma città aperta* by Rossellini. Fellini is a co-scriptwriter.

1946—Fellini is co-scriptwriter and assistant director of *Paisà*. **June 2:** Italy becomes a Republic by referendum. A Constituent Assembly is elected.

1947—Einaudi publishes Gramsci's *Lettere dal carcere* (Prison Notebooks). **February 16:** Flaiano wins the Strega literary prize for his novel *Tempo di uccidere* (A Time to Kill). **March 13:** Fellini nominated for an Oscar for his contribution to *Roma città aperta*. **June 15:** Almirante becomes the secretary of the Italian Social Movement, newly formed from the ashes of fascism.

1948—Ernesto De Martino publishes *Il mondo magico* (The World of Magic) with Einaudi. **April 18:** The Christian Democrats defeat the Communist Party and Socialists in the first Republican elections. De Gasperi becomes prime minister. **September 5:** Release of *Senza pietà* (Without Pity) by Lattuada; Fellini is co-scriptwriter and assistant director. **October 30:** Release of *L'amore* by Rossellini; Fellini writes and appears in *Il miracolo* (The Miracle) with Anna Magnani. **November 24:** Release of *Ladri di Biciclette* (Bicycle Thieves) by Vittorio De Sica.

1949—March 16: Italy joins NATO.

Essential Chronology

1950—December 6: Release of *Luci del varietà* (Variety Lights), co-directed with Lattuada.

1952—September 6: Release of *Lo sceicco bianco* (The White Sheikh).

1953—August 17: De Gasperi is replaced by Pella. **September 4:** *I vitelloni* wins the Silver Lion.

1954—Fellini begins and immediately discontinues therapy with the Freudian analyst Emilio Servadio. **January 3:** The state broadcaster, RAI, begins regular TV transmissions. **January 18:** Fanfani becomes prime minister. **September 7:** *La strada* wins the Silver Lion.

1955—Norberto Bobbio publishes *Politica e cultura* with Einaudi. **October 7:** Release of *Il bidone* (The Swindle). **December 10:** The Radical Party is founded.

1956—November 4–10: The Soviet Union invades Hungary. Togliatti and the PCI support the invasion, losing the backing of many intellectuals.

1957—March 25: The Treaty of Rome starts the process leading to the European Union. **March 27:** *La strada* wins the Academy Award for best foreign picture. **October 7:** Release of *Le notti di Cabiria* (Cabiria Nights); Pasolini helps write the dialogue.

1958—March 26: *Le notti di Cabiria* wins the Academy Award for best foreign picture. **October 9:** Death of Pope Pius XII. **October 28:** John XXIII becomes pope.

1960—Probable beginning of Fellini undergoing Jungian analysis with Ernst Bernhard. **February 5:** Release of *La dolce vita*. **May 20:** *La dolce vita* wins the Palme d'Or in Cannes. **June 29:** Release of *L'avventura* by Antonioni. **June 30:** Street demonstrations in Genoa cause Tambroni to resign, paving the way to a center-left government. **August:** Olympic Games in Rome.

1961—November 4: RAI inaugurates a second channel. **November 22:** Release of *Acattone* by Pasolini.

1962—February 22: Premiere of *Boccaccio '70*, including *Le tentazioni del dottor Antonio* by Fellini. **October 11:** Opening of the Second Vatican Council, beginning profound renewal in the Church.

1963—February 14: Release of *8 ½*. **June 21:** Election of Pope Paul VI. **July 18:** *8 ½* wins the Moscow Film Festival. **December 4:** Aldo Moro leads a government that, for the first time, includes the Socialists.

Essential Chronology

1964—Fellini tries LSD under Servadio's supervision. **April 13:** *8 ½* wins the Academy Award for best foreign picture. **August 21:** Togliatti dies in Yalta and is succeeded by Longo.

1965—**June–August:** Fellini and others write the script for *Il viaggio di G. Mastorna* (The Journey of G. Mastorna), based on an idea by Dino Buzzati. **June 29:** Death of Bernard. **October 22:** Release of *Giulietta degli spiriti* (Juliet of the Spirits).

1968—**May 17:** *Tre passi nel desiderio* (Spirits of the Dead), including Fellini's *Toby Dammit,* presented at Cannes. The festival is interrupted by the student uprising in Paris. **August 20–21:** The Soviet Union invades Czechoslovakia, crushing the Prague Spring. The PCI distances itself from the invasion without condemning it. **November 5:** Fellini moves to Via Margutta 110. **December 21:** Release of *C'era una volta il West* (Once upon a Time in the West) by Sergio Leone.

1969—Formation of the MLD, the Women's Liberation Movement, as part of the Radical Party. **April 11:** NBC broadcasts *A Director's Notebook.* **July 23:** Release of *Tre passi nel delirio.* **September 18:** Release of *Fellini Satyricon.*

1970—Carla Lonza publishes the Manifesto of Female Revolt based on the idea of separatism. **Winter:** Franceschini and Curcio establish the Red Brigades. **December 1:** Divorce becomes legal. **December 25:** *I clowns* is broadcast by RAI.

1972—**February 17:** Andreotti becomes prime minister. **March 8:** Violent demonstrations by feminists in Rome, suppressed by the police. **March 16:** Release of *Roma.* Enrico Berlinguer takes over leadership of the PCI. **April 6:** First broadcasts of Telebiella, Italy's first private television station. **November 20:** Death of Ennio Flaiano. **December 16:** Release of Bertolucci's *Last Tango in Paris.*

1973—**September 20:** Adele Faccio establishes the Italian Center for Sterilization and Abortion, which carries out abortions illegally. **December 18:** Release of *Amarcord.*

1975—Renzo De Felice publishes *Intervista sul fascismo* (Interview on Fascism) with Laterza. **April 8:** *Amarcord* wins the Academy Award for best foreign picture. **April 14:** End of state broadcasting monopoly. Hundreds of private local stations spring up in the following years. **September 24:** RAI broadcasts *La dolce vita* for the first time. **November 2:** Pasolini murdered by Pino Pelosi. **December 6–13:** Feminists in Rome clash with Lotta Continua.

1976—Giorgio Amendola publishes *Intervista sull'antifascismo* (Interview on Anti-Fascism) with Laterza. The feminist movement occupies the Women's Home in Rome. **June 20:** The PCI erodes the support of the Socialist Party (PSI), making significant electoral gains. **July 16:** Bettino Craxi becomes the secretary of the PSI. **July 29:** Andreotti's third government initiates so-called "national solidarity." **December 7:** Release of *Casanova*.

1977—**January 1:** The program *Carosello* is abolished and television advertising is extended to all programs. **February 1:** RAI broadcasts in color. **February 17:** Autonomia Operaia, an extra-parliamentary left-wing movement, violently challenges the trade union leader Luciano Lama. **March 11:** A student is killed in Bologna, leading to a lengthy period of disorder. **September 24–26:** The "Conference against Repression" in Bologna brings together the student and feminist movements.

1978—**March 16:** the Red Brigades kidnap Aldo Moro. **May 9:** Moro's body is found in Via Caetani in Rome. **May 22:** Law 194 legalizing abortion. **October 19:** Premiere of *Prova d'orchestra* (Orchestra Rehearsal) at the Quirinale Presidential Palace in the presence of the newly elected president, Pertini. **October 22:** John Paul II becomes pope.

1979—**February 22:** Release of *Prova d'orchestra*. **April 10:** Death of Nino Rota.

1980—**March 28:** After lengthy and troubled production, *La città delle donne* (The City of Women) is released. **September 30:** Berlusconi's first television station, Telemilano, changes its name to Canale 5.

1981—**March 17:** Lists of members of the P2 Masonic lodge are found, causing the fall of the government led by Forlani. Craxi, Andreotti, and Forlani usher in the new phase of five-party government. **June 28:** Spadolini becomes the first non-Christian Democrat prime minister of the Republic.

1982—**May 6:** De Mita becomes secretary of the DC. **November 30:** Rusconi sells Italia 1 to Berlusconi's Fininvest.

1983—**August 4:** Craxi becomes prime minister. **October 7:** Release of *E la nave va* (And the Ship Sails On). **December 21:** Fellini takes a cameo role in Sordi's *Il tassinaro* (The Taxi Driver).

1984—**June 11:** Death of Berlinguer, who is succeeded by Alessandro Natta. **June 13:** Fellini is part of the guard of honor at Berlinguer's funeral. **August 27:** Berlusconi's Fininvest purchases Rete 4, becoming the leading private TV station in Italy.

Essential Chronology

1985—March 11: Gorbachev becomes the leader of the USSR. **September 6:** Fellini is awarded a career Lion. **December 15:** *Ginger e Fred* premieres at the Quirinale and is reviewed in *Corriere della Sera* by Andreotti.

1986—January 22: Release of *Ginger e Fred*.

1987—May 19: *Intervista* (Interview) wins the 40th Anniversary Prize of the Cannes Film Festival. **September 28:** *Intervista* is released.

1988—April 13: De Mita becomes prime minister. **June 10:** Occhetto becomes secretary of the PCI.

1989—February 14: Fellini takes part in the demonstration organized by the PCI against interrupting films with television commercials. **July 22:** Andreotti becomes prime minister for the sixth time. **November 9:** Fall of the Berlin Wall, Occhetto takes the Communist Party toward social democracy.

1990—February 1: Release of *La voce della luna* (The Voice of the Moon), which wins three David di Donatello Awards on June 2. **August 6:** The Mammi Law ratifies the duopoly RAI-Fininvest.

1991—February 3: The PCI becomes the Democratic Party of the Left (PDS). **April 12:** Seventh Andreotti government begins. **December 8:** Dissolution of the Soviet Union.

1992—February 17: A member of the Socialist Party, Mario Chiesa, is arrested in Milan and the so-called Tangentopoli investigation into corruption gets under way, leading to the end of the first Republic and of the Christian Democrats as a political force. **April:** Fellini gives Damien Pettigrew a long interview which, in 2002, becomes the film *Fellini: je suis un grand menteur* (I Am a Big Liar). **December 15:** Craxi is indicted for the first of eleven crimes relating to corruption.

1993—February 11: Craxi resigns as secretary of the PSI. **March 27:** Andreotti is indicted for association with the mafia. **April 30:** Craxi targeted with coins thrown by an angry mob outside the Hotel Raphael in Rome. **August 3:** Fellini, in Rimini, suffers a stroke. **October 17:** Fellini goes into irreversible coma. **October 31:** After fifteen days in a coma, with television cameras and the press anxious to film and report on his dying moments, Fellini passes away in the Umberto I General Hospital. **November 2:** Homage is paid to Fellini's body, at the center of a Felliniesque set in Studio 5, Cinecittà, by thousands filing past in line.

1994—March 23: Giulietta Masina dies in Rome.

Introduction

Political Fellini?

This book sets out a "political" reading of Fellini and discusses the relationship between his films and Italian ideology.

In the popular mind, Fellini is synonymous with dream, creative freedom, visual inventiveness, poetry. The notion of a political Fellini might therefore seem rather odd.

And yet, at the filmmaker's funeral, Ettore Scola said that, in his opinion, Fellini "contrary to all appearance" had been "the most political Italian film director." Scola did not seem to mean that Fellini's films espouse a political thesis or enshrine specific political ideas. What he appears to have been suggesting is that Fellini's imaginative "elsewhere," beyond any sort of political grouping or affiliation, shows a deeper and better understanding of the essence of the Italian identity than other filmmakers had been capable of demonstrating.

Fellini is part of a long line of intellectuals and artists, from Leopardi to Pasolini, who investigated the relationship between the Italian identity and modernity in its many social, cultural, and political manifestations.

Fellini's lack of interest in politics is well known and is an essential part of his myth. In the history of Italian cinema, Fellini was the least "engaged" director. In some ways, the insistence of critics and of Fellini himself on this aspect of his work served to justify the anomaly of his films within the rather regimented context of postwar Italian cinema.

Camouflaged behind the myth of the artist outside history, Fellini was the great exception in Italian culture. When in *Amarcord* he told the story of Italian fascism as no political film had ever managed to do, or in the allegory of *Prova d'orchestra* he portrayed the profound crisis of Italian democracy, he demonstrated what he had always been: an auteur whose imagination fed off the conflicting trajectories of Italian modernity, a kind of seismograph, able to pick up even the faintest tremors in customs and the political and cultural life of the country.

Seen in a political light, the motifs of his work, the nostalgia for childhood, the phantoms of femininity, the invention of memory, the dreamwork—dwelled on at length by the critics—take on a pathological connotation, i.e., they become the allegory of a nation unable to leave its adolescence behind it, trapped by its own history in an immaturity that is uniquely Italian.

The apparent repression of the "political" in his work has an emblematic significance:

> I realize that mine may be a neurotic attitude, a refusal to grow up, determined perhaps in part by growing up under fascism and hence uneducated, disinclined to take part in any form of politics that was not demonstrative, people parading in the streets; while feeling throughout that *politics is for grown-ups* …. The whole Anglo-Saxon mythology of *democracy*, this lesson of civilization and political awareness, has perhaps passed us by, has not been an integral part of our culture, and in some way has left us with the conviction that politics is always something done by someone else, people who know how.[1]

While Italian comedy investigated these motifs above all sociologically, Fellini turned them into powerful visions. The symbolic forms, such as the figure of Christ lifted by helicopter and the monstrous fish in *La dolce vita*, the transatlantic liner *Rex* in *Amarcord*, the obscure wrecking ball in *Prova d'orchestra*, the rhinoceros in *E la nave va*, and similar examples, are—among other things—a commentary on the traumatic dimension of Italian modernity.

* * *

At the end of the sixties, the theoretical journal of the Soviet Communist Party, *Kommunist,* attacked the prevailing criticism of Fellini's films, affirming that the subjective deformation of the world by no means concealed "the acute representation of the agony of capitalist civilization." The journal took issue with Fellini himself and the way he talked about his films. "There is an objective sense to his films," the house organ of the PCUS went on, "which opens up far vaster horizons than those the director himself wishes to deal with, even at the expense of—and contradicting—his own artistic conceptions."[2]

These horizons, I think, have not been investigated systematically by criticism.

Introduction

In a book by Peter Bondanella, one of the leading experts in the field of Fellini literature, there is a chapter on *Amarcord* and *Prova d'orchestra* entitled *Fellini and Politics*; there are some hints of politics in Tullio Kezich's biography of Fellini; look hard and something comes to light from the essays and almost endless amount of material dedicated to individual films and aspects of his cinema. Interesting is a piece by Pietro Angelini, published in 1974, with the significant title *Controfellini* (Counter-Fellini) which, in line with the cultural Marxism of the time, analyzes the ideological ambiguities of Fellini's cinema. Of a more documentary nature is Angelo Olivieri's booklet on Fellini's work as a political cartoonist from 1938 to 1947 for some satirical and humorous newspapers of the period, notably *420*, *Marc'Aurelio*, and *Il Travaso delle idee*. It shows how in the postwar period Fellini managed to work both as a neorealist screenwriter and as an anti-Communist satirist for *Il Travaso*.

This book does not attempt to interpret the whole of Fellini's work. What I seek to do principally is to outline an area of investigation that has been largely neglected and that I hope may stimulate further research into Fellini and the cultural history of Italian cinema.

Some films, such as *I clowns* and *Toby Dammit* (an episode in *Tre passi nel delirio*) are barely mentioned. Others, for reasons of space, are discussed only briefly. I do not deal with the films chronologically. I have decided to focus on just a few topics. For example, *La dolce vita* crops up repeatedly and many different aspects of the film are analyzed in chapters 1 and 4, as well as in the chapter dedicated to it.

I have looked at contemporary sources, the newspapers and journals of the day—not only specialist publications—and I have attempted to reconstruct some of the important debates that accompanied the films. They include the discussion of *La strada* in the mid fifties and the raging polemics that were prompted by *Prova d'orchestra*, *La città delle donne*, and *Ginger e Fred*. Today, these indicate how paradoxical and emblematic the artistic trajectory of Fellini was, from fascism to the symbolic end of the First Republic. Where *La strada* indicated the political point of no return for neorealism and for the engagement of Communist intellectuals, *Ginger e Fred* can be considered the first anti-Berlusconi parody, ten years before Berlusconi entered the political arena.

Chapters 1, 2, and 4 are more theoretical. From a number of different points of view, the introductory first and second chapter set out the essential thesis of the book, i.e., the political dimension of the perpetual childhood represented in Fellini's films. If Fellini is now a major figure in the anthropological history of the country, and emblem of what is quintessentially "Italian"—alongside Dante and, say, Ferrari sports cars—the ways, reasons, and mechanisms involved in this process of symbolic acquisition are far from simple and should not be taken for granted, particularly in view of the fact that Italian culture has always been so closely related to politics.

Chapter 4 focuses on the "elective affinities" between Fellini and Rome, and revisits them in the light of the visual culture of fascism and the mirroring effects of the relations between Fellini's imagination and the pursuit of the myth of Rome harbored by Mussolini.

Three chapters constitute a reading of Italian modernity, partly stimulated by, and borrowing from, Giulio Bollati, Silvana Patriarca, and Suzanne Stewart-Steinberg in relation to the construction of national character and identity, as well as the important studies of fascism by Emilio Gentile.

The Appendix at the end of the book includes intriguing materials and documents from the Andreotti archives, including the correspondence between Fellini and the many-times prime minister of Italy.

Notes

1. F. Fellini, *Intervista sul cinema* (Interview on the Cinema), ed. Giovanni Grazzini, (Rome/Bari: Laterza, 2004 [1983]), 15–16.

2. The opportunity arose from the publication of a book edited by Georgi Bogemski, *Federico Fellini: Stat'i: Interv'ju: Recenzii: Vospominanija* (Moscow: Isskustvo, 1968). Also see C. Fracassi, "Così vedono Fellini in URSS. Un realista suo malgrado" [How They See Fellini in the USSR: A Realist Despite Himself], *Paese Sera*, 22 September 1969.

Chapter 1

Fellini and "Italian Ideology"

We followed the "Alcina-like seductions" of Justice and Freedom; we've produced little justice and perhaps we're losing our freedom.
—Norberto Bobbio

Certainly the Catholics have a damnable vice: to think of the force of modernity and not know how this modernity, in as much as it believes that it seeks to negate religious transcendence, is at the culmination of its most acute crisis.
—Augusto del Noce

Question: If President Pertini asked you to form a government, what would you do?
I would try to set up a Ministry of the Italian identity to ponder what Italy is, our psychology, our historical secretions, Catholicism, the regions that make up the country, who Sicilians are and what Venice is. Which, over and above the personal culture of its components would seek unstintingly to put before us what the real country is, its culture, how it expresses itself, at what level. I mentioned this to Andreotti once ... he didn't reply, just cracked a thin smile and looked at me through those eyes that seem as if they belong in who knows what kind of dark laboratory.
—Federico Fellini

A Singular Modernity

Indisputably, the cinema has been a powerful tool in the production of Italian identity. Through film, the country has investigated and told a story about itself; at the same time it has commented on the story being told. One of the fundamental motifs of Italian modernity is the close relationship between culture and some of the most important forms of politics in the twentieth century: fascism, Christianity as a social force, and communism (Gramsci's brand of it).[1]

What the historian Brunetta called the "literary, didactic and vaguely Socialist"[2] vocation of Italian cinema is the result of the specific character of national history, the backwardness of the country, its sudden and incomplete industrialization, the lack of a middle class, and the famous gap between the people and the "cast" of intellectuals, as Gramsci called them long before the phrase became a buzzword.[3]

More than other places, Italy developed the natural propensity for film as a popular form of entertainment. At the same time Italian cinema has allowed itself to become permanently politicized, a peculiarity of Italian culture. After the fall of fascism, a battle raged between the two hegemonic ideologies of the country, Catholicism and communism.

If a place exists where Italian communism and Catholicism can be seen as contiguous—through their "metaphysical" heritages (the word belongs to Giorgio Galli),[4] their anti-modernism, and a shared diffidence toward democracy—it is in the history of Italian cinema, a congruence that persists, to some extent, still today.

The case of neorealism is a notorious example.

In Italy, the unending debate on neorealism was above all a head-on collision between the two forces, a perfect instance of "cultural cold war" that the *Don Camillo e Peppone* films served up, in fraternal conciliatory and national-popular form, as a trade-off.

It could even be thought that the ideology of fascist propaganda, which considered cinema "the most powerful weapon," was continued into the hyper-politicization of neorealism, albeit on the opposite side of the political spectrum: "on the one hand [neorealism] overturned the political set-up and characters of the fascist imagination yet, on the other, it inherited from fascism the structure and some of the mechanisms by which it worked." From opposite starting points, "the authoritarian character of the message was the same." A different ideology, for sure, but one that enrolled cinema into the fight "for progress and the creation of a new society, now openly Socialist and inspired by populism."[5]

In generating its imagination, Italian cinema has admirably converted the failings of the country into something immediately recognizable, sometimes even into strengths. The uncertain national identity has allowed the country to assimilate the way others have thought about Italy, which, within the broader Italian cultural heritage, has generated unusual new forms of imagining the national identity.[6]

In Fellini's films, first and foremost there is the structural datum of the Italian imagination, tottering between universal myths—the Church, the Roman Empire—and hyper-local myths (the city-states, strong regional identities, and a sense of local rather than national belonging). The universal nature of his visual creations is systematically interwoven with the particular and peculiar nature of specific localities, passed on from one generation to another. Like the effects of a spell, this cultural heritage seems to be evoked from the depths of the Italian unconscious.

Rather than the well-known visions of Fellini, think of the voice in his films, the extraordinary mixture of local dialects mixed with foreign languages, creating an indecipherable texture of sound, both ancient and modern.[7]

A singular modernity, as Kezich pointed out, explaining Fellini's disinterest in politics and the particular nature of his films within the ideological climate of the fifties; "an artist who lived modernity as absolutely natural," whose work "accompanies and often predates changes in society."[8]

In the seventies, the most hard-line and radical ideologues of the left criticized Fellini for political apathy and the reactionary forces hidden in his work—for his petty-bourgeois individualism. In his pamphlet against Fellini, Pietro Angelini wrote: "to political propaganda Fellini ends up preferring another sort of propaganda, that of his own world, the utopia of a society made to measure for him."[9]

It is precisely the presence of these two strands in the fabric of his films that leads us to think of Fellini as a universe in which the heterogenesis of Italian modernity can be seen.

Criticism of the Neorealist Paradigm

In spite of his oft-repeated disinterest in politics, the films of Fellini, no less than those of other filmmakers, express the superimposition of two visions of the world, a Catholic and a Communist vision, opposites yet *inseparable* in the broader context of "Italian ideology." An ideology from which—as he showed in *Amarcord*—the memory of fascism cannot be excluded.

If Italian postwar cinema represents the meeting and mutual influence of the two great populist cultures of the country, the position established as a result of this ideological standoff was complexly reconfigured in the debates sparked by Fellini.

In these discussions in Italy, the Catholic world addressed a mixture of problems of a spiritual (but also concrete) nature, pointing to the failings of communism in this area, and, vice versa, communism accused the Catholic world of being unable or unwilling to accommodate promptings for the renewal and transformation of society.

In other words, in his own way, concealed behind the myth of autobiography and independent artistic creation, Fellini worked through this paradox in Italian ideology no less than others. He redefined it in work that was to become increasingly national and less and less populist (and popular), ending up as purely "monumental."

Maurizio Grande, a researcher attentive to the polysemous nature of Italian realism, recalled that the period of neorealism in Italy coincided not only with the international success of its cinema, but also with "the height of ideology in the relationship between cinema and reality."[10]

Fellini's allergy to providing any theoretical framework to his work does not mean that in his films there was no implicit criticism of the ideologies of realism. In this respect, Fellini brought new compositional and interpretative resources to Italian cinema (for example, the exploration of the unconscious, almost entirely absent from Italian culture in the late fifties and early sixties).

In one of the early scenes of *La dolce vita,* at the press conference arranged for Sylvia (the American star who is in Rome to make a film, played by Anita Ekberg), a journalist asks her point-blank: "Do you think Italian neorealism is alive or dead?" A little at a loss, the actress looks toward her assistant. Instead of translating the question, he simply tells her: "Say alive." The questioner is duly satisfied and the starlet can go back to assuring her audience about her love for pizza and cannelloni.

Although this is 1960 and we are a long way from the ideological bluster surrounding films like Visconti's *Senso* (1954) and *La terra trema* (1948) or De Sica's *Umberto D* (1952), the sarcastic treatment of one of the most enduring questions of Italian culture is unmistakable. For Fellini, in a country self-absorbed in its *unexpected belle époque*—as Calvino called it in 1961[11]—the myth of neorealism had become empty and formulaic, kept alive artificially solely in the name of a political battle.

Fellini's irony doesn't spare the final, twilight phase of the debate, the "keyhole" and "shadowing" films and furtive images of the most unstinting promoter of neorealism, Cesare Zavattini, prefigured in an article published in 1941 in which Mario Alicata and Giuseppe De Santis affirmed: "one day we'll make our best film following a factory worker home, narrating the sheer poetry of a new, pure life which has at its heart the secret of an aristocratic beauty."[12]

In *Giulietta degli spiriti,* this factory worker on his way home who is elevated to poetry becomes the adulterer tailed everywhere by a detective, armed with a movie camera, sleuthing for his wife.

When Giulietta is shown the film of her husband with his lover, the investigator makes a comment that is half refutation of Zavattini's theoretical stance and half "biographical self-absolution" (at the time, a jealous Giulietta Masina was, in fact, having Fellini followed):[13] "You see, dear lady, I always advise my clients to view what we show them with a certain detachment. Ours, you understand, is an objective point of view, and is therefore *limited*. Reality may be something else. More innocent. This is Lake Bracciano, isn't it Remo? (talking to his assistant)...No, it's a meadow beneath the 'Castles.'"

For all that it may seem grotesque, it is in this mirroring between fiction and reality—over which the lengthy shadow of Pirandello is cast—that Fellini renews the neorealist spirit. As in Pirandello's *Quaderni di Serafino Gubbio operatore*, in which the diary and story are mixed together and "the drama takes place as a film is being edited," for Fellini neorealism was an opportunity to rethink the relationship and continuity between film and life, as he was to do most famously in *8 ½*.

As we know, he developed this procedure as a result of his apprenticeship with Rossellini, as he observed the older film director's do-as-you-please attitude to the production process, the chaos orchestrated by Rossellini from an idea he didn't immediately know what to do with or where it would take him. Similarly, Fellini started with a sketch, a photo or a face he'd seen in the street; both filmmakers came to the set without a completed script (and the myth of "improvisation," actually far from true, was the main cause of the narrative aphasia afflicting Italian cinema for years to come).

The pages of the book, *Fare un film* [Making a Film] that Fellini dedicated to Rossellini indicate an artistic proximity between the two directors that would barely be suspected from viewing their films, apparently so radically different:

> I was more at ease in films made outdoors, in the open air. In this Rossellini was a pioneer ... From Rossellini I believe I learned—in lessons from him and an apprenticeship of mine that he never translated into words, never expressed, never made schematic—how to walk a tightrope in the toughest, most adverse, circumstances, which at the same time he naturally turned to his advantage, transforming them into feeling, emotional values, a point of view. This is what Rossellini did: he lived the life of a film as an adventure simultaneously to be lived and narrated. ... Isn't this neorealism? So, if you talk about neorealism, you can only be referring to Rossellini. The others made films of realism, *verismo*, or tried to translate a talent, or vocation, into a formula, a recipe.[14]

Some time later, to express his spirit, Fellini was to take everything indoors, into the studios of Cinecittà, but this changes little.

The "others" included the Visconti of *La terra trema* and *Senso*, who—with the applause of the Communist Party and massed ranks of critics, headed by Aristarco—was painting a fresco of the "rise of the subordinate classes" and an interpretation—in the spirit of Togliatti—of Gramsci's concept of national-popular culture, with the inevitable myopia and paradoxes of Italian communism at the time, backed up where necessary by government boycotts.

These events are well known. Without them, Fellini's arrival on the scene, which knocked askew and undermined all the positions in play, cannot be understood; nor can it be understood how he reawakened a climate in which the degree of realism functioned as the coefficient of the quality of the work and its ability to "stir" consciences (an attitude that persists in Italian criticism even today).[15]

Now behind the camera, the neorealist scriptwriter of *Roma città aperta* and *Paisà* begins to narrate the world of vaudeville and the shows put on in theaters as curtain raisers, the way women are enchanted by photo-romances in magazines, the idleness and permanent childhood of somnolent provincial life. He does so in his first three films (*Luci di varietà, Lo sceicco bianco, I vitelloni*), revealing a dreamy and melancholic gaze deeply rooted in Italian psychology and by showing the artistic debt to low rather than high culture, to popular forms of entertainment instead of literature, to cartoons and caricatures rather than painting.

This shook up Gramsci's concept of the "national-popular," as it was being played out in those years, following Togliatti's astutely managed "Operation Gramsci."[16]

In relation to the publication in 1950 of a book entitled *Letteratura e vita nazionale* (Literature and National Life), it has been pointed out that: "Even this volume, which apparently lent itself less to political aims, was considered very important by Togliatti …. In fact it wasn't only a debate on Gramsci, nor a dry discussion of literature by the literati: 'Questions about the lack of a national-popular character to Italian literature involve 'walking in the shoes of workers' in other words 'saving Italian culture from decadent mysticism.'"[17]

"Decadent mysticism": precisely the term used in the years to come, by both sides of the political spectrum, to dismiss Fellini.

During the fifties, Italian Marxist critics targeted both Fellini and Rossellini. Focusing on the social themes of the films, rather than on their cinematic language or formal inventiveness, their criticism was utterly unlike that of their French counterparts, which was inspired by André Bazin and his idea of cinematic modernity, i.e., a radical revolution in film language.

Brunello Rondi, a critic, scriptwriter, film director, and subsequently collaborator of Fellini, was a rare exception. So particular significance can be attached to the preface written by Fellini to a book by Rondi, *Cinema e realtà*, published in 1957, in which the critic distanced himself both from the Marxist-Lukacsian paradigm and from Croce's form of idealism, preferring a form of realism close to the phenomenological-spiritual perspective of French criticism, which the films of Rossellini and Fellini had adopted, without being understood in Italy.[18]

For Rondi and Fellini alike, neorealism should have eschewed didactic and political aims and old ways of thinking unable to capture the attention of a fan of comic books (like Fellini) or the general public.

In relation to the massive audiovisual project—with similar didactic and humanistic aims—that took up much of Rossellini's attention from the mid sixties onward, Fellini was skeptical. The pseudo-documentary turn taken by his cinema in the seventies with that (phony) language of television investigative journalism—in *I clowns, Roma, Prova d'orchestra*, and *Intervista*—was a parody both of "cinéma-verité" and of Rossellini's utopian vision.

During the Venice Film Festival of 1966, responding to Rossellini's declarations about the death of "artistic" cinema, which was supposed to make way for a "didactic-informative" cinema, Fellini said:

> ... it is what Stalin believed, making Soviet cinema pedagogical and scholastic .... Roberto's ideas are acceptable if he, in all sincerity, is speaking about himself and says humbly that he wants to dedicate himself to making educational films, but he cannot make declarations that involve the cinema as a whole ... [T]ake the photos of the moon published by newspapers ... what do think of them? I think they look like the surface of a piece of cheese...*the first decent photographs of the moon will be shot by a filmmaker who knows how to express a feeling, let's say of nostalgia for the earth, the anguished sense of the enormity of space.*[19]

The opposite is also true, of course: "the anguished sense of the enormity of space" can be represented by a piece of cheese against a black background. This motif is at work in all of Fellini's films, in which the filmmaker conjures a sense of nostalgia and wonder, well aware that they are fictions—as in the most emblematic set Fellini ever constructed, the *Rex*, a huge transatlantic liner, made of cardboard, cutting through an ocean of plastic.

The PCI against *La strada*

"A critical anthology of *La strada*," writes Brunetta, "might be the best proof of just how visually obtuse left-wing criticism had become in the mid-fifties."[20]

The Italian Communist Party (PCI) was unlikely to be sympathetic to the kind of thing on offer in the itinerant tale of Zampanò and Gelsomina, where the obvious social implications of poverty were kept in the background in order to bring to the fore its more extravagant aspects. However, to say that left-wing critics were obtuse is unfair; in terms of the cultural cold war being waged at the time, their position was entirely understandable.

Just as Togliatti accused Vittorini and "Il Politecnico" of an "abstract search for the new, the different, the surprising," in subsequent years the writers, artists, and filmmakers who did not toe the party line were similarly ostracized. Morandi was accused of "formalist self-indulgence," his "dusty bottles" serving no purpose in the "struggle for progress."[21] Not coincidentally, his are the paintings found in the drawing room of Steiner, the intellectual who commits suicide in *La dolce vita*. "I see you have a marvelous Morandi," Marcello says to his friend. "He is my favorite painter," Steiner replies, "the objects are subsumed in a dreamy light, and yet they are painted with such detachment and precision, such discipline that they are almost tangible. It is an art in which nothing is accidental."[22]

In April 1952, the National Cultural Committee of the Communist Party pondered—among other things—"mass culture" and produced a document to encapsulate the fundamental motivation behind the cultural policy of the PCI. In his report, Carlo Salinari, head of the Central Cultural Section, spoke of the corruption of the cultural movements which, in the postwar period, had aspired to avant-garde status: "in thousands upon thousands of pages sold in Italy," he said, "from glossy magazines to cartoons, we see the degradation of culture."[23]

As Misler pointed out in the seventies, the overall impression is that the PCI was troubled by what it saw as the "rebirth of irrational currents in Italian culture." In his report, Salinari stigmatized the phenomenon with a hint of disdain: "Existentialism came along, starting life as a form of clothing. The various currents of spiritual and national rebirth are nurtured by diverse, even bizarre means, from so-called poetry nobody understands or knows the meaning of, to serious investigations of the epistemological validity of witchcraft or the analysis of the active and passive pederast's soul."[24]

The polemics regarding *La strada* can only be understood in relation to this "call to order." The call came from a journal founded shortly before, and more open and receptive to the new than, say, *Rinascita*, which owed its allegiance to Togliatti. Headed up by Romano Bilenchi, Antonello Trombadori, and Salinari himself, *Il Contemporaneo* began publication in 1954. It was intended as a left-wing response to the cultural eclecticism of *Mondo*, the famous journal of Mario Pannunzio; as Ajello recalls: "its 'openness' was most evident in artistic and literary matters. Except for an initial declaration against abstract and decadent art in favor of neorealism, Salinari and Trombadori took a position of tolerance."[25]

In light of the battle at the Venice Film Festival between the opposing factions supporting, on the one hand, *La strada* and, on the other, the epic/Risorgimento-inspired realism of *Senso*, this tolerance was evidently in rather short supply.

An article on *La strada* in the Communist Party newspaper *l'Unità*, dated 2 October 1954, remarks on its "mystique-making philosophemes" and "useless pseudo-existential questioning"; the failure of the film was attributed to following Rossellini too closely.[26] Gian Luigi Rondi commented on its "deep spiritual echoes and delightful meanings" and considered the film "one of the most significant works of the new Italian cinema,"[27] while Chiarini wrote peremptorily in *Il Contemporaneo*: "The confusion of ideas (elevating to a symbol of Italian society today the incomprehension and lack of solidarity between men strikes me as a serious error since clearly there is both understanding and solidarity, to good and evil effect: not only, I mean, within the masses who advance, aware of their human rights, but also within the classes that seek in every way to prevent this advance) is not alleviated by the force of feeling (this, too, an inner clarity) but adds to the sentimentalism reigning over the whole film, which is half-mystical, half-skeptical."[28]

The squabbling might have ended there. But it should be remembered that *La strada* was received in two very different ways: with indifference in Italy (where the film was not among the top ten box-office hits of the season) and enthusiastically in France, by critics from Sadoul to Bazin. The film went on to win the Academy Award for best foreign picture in 1957, inaugurating an intense elective affinity between Fellini and the world of American cinema.

The discussion was resumed after the critical and public acclaim of the film in France. The polemics triggered by Massimo Mida were influenced by the huge international success of the film.

Mida spoke of an "irrational and pathetic adherence to mannered sentimentality, the simple and derelict souls of Hugo, beloved by readers of comics and today's novelistic soap operas";[29] Trombadori, on the other hand, described the film as a "confused attempt to blend a sort of mystic and Franciscan pantheism with the disconsolate theories of existential angst."[30]

In his defense, Fellini cited the personalist philosophy of Emmanuel Mounier, which he probably hadn't read but he understood that it was in the cultural orbit of defenders of the film. For the critic Renzo Renzi, *La strada* was symptomatic of a broader failing of Italian culture and a "return to the climate of 1940." A French critic, Michel Lang (subsequently a director of film comedies and then in television), immune to the esteem of his fellow citizens for Fellini, accused him of pretentiously borrowing from Mounier without understanding a word he had written. He went on to attack the film's generic and decadent betrayal of neorealism: "Your cinema has meant for us the opposite of replacing concrete problems with the hokum of spiritual solutions ... what Fellini is doing here runs the risk of taking Italian cinema back to trite generalities, soaked in *verismo* and soft spirituality, precisely what ruined French cinema even where it was most successful."[31]

Toward the end of May, Fellini defended himself with a cunning piece of diplomacy, evoking both the "atmosphere of the CLN" (the National Liberation Committee of the Resistance Movement), and echoing the Pope's recent appeal to "Man" in an address to filmmakers on the subject of the *ideal* film.[32] Fellini wrote:

> I do not think neorealism can be broken down into this or that precise ideology or should be confined to being the heir of this or that theoretical stance, forcing it in terms of creative methodology to rehash "systems" applied in the past and elsewhere. Today it is thought that after the preliminary unity of the postwar period and the atmosphere created by the CLN, neorealism has once more shattered into tiny little pieces and opposing parts, previously smoothed over and held together. It's an excellent way to negate the best works of neorealism ... neorealism is a movement with the "highest" ambitions: it seeks to become an organic sense of life, a new "vision." There has been a Renaissance sense of the world, an Enlightenment relationship with things, a baroque feeling, a Romantic vision, and today—can we say so?—there is, or there is an attempt to create, a "neorealist" relationship with the world. This is the essential point: I welcome films that, even shabbily and crudely, without a weighty narrative apparatus, discover and invent this "new relationship."

Here Fellini recalls the Foucault of "episteme." He then headed toward a masterful crypto-ecumenical conclusion: "it isn't out of a vague spiritualism, but from a love of man and life, that we are humbled by the *Mystery*."[33]

Although unconvinced, Trombadori was to become Fellini's lifelong friend. Massimo Mida, on the other hand, praised both sides of the argument and ended it with a no less ecumenical appeal to a sense of fellow feeling "under the common banner of anti-fascism."

Fellini, De Martino, and the "Irrational Currents in Italian Culture"

The attacks on *La strada* were symptomatic of the utter rejection of any art form that attempted to represent the "magical" or "folklore," the position of the Italian Communist Party since the end of the forties. It was a rejection that was to weigh heavily on Italian culture and was in open contrast—as some may recall—with Gramsci's appreciation of the importance of these phenomena.

Although sympathetic to the party line, Ernesto De Martino was ostracized after publishing, with Einaudi, *Il mondo magico. Prolegomeni a una storia del magismo,* an investigation of magic and the culture of southern Italy. The book came to represent one of the most significant episodes in the party's fight against the so-called irrational currents of Italian culture, and testified, among other things, to its fervent espousal of Marxist materialism wedded to the Crocean tradition of idealism.

De Martino's highly original investigation and analysis of the backwardness of southern Italian culture was bound to raise a few eyebrows.[34] The attention given to the archaic dimension of Italian religious rituals, as "unmanageable" experiences within the official framework of faith, was part of a larger cultural strategy: "Albeit choosing the South as the privileged terrain for his research, he is in fact preparing a far broader work, updating Italian culture with regard to studies of folklore, psychology, religion and myth, indeed anything relating to historically distant phenomena of this kind: as can be seen from the title of a series of books published by Einaudi, which he edited between 1948 and 1955."[35]

The series included works by Jung, influential on Cesare Pavese in the forties.

If neorealism was not to be contaminated by fable and the oneiric, the study of the South, with its concrete problems of poverty and backwardness, could not confine itself to an analysis of the irrational or a specific anthropology, and the "magical" was certainly to be kept as far away as possible.

In relation to the fierce criticism dished out to *La strada,* in his biography of Fellini, Kezich noted the similarity between Fellini and De Martino and the "inability of hegemonic culture to accept narrative fable," in which he saw the left negating a different Italy and an "anthropology which, following in the footsteps of Carlo Levi and his *Cristo si è fermato a Eboli,* comes to the fore in Ernesto De Martino's investigations of the South."[36]

The connection between Fellini and De Martino has been made all the stronger by the recent discovery of an unpublished work by the filmmaker and Pinelli, probably prior to *La strada* (the exact date is as yet unknown),[37] a story of magic, legends, and primitive rituals, almost an anthropological exploration that, in its adaptation for the cinema, was to become a journey not unlike that of Zampanò and Gelsomina, but set in the mythical depths of the South of Italy.

From the first scene of the typed script ("a barefoot man, long hair, loose, as in some depictions of Christ, walks into a small village in the south of Italy"), the atmosphere is a mixture of magical realism and ethnographic documentary. Fellini and Pinelli give the main character the name Salvatore Incòrpora; he is a wandering healer who "in mystical and pagan excitement, enters unlit rooms, turns upon the sick an intense magnetic gaze, places his hands upon them, reciting under his breath *prayers mixed with incomprehensible words.*" The female character is called Regina Macallè, a starving nymphomaniac, utterly dominated by sex, with "*magical powers and the ability to move objects.*" In Fellini's tried and trusted narrative manner, the story unravels in pictures, the couple—as in *La strada*—wandering from farm to farm, village to village, in a countryside that is "*increasingly ancient and mysterious, full of remote echoes,*" with witches, ghosts, apparitions of the Madonna, voices from the depths, and so on.

There is much of De Martini in this, his observations of Lucan rituals and more generally the mix of superstition, popular Catholicism, and magic that permeates the South, as indeed investigated by De Martino.

While Dino Buzzati (above all in *Lo strano viaggio di Domenico Molo*, the story adapted by Fellini in the *Mastorna* project) prompted the mystery in Fellini's oeuvre, De Martino showed him how this mystery was related to Catholicism and religion in Italy:

> ... the connections between magic and the hegemonic form of religious life are evident in popular Catholicism, in private non-liturgical prayer, in the cult of religious relics, in the pilgrimages to the sanctuaries of the Virgin Mary in Viaggiano, Pierno, Picciano, and Fonni, in miraculous healings, and other phenomena in the Lucan area which accentuate the "exterior," "paganism," and "magic" within southern Catholicism: and yet, even here, it should not be forgotten how this "magic" potentially mediated Christian values, albeit in a very narrow and elementary fashion.[38]

In Fellini's films, the dimension of the magical is placed systematically in relation to Catholicism.

In *8 ½* and *Giulietta degli spiriti* we could think of the dream sequences of Guido and Giulietta and the visual phantasmagoria with which Fellini represents their memories. Open to the paranormal and the Jungian unconscious, they nonetheless always run into a Catholic "primary scene" (for Guido the College of the Priests, for Giulietta the school play in which a woman undergoes martyrdom by being burned alive).

In turn, these Catholic rituals evoke an atmosphere of pagan fascination (from *La strada* and *Le notti di Cabiria* to the ecclesiastical procession in *Roma*). Above all, in the films of the fifties and the sequences of the Marian processions in *La strada* and *Le notti di Cabiria,* Fellini shows himself to be close to the thinking of De Martino. These films demonstrate a sense of the archaic and the workings of popular magic beyond the Catholic management of mystery.

In February 1960, in a discussion on *La dolce vita,* De Martino unsurprisingly focused his attention on the phony miracle episode, emphasizing its "ethnographic truthfulness."[39] At the beginning of the sequence, in fact, a woman shouts: "it doesn't matter if it is the Madonna, if she is there or not! ... it doesn't matter. Italy is a country of ancient cults, abounding in natural and supernatural places. Everyone feels their influence ... if you look for God you find Him, wherever that is." Especially, in Italy, if you are looking for the Madonna. In Italy, due to its popular origins and the promise of immediate access to the sacred, the cult of the Virgin Mary is second only to that of Christ, less in the hands of the Church, and with a form of intercession that has a familiar and spontaneous nature: "the Madonna appears almost always in the countryside, to humble people and her sanctuaries are generally far from city walls."[40]

The pilgrimage to Divine Love in *Le notti di Cabiria* is an excellent example. The construction of the scene, the quickening pace of the editing, the close-ups of the faithful as the songs to the Madonna can be heard in the background, with the almost hysterical invocations of the pilgrims, provide the popular and mystical atmosphere of a cult of worship. There is a similar reutilization of the neorealist visual paradigm in De Martino and Fellini (Franco Pinna, the photographer who accompanied the ethnologist on his explorations of the South, became Fellini's chosen photographer for the sets of his films in the sixties). According to the anthropologist Francesco Faeta, De Martino's basic disinterest in visual materials did not exclude a predilection for images able to restore a "virgin terrain," which the neorealist paradigm—"the dominant iconic code inspiring his research"[41]—was able to provide him with.

De Martino and Fellini should also be placed alongside the framework Faeta calls the "domestic paradigm" of Italian ethnography, particularly that of De Martino, meaning the interdependence of national culture and ethnographic research: the idea that an anthropologist need not go to the ends of the earth for research but can investigate society by turning the attention away from the exotic and toward one's own culture and oneself.

The renowned search for the "exotic" in Rome or as reconstructed in the studios of Cinecittà shows Fellini carrying out the same ethnographic research to understand his own culture.

Light is shed on Fellini's own "domestic paradigm" by De Martini's well-known remark (here quoting Lévi-Strauss): "... my recent passion for itinerant ethnography in the South of Italy ... involved *questioning the system into which one is born and in which one grows up,* symbolizing *expiation and redemption."*[42]

The Aestheticizing of Christianity

The above considerations lead us directly to an examination of what is recognized as the central role of Catholicism in Fellini's poetics, a complex issue that permeates his work at various levels.

Beyond the films and the polemics—for example the brouhaha over *La dolce vita* and the rift it caused in the Catholic world[43]—Fellini maintained close relations with the ecclesiastical environment, a fact that should not be ignored. At the same time it would be quite wrong to consider Fellini's films only in this light.

The social and political fragmentation of Catholicism in Italy did not begin with the passing of the Christian Democrat Party at the beginning of the nineties but had been ongoing for many years. During those years, Fellini's films investigated the relationship between Italian culture and Catholicism, the tension between the secular and the spiritual, accompanying and foreshadowing the enormous changes in Italian society today.

Like it or not, Fellini's oeuvre is part of Catholic culture, and as such it speaks to the repositioning of Catholics within Italy and as representatives of the country, a topic that is today the object of fierce debate and rethinking.

From a "political" point of view, in relation to the Church, Fellini was utterly canny. He cultivated personal relations that were useful in defending his films against censorship (as was the case with *Le notti di Cabiria*)[44] without shying away from portraying the castrating nature of Catholic education, particularly in relation to sexuality. Despite condemning this type of upbringing, his investigations were of a spiritual nature, involving the search for the sacred and its relationship with Italian identity within the interpretative framework of Catholicism.

The fact that Fellini could be fiercely critical of the Catholic Church while seeking its support for his ambitious films is part of an Italian intellectual tradition dating back to Guicciardini.[45] Rossellini worked with Father Felix Morlion (an influential and somewhat shady Dominican intellectual), while one of Fellini's closest advisors was the Jesuit Father Angelo Arpa. Neither filmmaker, however, can be regarded as being part of the "Catholic avant-garde" for all that it was interested in cinema and close to intellectuals not aligned with Marxist culture.

Angelo Arpa made a vital contribution to Fellini's career and cultural development. An eclectic intellectual and the force behind the cinematography of the Arecco Institute in Genoa (copied from the cinema club founded by Father Morlion in Rome), Arpa met Fellini in 1954 and became a key figure in the complex ecclesiastical mediation for *Le notti di Cabiria* and *La dolce vita*. He said of Fellini and his unresolved relationship with religion: "Like every Italian given a Roman Catholic upbringing, Fellini was a Catholic, but his religious universe gradually took on a less codified form, more inwardly free-and-easy... Fellini never dried up as nonbelievers do, still less did he become condescending according to the dictates of the so-called secular spirit."[46]

While it may be true that "Fellini's attention to the sacred, which critics often mention, seems to focus on the dimension of ritual and spectacle,"[47] it is also true that the sacred is not investigated only for the elements of spectacle.

The priests, nuns, and countless ecclesiastical extras populating the frescoes of his films, which are inseparable from Fellini's imaginary world, express above all the Italian identity. This is an export-oriented Italian identity, one of the greatest strengths of which was Fellini's recognition of the importance of these figures for the proper understanding of Italian culture in the world (and of the entirely surface fascination in them felt in the rest of the world). Indeed, the pomp and spectacle of religion in the rituals of the Catholic Church came to characterize Fellini's *mise-en-scène*. The choreography of the Catholic Church attracted him due to "its unchanging, hypnotic representations ... the enormous mortuary apparatus." Naturally there are many examples, but the most well known is undoubtedly the ecclesiastic parade in *Roma*.

While the college priests in *8 ½* and the attempts in *Amarcord* to contain the testosterone-driven turbulence of adolescence are criticisms of a repressive religious education, the parade in *Roma* has an altogether different feel. It shows Fellini's fascination with Catholic drama and with the incantatory force of its scenery and rites. The ecclesiastical fashion parade in *Roma* is far more a homage to the Church's ability to put on a show than a parody or condemnation of the worldly corruption of its orders.

In his review of the film, Moravia wrote: "With this parade, Fellini tells us semi-seriously and half-facetiously that the Church has become nothing more than ceremonial and decoration, without content. Corruption explains the emptiness of the Church; and in turn the emptiness of the Church explains its corruption. Some have criticized this sequence for its coldness and frivolity. I found it rather beautiful. It is cold and frivolous, certainly; but that is because, in this scene, Fellini—like Leopardi—joins together death and fashion."[48]

These are the years in which Michel de Certeau was formulating his ideas about the gradual transformation of Christianity into folklore, a phenomenon that involved the proliferation of religious signs everywhere within culture and sanctioned its separation from the authentic experience of faith.

Published in 1974, *Le Christianisme éclaté*[49] is a short but concentrated essay in which the French intellectual describes a fundamental change that started in the sixties.

What is faith today?—de Certeau wondered—now that "Christianity has taken the form of cultural exoticism" and "in the mass media, priests and bishops have the role of gurus of the spirit"? "Today what appears to characterize Christianity is its aestheticization. The *corpus* of Christian writings and rites is perceived, and hence used, as a collection of works of fine art, poetic, evocative; churches, texts, the liturgy provide material for theatrical creativity, for poetic secrets from readings and a recomposing of the social imagination. They no longer bear witness to a revelation, a truth handed down through the Christian faith, but are like the admirable ruins of a system of symbols which can be used for all kinds of invention and forms of expression."[50]

This landscape of "admirable ruins" of the Church, so skillfully evoked by de Certeau, and the idea of a huge phantasmagoria now redundant except for its ability to seduce through beauty, is what most attracted Fellini's Catholic imagination. Like the French Jesuit, Fellini wonders how it is possible to be Christian in contemporary society and "how to express the community experience of faith within the heart of modernity."[51] In *8 ½* the all-important meeting between Guido and the Cardinal, both of them in treatment in the health spa, is a clear indication of this.

Hinted at from the outset of the film and postponed almost for the sake of "suspense," Guido's visit to the Cardinal—from whom he wishes to obtain the concrete sense of an existential crisis, its resolution, and his salvation—ends up in an incomprehensible soteriology. In the grottoes, amid hot springs and mud packs, the first image of the Cardinal is indicative: his shadow is leaning forward on a chair placed behind a white sheet held by two priests to protect his eyes from Guido, while the meaning of the reference to the homilies of Origen of Alexandria is lost in the steam and vapors.

In Fellini, imagination, dreams, and the creative act do not close the door on religious experience, far from it. His rejection of religious dogmatism and inability to abandon a spiritual search led him to a personal "reuse of the religious repertoire," which de Cerceau regarded with suspicion but which seems—after the storm over *La dolce vita* had died down—to have interested the ranks of the Catholic Church.

In an essay on the reaction to *8 ½*, Mauro Giori pointed out that the film partially healed the rift with Catholicism prompted by *La dolce vita*:

"if some admiring reviewers go so far as to ignore the sarcasm and polemics behind the representation of the Cardinal and the flashback to the college, even the most diffident of them see in the introspection of Guido/Fellini a spiritual search worthy of the name ... the Catholic Center for Cinematography may regret the unilateral and unjust presentation of a certain form of Catholic education and an archaeological Church absent from the modern world, but it admires the film's undoubtedly positive ferment."[52]

From this point of view the "undoubtedly positive ferment" of Fellini might be thought of as *religious skepticism,* in the terms recently put forward by the philosopher of religion John Schellenberg. "Faith," "belief," and "imagination" are all terms that need to be reexamined within the framework of skepticism, which does not negate, but revitalizes religious experience. The Canadian philosopher believes that it is precisely skepticism that may, in the future, give rise to "a new form of faith based on the *imagination*" rather than faith. This would be a new phase for religion with a much looser hold on dogma but a stronger sense of its own imagery and mythical/poetic force, upon which an experience that cannot be reduced to pure consciousness is based.[53]

The Christ of Modernity

The statue of Christ transported by helicopter over Rome—in the opening sequence of *La dolce vita*—is certainly one of the best known of the many icons in Fellini's films.

In his detailed work on the visual sources of Fellini's cinema, Sam Stourdzé[54] points out the debt of this inventive scene to an event dating back to the celebrations for Labor Day in 1956, captured in a CIAC newsreel.[55]

On that occasion, a statue of Christ, "a gift from Milan to his Holy Father" was taken by helicopter from Piazza del Duomo in Milan to the Vatican. As curious and festive onlookers gather around, the statue of "Christ the Worker" is lifted against a background of huge advertising billboards all around the square.

There is no doubt that Fellini drew his inspiration directly from this event, attracted by the modern, unusual blending of the sacred and profane (if further proof were needed, the helicopter used for the opening sequence of *La dolce vita* was a Bel 47, the same that can be seen in the newsreel).

While the newsreel documents the historical event, Fellini's imagination goes well beyond it. As the newscaster makes clear, "Christ the

Worker" is the symbol of the "throng of like-minded Christian workers" on Labor Day; the embrace between the "skilled workers who built the magnificent Italian aircraft in the Augusta factory" and the Catholic Church, whereas the Christ that flies over Rome, recreated by Fellini, was one of the most scandalous scenes of the many that caused a stir in *La dolce vita*. The statue flies over a terrace where some young women are sunbathing in bikinis, and Marcello and Paparazzo try to chat them up from the whirring helicopter; some were moved to condemn the entire film on the sole basis of this opening sequence.

Giovanni Colombo, on the staff of Archbishop Giovanni Battista Montini of Milan (and his successor), associated the opening scene symbolically with the end of the film (the scene on the beach with Marcello unable to hear the voice of the girl on the other side of the canal). He wrote: "the first and last sequences tell us that there can be no dialogue between this 'dolce vita' and the world of religion (Christ flies over the *carnal terraces*) and purity (the young serving girl, still untouched by evil, is on the other side). The noise of the helicopter and of the waves drowns out every word."[56]

The stripping away of the sacred from the figure of Christ is evident in one shot of the statue suspended in the sky, followed by the close-up of a dancer in a Rome nightclub. A brusque, sudden change of shot, as in montage.[57] Often mentioned, whatever the particular inflection of the reading of the film, the intermingling of religion and spectacle is one of the most significant vehicles for meaning in *La dolce vita*.

Yet it does not cancel out the so-called religious undercurrent of the film, as a small number of Catholic critics noted. Indeed, Pasolini called it "the highest and most absolute product of Catholicism in recent years."[58]

In the same way, the initial sequence of the film cannot be pinned down to one simple meaning, such as sensationalism, as Catholic critics suspected. As I will try to show, the statue of Christ in the film is a symbol open to numerous interpretations, characteristic of artistic inventiveness in relation to religion.

As de Certeau put it: "An entire population of symbols shifts; each sign takes its own route, is cut adrift, makes itself open to different forms or to reutilization, as if the words of a phrase ran riot on the page and could be rearranged into other sentences ... Specifically, the religious repertoire provides a way to express the problems arising from the breakdown of traditional society ... in other words, it shows the transition from one society to another."[59]

An "epoch-making" film, according to popular wisdom, *La dolce vita* does not only portray the transition from one era to another, from rural to modern Italy, but reutilizes the entire repertoire of Italian modernization—cars, fashion, the cinema, the cynicism of new customs, and the "society of the spectacle"—and suggests that these two eras, one passing and one asserting itself, are not so much in conflict as continuous. It is a negotiated transition and a process in which trauma can be reduced to a minimum, and hence seeks to soothe the feelings of insecurity that change inevitably brings about, along with the impact of the annihilation of an entire system of beliefs and meanings.

Hence, the image of the helicopter, the symbol of Italian modernity, together with the icon of Christ, not only sucks the sacred out of religion, but it gives symbolic form to the transformation of Italy and the Italian identity, indicating not a clean break but essentially a continuity.[60]

In this connection, the composition of the opening sequence speaks loud and clear: the helicopter flying over the countryside near Rome passes by the ruins of an aqueduct, so the symbolic overlapping and hence the continuity between the "ancient" (the ruins of Rome) and "modern" is *mediated* by the figure of Christ.

Mussolini had attempted to bring together fascism and Catholicism in the name of a renewed "Roman civilization," but this sequence shows something quite different at work in Fellini's imagination. According to Jacqueline Risset,[61] Fellini's style consists in joining the beauty of illusion (image, dream, appearance, momentary as if in a flash) with the knowledge of deception, the emptiness of the illusion. However, the vacuity does not cancel the wonder. In the tangle of two opposites, Fellini holds enchantment and disenchantment in perpetual suspension. In the combination of nostalgia for the old and euphoria for the new, the opening scene of *La dolce vita* also has a political dimension. The symbols representing them do not find their way onto the screen by chance and, indeed, the entire film is bathed in affection for the old, shot through with the joy of an impetuous leap into the future. This is immediately evident in the powerful visual synthesis of the opening shots. In my opinion, this is how the entire film should be viewed.

Fellini often expressed his regret about the reaction of Catholics and, in general, audiences to his film, unable, as he saw it, to appreciate its more "elevated" aspects.

Its spirituality was noted by Pasolini and by Father Nazareno Taddei, who reviewed the film in *Letture* in March 1960.[62] Over the coming years Pasolini was to speak increasingly about the relationships between rural culture, modernization, and Christianity, all of which are evident in the opening scene of Fellini's film. Indeed, the film may have prompted Pasolini's line of thought, especially if the notion of Pasolini as an opponent of modernity is dropped, as recommended by the philosopher Giacomo Marramao.

This is worth looking into at some depth, not so much by rereading the (well-known) review by Pasolini as by analyzing what Marramao has to say about some remarks of Pasolini from 1974, later included in *Scritti corsari*.[63]

He stresses the absolute modernity of Pasolini's Christianity, emphasizing the relationship between pagan and Christian times. According to Pasolini, the transition from a peasant culture, with its mythical models, to a culture of modernization corresponded to a change in the conception of time. The rural world was closed, with "cyclical time" (based on the *eternal return*) as opposed to linear time based on the idea of an "end," i.e., the Christian eschatology of salvation. Compared to all other religions, this is the *original* moment of Christianity, the "original excess compared to the balances of classical cosmologies." The introduction of a new (linear) conception of time, says Pasolini, finds expression in leaving peasant and rural culture behind, abandoning the cyclical conception and pagan version of time measured by the repetition of the seasons.

As Marramao says:

> The compromise strategy of the "official Church" consisted in this interminable *interim* over two thousand years, in which equivocation was accepted: "Christianity could not exist except in a peasant culture." However, the giddy acceleration of the processes of modernization brought about an unexpected, drastic change, in which the essentially modern and urban vocation of the Christian revolt emerged: "Now, suddenly, the countryside is no longer religious. Cities are. No more does Christianity belong to an agricultural community, it has become urban. One feature of all urban religions—and hence of the dominant elite—is the way the cycle of return is replaced by an end... Therefore an urban religion, as a scheme of things, is much better equipped than any rural religion to accept the model of Christ."[64]

The opening scene of *La dolce vita*, with the transfer of the statue of Christ from the countryside to the city, appears to exemplify Pasolini's analysis. Hence, the opening scene of the film could be seen not only as showing how the sacred is turned into a spectacle but how the icon of Christ may be a symbol of the radical *modernity* of Christianity.

Fellini and Italian Intellectuals

"I haven't read Proust, haven't read Joyce, know fuck all ... You don't have to have read Joyce or seen Picasso's paintings to know them. They are so much part of life that just being alive means you absorb them."[65]

This is one of the many examples of Fellini's "manifesto of anti-intellectualism" (as Calvino called it), written at the beginning of his career and never abandoned.

Naivety, candor, and stupefaction in relation to the world—as opposed to the cold rationalism and cynicism of the intellectual—are a major part of the myth of Fellini's art. As has been observed, from *8 ½* onward, he used the anti-intellectual stance partly as a provocation, particularly in relation to the development of his films in a certain direction, i.e., the fun and games began just as Fellini was becoming Fellini-esque and his films were getting more and more "difficult."

In relation to *La dolce vita* Moravia spoke of Fellini as a new Petronius; Montanelli described his *mise-en-scène* as a painting by Goya. Now *8 ½* came along to ruffle other hallowed names: Joyce, Proust, the French *nouveau roman*, informal art, and so on.[66]

With *8 ½* Fellini may have managed to heal the rift with the Church but not so with the film-going public (which, with the sole exception of *Amarcord*, abandoned him). Never again was he able to fill theaters as he had for *La dolce vita*. He became an anti-intellectual loved by intellectuals. Toward the end of his career, now a monument to himself, his following dwindled to the most cultured and refined portion of the bourgeoisie, a situation put in a nutshell by Kezich: "magnificently received by the critics, the movie theater empty."[67]

In this sense, *8 ½* was a key film, a huge misunderstanding, one might say.

Fellini believed he had made a film about the "crisis of every man" and the importance of learning to accept the chaotic flow of existence, and so on, until the final epigraph: "it is a feast of life, let's live it together." Not that he imagined it was a popular film, surely not, but nothing could have been further from his intentions than meta-art, or the "open-ended opus" theorized by Umberto Eco at the time. Just think of Nino Rota's brass band and the conjurer, the references to comic strips, and the whole array of elements from the "vernacular" in *8 ½*.[68]

But before long, *8 ½* was to become the epitome of auteurial filmmaking, the open-ended opus with directors telling us about their confused states of mind, and a cliché and *topos*, the stock response of amateur intellectuals when asked about their "favorite film." Whereas Fellini wondered out loud: "Is it true that the film is a little difficult to understand straight away? It must be, because a lot of people have understood sod all. All I can say, and I've said it a thousand times, is that you don't need to understand the film, you have to feel it."[69]

What this boils down to is Fellini's insistence on the need for an instinctive relation to film, less mediated by the poses of cultural consumption. It was, precisely, an example of Fellini's naïveté but raised the eternal question of the relationship between the general public and an "art-house film," reflecting the fracture between the Italy's "masses" and its "intellectuals," as described by Gramsci in a well-known remark in the *Prison Notebooks*: "There is popular feeling but not necessarily popular understanding or knowledge; intellectuals often 'know' but don't understand or 'feel'... The intellectual's mistake is to think he can *know* without understanding and, above all, without feeling, without passion (not for knowledge in itself but for the objects of knowledge), i.e., the notion that an intellectual can be such (and not a mere pedant) if he is distinct and detached from the people/nation, untainted by their elementary passions."[70]

Calvino had already noticed that intellectuals—victims of their cold detachment and inability to "feel"—invariably come to a bad end in Fellini's films, like Steiner, who kills himself and murders his own children in *La dolce vita*. Or Daumier, the writer/consultant imagined being hanged in *8 ½*. Victims of their obtuse egocentricity, like Leopoldo, the intellectual in *I vitelloni* who, pursuing dreams of glory, doesn't realize that the great actor who has come to the provinces is interested in his mediocre plays for reasons that have little to do with art. According to some commentators, Daumier was a parody of a left-wing film critic, the Marxist Guido Aristarco. His barbed comments, brilliantly packaged by Fellini, Flaiano, and Pinelli in this blistering and withering attack, run counter to everything Fellini stood for in film: "If you really want to do something radical on Catholicism in Italy, then, believe me, my friend, a much higher cultural level is required, in addition to a logic of inexorable lucidity. Forgive me but... your tender ignorance is entirely negative, your puny memories drip with nostalgia, your inoffensive evocations, essentially emotional in nature, are complicit... You set off wanting to denounce and end up aiding and abetting what you abhor. What confusion, what ambiguity, don't you see that?"

Almost fifty years after the release of *La dolce vita*, Alberto Arbasino returned to the topic of the portrayal of intellectuals, criticizing the unreality of these characters who "were supposed to be us" and calling their expressions "utter tripe."[71] What Arbasino sees is mystification under the guise of populism.

Montanelli was of a different opinion. In his review in *Corriere della Sera*, he discussed Steiner's milieu: "Let me say that, in all honesty, rarely have I seen anything as true as that intellectual circle. So much so that I, who don't belong to any of these circles, felt mortified, and had the vague urge to change jobs and take up, say, farming. Good heavens, what sadness, what wretchedness, those conversations, those faces, all that falsehood! Is that what we're really like? Yes, God help us. Those are the things we go around saying (unthinkingly) when we get together. Those are our lies. That is our vanity."[72]

Among the intellectuals playing themselves in the sequence of *La dolce vita* were the painter Anna Salvatori, a prominent figure in the cultural gatherings in Rome in the postwar period, and the writer Leonida Règpaci. The latter, rather than for his weighty volumes—novels, plays, and essays—is famous for founding (with Renato Angiolillo) the daily newspaper *Il Tempo* and, above all, for creating the Viareggio Prize. It was his decision, in 1947, to select Gramsci's *Letters from Prison* for the award, an unprecedented decision, given that "the work was not strictly literary and the author was dead."[73] Without this prize, Gramsci would have been read much less in Italy.

Although Togliatti did not exercise any direct pressure on Règpaci, the Einaudi edition of the *Letters* was practically his book; it was an expert selection of passages chosen by the Communist leader, the de facto editor. In this first edition, some of the pages omitted referred directly to Règpaci. He and Gramsci had met in Turin and had been comrades in the class war for a brief period. Running parallel to his political commitment, Règpaci became increasingly interested in writing and sought to cultivate his talent. Gramsci's opinion was implacable: "Règpaci has no creative imagination; he is able to give a somewhat mechanical gloss on a few events in his family, which serves as the 'myth' for his art… He would be willing to commit incest in order to write a novel on incest and show that his family is the protagonist of all Greek tragedies, from Phaedra to Oedipus."[74]

It is not difficult to understand why Togliatti removed these references from the edition given the Viareggio prize by Règpaci himself, blithely unaware of the excised passage. In certain respects, it is an emblematic episode in Italian intellectual life that seems to support the critique of Montanelli rather than that of Arbasino.

In light of Gramsci's criticism, Fellini's decision to use Règpaci to illustrate the hypocrisy of intellectual circles at the end of the fifties is particularly effective. With Steiner's circle he gives us an extraordinary portrait of the intellectual milieu of the time, unchanged today.

Notes

1. "Nowhere more than in our cinema," wrote Ernesto Galli della Loggia, "have these three forces intertwined and blended together, expressing overall what has been called *the Italian ideology*, with its basic anti-bourgeois populism, which neo-realism encapsulated, but which continued into Italian comic films, as well as in Pasolini and Moretti." From "Il paese del cinema" [The Country Seen through Its Cinema], *Corriere della Sera,* 29 August 2007. See also Galli della Loggia, *L'iden-*

tità italiana (Bologna: Il Mulino, 1998), and particularly the Afterword in the 2011 edition.

2. G.P. Brunetta, *Gli intellettuali italiani e il cinema* (Milan: Mondadori, 2004), x.

3. "...In Italy, intellectuals are distant from the people, i.e., from the *nation* and have a tradition of cast, which has never been broken by a political or national movement from below, however strong." A. Gramsci, *Concetto di nazional-popolare* [Concept of the National-Popular] (Quad. 21, 17, 5), in *Il lettore in catene. La critica letteraria nei "Quaderni"* [Reader in Chains: Literary Criticism in the Notebooks], ed. Andrea Menetti (Rome: Carocci, 2004), 95.

4. Giorgio Galli remarked that the Christian Democrat and Communist Parties inherited a metaphysical stance of distrust in democracy and liberalism that made them both anti-modern and anti-capitalist forces. See G. Galli, *Il bipartitismo imperfetto. Comunisti e democristiani in Italia* [Imperfect Bi-partisan Relations: Communists and Christian Democrats in Italy] (Bologna: Il Mulino, 1966).

5. P. Bertetto, "Storia del cinema/storia della cultura in Italia. Percorsi di interpretazione" [History of Italian Cinema/Culture: Paths of Intepretation], in *Storia del cinema italiano. Uno sguardo d'insieme* [The History of Italian Cinema: An Overview], ed. Bertetto (Venice: Marsilio, 2011), 13. (All quotations are from this book.)

6. See G. Canova, *Cinema italiano e immaginario collettivo* [Italian Cinema and the Collective Imagination], in P. Bertetto, *Storia del cinema italiano. Uno sguardo d'insieme*, 43–56, and C. Lizzani, *Il mio lungo viaggio nel secolo breve* [My Long Journey in the Short Century] (Turin: Einaudi, 2007).

7. Recently Luciano De Giusti has returned to this question of the voice in Fellini, in his introduction to the writings on the cinema of the poet Andrea Zanzotto, *Il cinema brucia e illumina. Intorno a Fellini e altri rari* [The Cinema Burns and Illuminates: On Fellini and Other Rarities] (Venice: Marsilio, 2011), 9–38.

8. T. Kezich, *Federico Fellini, la vita i film* (Milan: Feltrinelli, 2007), 130.

9. P. Angelini, *Controfellini. Il fellinismo tra restaurazione e magia bianca* [Counter-Fellini: Fellini-ism between Restoration and White Magic] (Milan: Ottaviano, 1974), 68.

10. M. Grande, *Lo spazio del reale nel cinema italiano* [The Space of the Real in Italian Cinema], in *La cultura italiana negli anni 1930-1945* (Naples: Edizioni Scientifiche Italiane, 1984), vol. II, and subsequently in M. Grande, *La commedia all'italiana* (Rome: Bulzoni, 2003), 7.

11. I. Calvino, "La belle époque inattesa" [The Unexpected Belle Époque], *Tempi moderni* no. 6, (July–September 1961).

12. M. Alicata and G. De Santis, "Ancora di Verga e del cinema italiano" [Once More on Verga and Italian Cinema], *Cinema* no. 130 (25 November 1941), quoted in N. Ajello, *Intellettuali e Pci 1944-1958* (Rome: Laterza, 1997), 207.

13. *Agenzia matrimoniale* (Marriage Agency) in Zavattini's omnibus film *L'amore in città* (1953) had already shown that Fellini's cinematic imagination was irreconcilable with investigation in the neorealist sense.

14. F. Fellini, *Fare un film* [Making a Film] (Turin: Einaudi, 1980), 44–46. Fellini borrowed from Rossellini the ability to get professional and non-professional actors to work together in a mix of "truth" and "fiction." See E. Dagrada, *Le varianti trasparenti. I film con Ingrid Bergman di Roberto Rossellini* [Transparent Variants: Ro-

berto Rossellini's Films with Ingrid Bergman] (Milan: LED, 2008, second enlarged edition).

15. In his reconstruction of the relations between intellectuals and the PCI, Nello Ajello speaks of neorealism as "a formula to stir consciences." Ajello, *Intellettuali e Pci*, 217.

16. F. Chiarotto, *Operazione Gramsci* (Milan: Mondadori, 2011), 49.

17. F. Chiarotto, *Operazione Gramsci*, 133. The phrase in quotation marks is from "Dibattiti su Gramsci," *Rinascita* 7, no. 5 (1951), 248–249.

18. See R. De Gaetano, *Teorie del cinema in Italia* [Italian Film Theory] (Soveria Mannelli: Rubbettino, 2005), especially 48–51.

19. F. Fellini, "Fellini contro Rossellini," *Tempo* (5 October 1966). My italics.

20. G.P. Brunetta, *Storia del cinema italiano, vol. 3. Dal neorealismo al miracolo economico 1945-1959* [History of the Italian Cinema, from Neorealism to the Economic Boom] (Rome: Editori Riuniti, 1993), 512.

21. See N. Misler, *La via italiana al realismo. La politica del PCI dal 1944 al 1956* [The Italian Route to Realism: The Policy of the PCI from 1944 to 1956] (Milan: Mazzotta, 1976 [1973]), especially 21–29.

22. "This is the kind of art I like," Marcello replies, "useful tomorrow, I think. An art that is clear, limpid, without rhetoric. That doesn't tell lies or adulate."

23. N. Misler, *La via italiana al realismo*, 81.

24. N. Misler, *La via italiana al realismo*, 82.

25. N. Ajello, *Intellettuali e Pci*, 318.

26. "Furthermore, a film like *La strada* seems out of its time, closed in itself and with no love for humanity (portrayed in the ravings of three lunatics), just where it shows so much love for the trees and the stones in Creation." A. Scagnetti, *"La strada," l'Unità*, 2 October 1954.

27. G.L. Rondi, in *Il Tempo*, 10 October 1954.

28. L. Chiarini, "I pericoli de *La strada*" [The Dangers of *La strada*], *Il Contemporaneo*, 9 October 1954.

29. M. Mia, "Lettera aperta a Federico Fellini" [Open Letter to Federico Fellini], *Il Contemporaneo*, 19 March 1955.

30. In N. Ajello, *Intellettuali e Pci*, 342.

31. See *Il Contemporaneo*, 28 April 1955.

32. His Holiness Pope Pius XII, *Discorsi sul film ideale. Primo discorso* [Addresses on the Ideal Film: First Address], 21 June 1955 (published in *Rivista del Cinematografo* on 7 July 1955 and now in *Storia del cinema italiano, vol. 9. 1954-1959*, ed. S. Bernardi (Venice: Marsilio, 2004), 593–597.

33. F. Fellini, "Conclusioni sul dibattito sul neorealismo" [Conclusions from the Debate on Neorealism], *Il Contemporaneo*, 28 May 1955 (letter from Fellini to Trombadori).

34. In relation to this, see V.S. Severino, "Ernesto De Martino nel PCI degli anni Cinquanta tra religione e politica culturale" [Ernesto De Martino in the PCI in the Fifties, Religion and Cultural policy], *Studi storici* 44, no. 2 (2003) 527–553.

35. N. Ajello, *Intellettuali e Pci*, 338.

36. T. Kezich, *Federico Fellini*, 153–154. In his book, *Fare un film*, Fellini speaks about De Martino in relation to his own travels across the length and breadth of

the country and his search for the "mysterious and paranormal" in Italy. Dino Buzzati had written an article on the same subject, collected in *I misteri d'Italia* [Mysteries of Italy] See "Fellini nel suo nuovo film ha fatto incontri paurosi" [Fellini's Frightful Meetings] (Milan: Mondadori, 1978). The film Buzzati is describing is *Giulietta degli spiriti*.

37. *L'espresso* revealed the news of the finding of the script on 4 March 2011.

38. E. De Martino, *Sud e magia* [The South and Magic] (Milan: Feltrinelli, 1959), 119–120.

39. The discussion took place in the Eliseo Theater in Rome on 21 February 1960, when Fellini was awarded a "Golden Chaplin." It was reported that "Ernesto De Martino confined himself, as a sociologist, to testifying to the truth of ethnography beneath the aesthetic truth of the scene of the false miracle." *Hanno riempito il teatro Eliseo sulla Dolce Vita* [The Eliseo Theater is Filled by the Dolce Vita], l'*Unità*, 22 February 1960.

40. E. Galli Della Loggia, *L'identità italiana*, 48.

41. F. Faeta, *Le ragioni dello sguardo. Pratiche dell'osservazione, della rappresentazione e della memoria* [The Reasons of the Gaze: Practices in Observation, Representation and Memory] (Turin: Bollati Boringhieri, 2011), 53. "To understand important aspects of De Martino's work," Faeta writes, "it is first necessary to thoroughly analyze the context of neorealism in dialectic relationship with the realist claims that unfailingly characterize ethnographic and anthropological consciousness." See also F. Faeta, *Questioni italiane. Demologia, antropologia, critica culturale* [Italian Questions: Demology, Anthropology, Cultural Criticism] (Turin: Bollati Boringhieri, 2005).

42. E. De Martino, *La terra del rimorso. Contributo a una storia religiosa del Sud* [The Land of Remorse: Contribution to the Religious History of the South] (Milan: Il Saggiatore, 1961), especially chapter 4 for its explanation of the "domestic paradigm."

43. For a reconstruction of the reactions of the Catholic world to *La dolce vita*, see T. Subini, "Il caso 'Dolce vita'," in *Attraverso lo schermo. Cinema e cultura cattolica in Italia* [Via the Cinema Screen: Film and Catholic Culture in Italy], ed. R. Eugeni and D. Viganò (Rome: Eds, 2006), vol. 2, 239–253, and T. Subini, "L'arcivescovo di Milano e 'La dolce vita'" [The Archbishop of Milan and *La dolce vita*], *Bianco e nero* no. 567 (2011), 33–43, which examines key documents for the understanding of the Archbishop and future pope's opinions, held by the Montini Foundation in the Historical Archives of the Diocese of Milan. See also A. Arpa, *Federico Fellini: La dolce vita. Cronaca di una passione* [Federico Fellini: *La dolce vita*, Chronicle of a Passion] (Cantalupo in Sabna: Edizioni Sabinae, 2010).

44. See T. Kezich, *Federico Fellini*.

45. See A. Prosperi, *Intellettuali e Chiesa all'inizio dell'età moderna* [Intellectuals and the Church at the Beginning of the Modern Age] (Turin: Einaudi, 1981), 161–252.

46. A. Arpa, *L'Arpa di Fellini* (Rome: Edizioni dell'Oleandro, 2001), 51–52.

47. P. Bertetto, "Fellini, la religione, lo spettacolo" [Fellini, Religion, Spectacle], in *Cinema e religioni*, ed. S. Botta and E. Prinzivalli (Rome: Carocci, 2010).

48. A. Moravia, *Un défilé col cardinale* [The Cardinal's Catwalk], *L'espresso*, 26 March 1972, 23.

49. The text was the result of a conversation between de Certeau and the director of the magazine *Esprit*, Jean-Marie Domenach, on 22 May 1973, in the *Dialogues* series of French public radio, broadcast by France Culture.

50. M. de Certeau and J. Marie Demenach, *Le Christianisme éclaté* [Christianity in Pieces] (Paris: Seuil, 1974).

51. Trans. by S. Morra of M. de Certeau and J. Marie Demenach, "Raccogliendo frantumi" [Collecting the Pieces], in *Il cristianesimo in frantumi* (Cantalupa: Effatà, 2010), 13

52. M. Giori, "8 ½ e il cinema come istituzione. Il film difficile di Fellini e la cultura italiana del suo tempo" [*8 ½* and Cinema as an Institution: Fellini's Difficult Film and the Italian Culture of the Day], in *Federico Fellini. Analisi di film: possibile letture* [Federico Fellini: Film Analysis: Possible Readings], ed. R. De Berti (Milan: McGraw-Hill, 2006), 76.

53. See Schellenberg's trilogy *Prolegomena to a Philosophy of Religion* (2005), *The Wisdom to Doubt: A Justification of Religious Skepticism* (2007), and *The Will to Image: A Justification of Skeptical Religion* (2009), all published by Cornell University Press.

54. See the exhibition catalogue edited by Stourdzé at the Jeu de Paume, Paris, Fellini la Grande Parade (20 October 2009–17 January 2010), published by Édition Anabet, Paris, 2010.

55. With *La settimana Incom*, one of the most important film journals of the postwar period.

56. From a folder held by the Montini Foundation and cited in T. Subini, "L'arcivescovo di Milano," 36. My italics.

57. See P. Bertetto, "Fellini, la religione, lo spettacolo," and A. Costa, *La dolce vita* (Turin: Lindau, 2010).

58. P.P. Pasolini, "*La dolce vita*: Per me si tratta di un film cattolico" [*La dolce vita*: For Me It Is a Catholic Film] (23 February 1960), now in Pasolini, *I film degli altri* [Others' Films], ed. T. Kezich (Parma: Guanda, 1995), 57.

59. M. de Certeau and J.-M. Domebach, *Le Christianisme éclaté*, 30.

60. Recently a Lacanian interpretation of *La dolce vita* has been put forward, according to which both Steiner—the intellectual who commits suicide—and Marcello's father are to be thought of as symptoms of a general nostalgia for the order of society before the war and hence for the "Law" enshrined in fascism. Hence the film has something to do with a sort of anatomy of the "death of desire" in the newborn, unregulated society of the spectacle Fellini portrays. See F. Vighi, *Sexual Difference in European Cinema: The Curse of Enjoyment* (Hampshire: Palgrave Macmillan, 2009). I am grateful to Claudio Bisoni for pointing me toward this book.

61. See J. Risset, *L'incantatore. Scritti su Fellini* [The Charmer: Writings on Fellini] (Milan: Scheiwiller, 1994).

62. Father Nazareno Taddei was attacked by the *Osservatore Romano* and by *Civiltà Cattolica* and was forced to leave the San Fedele Catholic Center in Milan, where he was running film courses. For details, see T. Subini, *Il caso La dolce vita*.

63. G. Marramao, "'Tempo pagano' e 'tempo cristiano' in Pier Paolo Pasolini" [Pagan Time and Christian Time in PPP], in Marramao, *Potere e secolarizzazione* [Power and Secularization] (Turin: Bollati Boringhieri, 2005 [1983]), 278–282.

64. Ibid., 281.

65. See *L'ultima sequenza* [The Final Scene], a documentary by Mario Sesti (ITA 2004). These statements were recorded by Gideon Bachman on the set of *8 ½*.

66. Alberto Albasino excelled in his article in *Il Giorno* on 6 March 1963. In relation to the film, in addition to the more obvious, he cited *Lola Montès* by Max Ophuls, Dostoevsky, Musil, Flaubert, Balzac, Dickens, Cocteau, Citati, and, as if that were not enough, Giacomo Devoto's observations in *Castello di Udine* in *Studi di stilistica*, edited by M. Giori.

67. T. Kezich, *Federico Fellini*, 365.

68. "Onomatopoeia is part of the complicity between Guido and Carla, who immediately on her arrival in the spa tells him the latest Donald Duck story she has read. Guido imagines her reading Pluto at the beginning of the sixth dream sequence and doesn't have scruples about mentioning the world of cartoons to others, for example calling Claudio's agent Super Tarzan." M. Giori, "*8 ½ e il cinema come istituzione*," 81.

69. See *L'ultima sequenza*.

70. A. Gramsci, "Passaggio dal sapere al comprendere, al sentire e viceversa, dal sentire al comprendere, al sapere" [Passage from Knowing to Understanding and Feeling, and Vice Versa from Feeling to Understanding and Knowing], Q. 18, now in Gramsci, *Il materialismo storico* [Historical Materialism] (Rome: Editori Riuniti, 1971), 136.

71. See the interview with Arbasino in the DVD made by Gianni Borgna and produced by the Luce Institute, *Vita culturale a Roma dal '44 al '68* [Cultural Life in Rome from 1944 to 1968] and *Parigi o cara* (1960) [Paris, My Dear].

72. I. Montanelli in *Corriere della Sera*, 22 January 1960.

73. F. Chiarotto, *Operazione Gramsci*, 23.

74. F. Chiarotto, *Operazione Gramsci*, 24.

Chapter 2

Mythical Biography of a Nation

> *Federico Fellini "remembers" but doesn't do autobiography.*
> —Alberto Moravia

> *In the world of* Amarcord *we can see ourselves and we can see Italy; those years seem to be evoked not out of private, personal, experience but from a sort of choral memory, singing at the top of its voice.*
> —Natalia Ginzburg

> *Who are you? — You're nobody. All of you! All.*
> —*I vitelloni*

Italian-ness as a Work of Art

Notoriously, the work of Fellini has been canonized with the adjective *Felliniano*, Fellini-esque, which the Treccani dictionary defines as referring to: "the particular atmospheres, situations and characters of his films, characterized by strong autobiography, the evocation of the life of the provinces with the grotesque tones of caricature, and by fascinating oneiric visions."[1]

The emphasis on autobiography and the life of the provinces immediately calls to mind *I vitelloni* and *Amarcord*, both dialect words that have entered into the Italian language thanks to Fellini, respectively as "a young man of the provinces, idle, indolent, who spends his time in amusements and has no ambition" and "a nostalgic re-evocation of the past." Yet *I vitelloni* is based on the memory of an imaginary province, albeit not as "fake" as the reconstruction in *Amarcord*, with its plastic sea and cardboard ocean liner.

Amarcord is a compendium of Fellini's aesthetic, the reinvention of a reality distilled from its archetypes, filmed with evident theatricality.

The twenty years between *I vitelloni* (1953) and *Amarcord* (1973) were years of decisive transformation. *Amarcord* is Fellini's first evidently political film. Albeit reinvented in memory, Fellini's autobiography, and its reevocation of everyday life under fascism, gains a collective dimension.

In relation to *Amarcord*, Angelo Arpa said that "it is apparently nostalgic about a world that has gone, but is actually about a continuing mental transformation"; "its intimate structure," that is to say, "is based on claims that we might say belong to the sphere firstly of political ethics and only secondarily of poetical realism."[2]

As we will see, *Amarcord* demonstrated what Fellini's films had always been about and would continue to be: the extension of autobiography into a massive *mytho-biography of the nation*. The expression recalls the work of Ernst Bernhard,[3] the Jungian psychoanalyst Fellini consulted at the beginning of the sixties; it also echoes the famous saying of Pietro Gobetti, according to which fascism was not so much a political movement as the "autobiography of the nation," something rooted in the mentality and character of Italians.

In bringing two such distant references together, I am suggesting that Fellini's attraction to the dreamwork, the unconscious, and archetypes is inseparable from his thinking about Italian identity, which in his films takes on increasingly political shades.

Fellini's insistence on the so-called archetype of the "Great Mediterranean Mother," developed theoretically by Bernhard, is relevant here.[4]

In an interview from 1965, Fellini spoke of this archetype (ignored by the adjective Fellini-esque) within the framework of a series of stereotypes of Italian identity with which he associated the recurring motif of his films: infantilism and the inability to leave adolescence behind, and hence their permanence in (Italian) life: "Italians don't want to know themselves or discover in themselves any home truths; they slam the door shut on any attempt to talk to themselves. Out of an almost animal laziness, they look elsewhere for protection: society, their mother, the Church, political parties. We are wrapped in infantile protective swaddling clothes, as if we couldn't let go of the large teat. We don't want to grow up, to become adults. Maybe it's part of Mediterranean civilization, this way of being a mummy's boy. Hence the omnipotence of the family and the lack of confidence in ourselves."[5]

This rhetorical use of the third person in discussions about national character was used by Francesco Cossiga for the title of a book: *Italians Are*

*Always Someone Else.*⁶ And, here, it is not clear whether Fellini is talking about himself or "others"; this confusion between his own autobiography and the biography of the nation is what inspires his inventiveness. His creativity, in which the unconscious, dreamwork, melancholy, and spectacle play such an important role, is part of an inner search belonging to a precise culture and mentality. On the death of Fellini, the film critic Goffredo Fofi, often very critical of Fellini in the seventies, confessed:

> I found this identification of the artist and the cultural humus of the country disconcerting and, at times, just dismissed it, because it shoved under your nose something that was so deeply a part of you that you wanted to be rid of it. Fellini was certainly generous with Italy, but that was because of a profound understanding and deep love of the country, with all its qualities and defects. Perhaps generosity is not the right word: he described the good and bad in Italy with feeling, and the proper reading of his films shows him to have been able to scrutinize, discuss, and analyze them from a point of view that was certainly not that of the Church nor one of parochialism and patriotism, and unlike that of social and economic research institutes or televised debates on the state of the nation, fashionable these days. Fellini understood *us*—us Italians—like *no other* contemporary artist.⁷

Fofi, who admitted that time had proven Fellini right about *Prova d'orchestra* (which he had panned), concluded his tribute by saying that Fellini's films were the "cornerstone of an anthropological reading of Italy, which Italy desperately needed."

In 1993, when Fellini was in Los Angeles for the career Oscar, Italian journalists asked him what he thought about the current political corruption scandals in his country. Fellini was angrier with the common people than with the politicians: "We should all think about what it means to be Italian, and we should understand that what happens happens because we made it happen. Day to day, do we not live with complicity, make compromises, demands and betray the trust of others?"⁸

The historian Luca Canfora replied: "Is Fellini depressed? Are Italians complicit because they voted for the Christian Democrats? He was the first to be complicit. It is inaccurate to say that Italians are corrupt by nature... I think Fellini was talking about the submissiveness of Italians who rewarded a certain political class with their votes. Perhaps he was saying, 'We should have got rid of them sooner.'"⁹

Perhaps. However, in relation to the scandals collectively known as Tangentopoli, what interested Fellini—increasingly critical of Italian society in his later years—was not political analysis but the anthropological aspects of the phenomenon, however that might have appeared to be politically disengaged. In his films, invective is subordinate to visual invention, which dominates. Fellini doesn't "describe" the virtues and vices of Italians. His cinema is not a "mirror of society" as the saying goes, and Fellini was not a sociologist. His films do not display the customs of the country as the comic tradition of popular Italian cinema does, but place his own Italian identity in full view, *as a work of art.*

This is true not only of his films. Fellini was keen on creating the public image of himself as a "magician," "witchdoctor," and "snake charmer" (just some of the terms used to describe him) as well as country bumpkin unable to free himself of a repressive Catholic upbringing.

His public image was therefore a mixture of two stereotypes about Italians: the creative artist and "maestro" and, by a sort of "reverse patriotism," a heap of irredeemable defects. But just how do the two adjectives Fellini-esque and Italian go together?

Italian Graffiti

Summer 2011. Larusmiani, a famous Italian trademark in the tailoring industry, launches a collection, calling it a "remake of *I vitelloni* by Federico Fellini." In the photos, elegantly dressed models are shown inside a famous Milanese bar, sitting at tables, exhibiting a carefree air, drinking, sharing a joke. Helped by the retro look of the bar, the scene—despite the additional luxury—is reminiscent of the idleness of Fausto, Alberto, Moraldo, Leopoldo, and Riccardo, who spent their afternoons lazing about in bars, as immortalized in the poster of the film, in which the characters are shown in relaxed attitude: the essence of Italian *laissez-faire*.[10]

October 2007. The Economics Minister Tommaso Padoa-Schioppa appears before the Joint Parliamentary Budget Committee; commenting on a measure aimed to help out young people with their rent, the minister talks at length about young Italians who—unlike their European cousins— "stay at home, do not marry and fail to become independent." And calls them "mummy's boys."

The remark causes an uproar. The minister is accused of overlooking the lack of jobs for the young and the precarious employment of those who do have a job, making it impossible for them to leave home. Some upbraid him for ignoring the fact that the problem is cultural, not economic; it is part of the Italian way of life, not a contingent reality based on the employment market.

Unsurprisingly, Fellini's film and neologism cropped up in discussions about the epithet used by the minister.[11] One scene from the film comes readily to mind: Alberto (Alberto Sordi) consoles his mother after the departure of his sister, who has eloped, "You'll see, mamma, *I'm not going anywhere*...I'm going to stay here with you." The framing of the shot opens up and shows us the armchair in the dining room into which Alberto later sinks. His mother asks him with concern whether he has found a job: "No," he replies as if astonished by the question, falling asleep with his feet up.

Larusmiani evidently used the film to evoke a relaxed, untroubled lifestyle of enjoyment and pleasure. The word used by the minister, on the other hand, recalls the connection between indolence and childishness in family-based Italian life and culture. In the first case, the relaxed lifestyle of Italians is something others admire and may feel they lack; but the second case is an example of what others certainly do not envy about Italians and which, perhaps, needs correcting. It is not a question of opposites—relaxation against babyishness—but of a mechanism that is often thought of as the basis of Italian national character.

As the most sophisticated cultural studies have shown, national traits are discursive *relational* formations. They are created, that is to say, by closely knit networks of thought, images, and motifs in which the idea that a nation has of itself is continuously placed in relation to what other nations think of it. This is particularly true of Italy where the sense of the nation is weak and the tendency to self-denigration strong, making for an inferiority complex based on the feeling that other countries are more modern and civilized.

A similar dynamic can be seen elsewhere in countries that came to nationhood late in life; in discussions about their identity they tend to accept the negative image imposed on them down through the ages by nations with a longer and stronger tradition. In this "trading of stereotypes," ideas about the Italian temperament, character, and customs, seen from outside the country, are particularly relevant: "Needing to build for itself an image in the teeth of the idea of other, more self-confident and historically stronger nations, Italian patriots and nationalists often wavered between two extremes, an arrogant affirmation of Italian cultural 'superiority' and a discouraging and deprecating sense of inferiority."[12]

And this is also true of *I vitelloni*, which portrays both the enviably relaxed Italian way of life and its childishness and feeling of inferiority in relation to other cultures. The ambiguity of Fellini's films and their extraordinary wealth of conflicting meanings is part of this dynamic.

Of all Fellini's films, *I vitelloni* (and, to a lesser extent, *Il bidone* [The Swindle]) is the closest to Italian comic cinema, which was just getting going at the time. Actually, it would be more accurate to say that the tradition of Italian cinema comedy owes something to Fellini rather than the other way around. Alberto Sordi became one of the most recognizable figures in the comic genre and "the actor who best exemplified the character of a nation of acrobats in life and history,"[13] because Fellini—against the wishes of the producers after the failure of *Lo sceicco bianco*—insisted on him for *I vitelloni*.

Where Italian film comedy told the story of the average Italian and of life transformed by the economic miracle, Fellini explored the archetypes of Italian identity. These included, on the one hand, the Catholic Church / myth of Rome, and on the other, his provincial birthplace, Mussolini, Casanova, Pinocchio, a kaleidoscope of symbols of the *bel paese*. Soon, of course, these symbols were to include Fellini himself, as the *Campari* commercial he made in the eighties shows: by then, he stood alongside other world-famous symbols of Italy embodying art (the Leaning Tower of Pisa), beauty (the countryside), and creativity (Fellini himself).

If, as Maurizio Grande has said, the *commedia all'italiana* is the "Iliad of a country that is frayed, provisional, roguish, indestructible and unchangeable," Fellini's films are its artistic counterpoint, writ large in dreams and "visions."

Unlike Antonioni, the ideal filmmaker of the crisis of the bourgeoisie, Fellini's anti-intellectualism and empathy with popular forms of entertainment express an anxiety about the nature of what it means to be Italian and turn this crisis into art, not the "art of getting by" featured so prominently in the Italian comic tradition, but Art as admired the world over, Art as the heir to the Renaissance, lyricism, and the sweet life.

To make his Art, Fellini transformed a whole range of stereotypes of Italian identity into poetics. It is not surprising that *I vitelloni*, Fellini's first success in Italy, was also the first of his films to be distributed internationally.

In 1954, in an article dedicated to *La strada*, Guido Aristarco famously said that the "Fellini phenomenon" was less about "the art of filmmaking than a way of life, a psychology and sociology." He wondered why his films, "starting from their titles—*I vitelloni* and the announced *Il bidone*—enter, or seem destined to enter, common parlance and become part of our everyday speech."[14] Six years later, with the extraordinary success of *La dolce vita*, Fellini entered the common parlance of the world, making the term synecdochal for Italian stylishness.

In view of his fascination with archetypes, investigating the relationship between Fellini's imagination and Italian character involves a "discourse on ideas, subject matter, topics and tropes that are recurrent and *have existed in Italian culture for a very long time*."[15] Fellini doesn't so much use his memory as draw on sediments of cultural memory and "make cultural and autobiographical memory coincide."[16]

Alberto or Effeminacy

In his study, Peter Bondanella says that Fellini distances himself from neorealism by a new and distinctive conception of film character.

While the leading characters in *La terra trema* and *Ladri di biciclette,* or *Riso amaro* and *Umberto D.,* "reflect specific historical conditions in postwar Italy and can be understood primarily in terms of their social surroundings," this is not the case in Fellini's films, which "offer characters that are atypical and willfully eccentric" and "exist in a particular Fellinian fictional world, an environment that privileges the interplay of illusion or fantasy with reality rather than the representation of economic and social realities." The protagonists of Fellini's first films "may well embody certain values typical of a particular historical period or a specific social class, but they are closer in conception to the stock character of the *commedia dell'arte* as well as the caricatures Fellini drew during his days with *Marc'Aurelio,* sketches capturing with a few strokes of the pen universal human qualities transcending a particular moment in time."

I have quoted at length[17] because I think it is worth highlighting one aspect of this analysis. Bondanella emphasizes the exclusivity of Fellini's creativity, an anomaly and absolutely original for Italian filmmaking at the time ("atypical, willfully eccentric") yet sees in this a conception that derives from the *commedia dell'arte,* in other words the quintessential Italian theatrical tradition of masks and stock characters. Bondanella and most commentators rightly emphasize the singular point of view of Fellini in relation to the social issues of the postwar period. Brunetta, for example, says that Fellini's characters "are not sought or found by chance in the streets"—as they were in the stereotypical version of neorealism—"but are the result of a legacy of *prior experience.*"[18] This prior experience is not confined to Fellini's personal life and his apprenticeship as a journalist, cartoonist, screenwriter, and writer for the radio. So where do the characters of *I vitelloni* come from if they have almost nothing in common with neorealism?

The newspapers of the time show that the critics were divided between a biographical reading of the film ("Fellini says he was once a *vitellone* himself and hence is ideally placed to tell the story of these youngsters and their strange ways and customs"[19]), and the version of the film as social analysis ("these *vitelloni* are Italian and provincial";[20] "children of the Italian bourgeoisie";[21] "life's perennial adolescents...provincial layabouts"[22]). In *l'Unità,* Ugo Casiraghi criticized the film for its failure to explicitly censor "sponging good-for-nothings, almost thirty years old but still kids."

The film entered into one of the liveliest discussions of the time, the debate about "mummy's boys," provoked by Corrado Alvaro (in a 1952 essay),[23] and by the anthropological research of Edward Banfield and his analysis of "amoral familism" in Italy.[24] Yet the film can also be seen in relation to two tropes of the Italian identity whose origins go back much further than the fifties: *idleness* and *effeminacy*.

Silvana Patriarca points out that idleness was considered by authors such as Balbo, Gioberti, and Carlo Lozzi (the latter having produced a mighty tome on the subject in 1870–1871) to be one of the great obstacles to the construction of the nation and national identity. Moreover, "in terms of the degeneration of the image of Italy, this idleness had a strong gender bias."[25] Idleness and effeminacy were the interwoven dual characteristics of the profound failings of the Italian character.

Could there be a more eloquent example of this Italian archetype than the cross-dressing sequence during the carnival scene in *I vitelloni*? As we know, it is a fundamental moment in the film:

> Alberto's moment of truth occurs during a masked carnival ball, an even more obvious arena for Fellini's presentation of the interplay of illusion and reality, mask and face. Fellini has Alberto dance about the ballroom in a drunken stupor, hugging a giant papier-mâché head while wearing an outlandish woman's costume, as if to set him apart from his stronger and self-reliant sister… Only while intoxicated does Alberto enjoy a moment of introspection or ask serious questions about the purpose of his life, as he turns to Moraldo and says: 'Who are you?… You're nobody. You're all nobody! … All of you. All.' … Alberto's illusions about himself are finally destroyed when he returns home from the ball and discovers that Olga has decided to leave with her lover, a married man.[26]

The same pose was struck by Sordi, embracing a huge papier-mâché mask, in a document produced by RAI state television in 1975 called *E il Casanova di Fellini?* (And Fellini's Casanova?). Scripted, the actor tries to convince Fellini to give him the role of Casanova, to whom, he says, he is able to bear "a striking resemblance." And what we see is a mirror image of the carnival scene from *I vitelloni*, with the added irony of the effeminacy of the mummy's boy set against the myth of the great Venetian lover and seducer.

Partly because of the famous gesture of derision directed at road workers (left hand brought violently to the forearm of the outstretched right arm, the equivalent of raising a middle finger), of all the characters in *I vitelloni*, it is Alberto who made an indelible mark on the collective imagination of Italian filmgoers. Alberto is the quintessential *vitellone*. He is a mummy's boy, petty, childish, cowardly, a mixture that Alberto Sordi would portray again and again throughout his career, earning him the reputation as the actor who best embodied the average Italian.

In his review, Moravia says that Alberto is "the most successful and original" character in the film, while *l'Unità*—with a premonition of where Sordi would take the character in the future—called him "a comic character that strikes fear into the heart." For Bondanella, Alberto is "the most pathetic of the vitelloni... a weak and slightly effeminate wastrel who lives with his mother off the wages of his sister Olga, while nevertheless pretending to know how to protect the family honor from any slip in *her* behavior."[27]

It is a description that recalls further deeply rooted stereotypes of Italian-ness:

> In one of the most authoritative texts of early Romanticism, *Corinne, ou l'Italie* (1807), Madame de Staël, the proud opponent of Napoleon, represented the sad situation of Italy through the tragic destiny of the eponymous heroine, portraying Italians as effeminate and idle: *in Italy, men are worth so much less than women because they have the defects of the women as well as their own*, says the leading male character, the Englishman, Lord Nevil; Corinne—half Italian—while defending her fellow countrymen, says: "Italians are as lazy as Orientals in everyday life... Life is nothing more than a long sleep full of dreams under a beautifully clear sky."[28]

Marcello

Madame de Staël's words sound like a definition *ante litteram* of the sweet life. Dictionaries define *dolce vita* as "a frivolous life of pleasure" and "a life of luxury, pleasure and self-indulgence."[29] In other words, *dolce vita* has a great deal to do with the *dolce far niente* commonly used to describe life in Italy in the nineteenth century.

Fellini takes the stereotype and uses it at the moment of transition from the fifties to the sixties in which Italy is becoming famous for its fashion, design, and architecture, and is generally thought of as chic. Being Italian means something.

In the wake of the myth of the "dolce vita," in 1964 the Italian-American journalist Luigi Barzini Junior published *The Italians*, a book that was to be a best seller for many years. In it he described the Italian character to the Anglo-Saxon world and earlier, in the fifties, he had had an idea for a film, *Happy Country*,[30] which Fellini and Pinelli wrote a script for, although nothing came of it. In *The Italians*, for the benefit of the many Americans arriving, he set out to give a historical and cultural guide to the country. The book boils down to a prolonged analysis of the vices and defects of the Italian character, unfailingly investigating the well-known stereotypes of theatricality, seductiveness, deception, the tyranny of the family, the "crypto-matriarchal" form of Italian society, everyone's chronic inability to govern the country, and so on.[31]

Nonetheless, in the wake of the "dolce vita," these inclinations were reexamined in light of the new incarnation of the *Latin lover*, Marcello Mastroianni. Sensual, with a mysterious air, shuffling around Rome with a perennially bored expression, he walks into a series of situations, all of them of the utmost elegance (as, later, James Bond would finish the most violent of scuffles with an immaculately pressed jacket).

Marcello's wanderings are a descent into the underworld updated to the times of Italian glamour and "Hollywood on the Tiber." The rhapsodic structure of the film has been compared to Dante's *Divine Comedy* (leading some critics to compare the creativity of the two artists), symptomatic of a perception that Italian style depended on "the unique ability of the country to bring the creativity of the past to bear on today's industrial production."[32]

In relation to idleness and sloth in literature, Salman Rushdie has recently written:

> Fellini, of course, is the supreme artist of enervated sloth. His protagonist is, almost always, some sort of a *vitellone*: a loafer, sometimes poor, sometimes affluent, always a wastrel, whose supreme incarnation is the Mastroianni of *La Dolce Vita* and *8 ½*, alienated, melancholy, drifting, passive, lost. There he goes, Marcello of the tired eyes, handsome and weak, a cigarette in his hand and a woman by his side, a woman he is in the process of losing. Along the via Veneto he wanders, down along dirty side alleys and up again into the world of the sweet life, into the homes of the rich. He meanders through slow, decadent parties, seized by inaction, by an inability to make choices or to move his life forward, a paralysis of the spirit.[33]

As is well known, Mastroianni in *La dolce vita* is literally an invention of Fellini's (just look at the same actor in other films of the period): fake eyelashes, slightly balding, heavy makeup to soften the facial features, cheekbones highlighted. His elegant manner, coupled with his effeminate yet dark features, made him the epitome of the *Latin lover*, an epithet Mastroianni often joked about, pointing out that in the film he fails to seduce a single woman.

Jacqueline Reich suggests that he represents *ineptitude* and is an antihero with weak masculinity, a character used by Italian cinema in the postwar period to exorcise the fascist model of the invincible male. The crisis of Italian masculinity in the period of the economic boom was symptomatic of a wider crisis in tradition: "the configuration of the masculine identity which reached its apotheosis—amid a thousand contradictions and ambiguities—in the 20 years of fascism, now changed in a period in which the undeniable sacredness of the tradition was receiving hammer blows from new and fascinating forms of modernity."[34]

In those years of rapid transformation in relation to consumerism, the feminization of Italian society was considered by some observers to be inevitable and, by the more progressive of them, desirable. A "reformed masculinity" was a consequence of the new subjectivity at work in modern urban society:

> During this period, an ideal classification of the popular view of the quintessential characteristics of masculinity would have seen the decline from their previous top positions of rough workman's hands, an austere work ethic and physical strength, and the rise of the ability to climb the social ladder, mass produced status symbols (primarily cars) and a degree of personal hygiene and tidiness: "Having a place in the world" in other words had become much less a question of virility; previously that had often been enough to guarantee a position of respect in the village, i.e., the world. Not many people knew much about anything outside the village.[35]

Embodying this metamorphosis in society, Marcello comes to Rome from the provinces and wants to be a journalist, a writer. But Fellini makes him do more than simply represent a new masculinity: the Mastroianni created by Fellini for *La dolce vita* is the export version of this new masculinity and new model of Italian elegance, "an icon packaged for the foreign (particularly American) consumption of Italian goods (fashion, design, tourism), including explicitly sexualized images of Italian masculinity."[36]

If Marcello is the incarnation of the devirilization of Italian society ("due to mass culture" wrote Giorgio Bocca back then, "the Beautiful Country is becoming more genteel, less virile"), he is also, I think, a "postmodern" reworking of another Italian archetype, as old as the hills, and often mentioned in relation to the Italian character, the *cicisbeo*, or gallant.

In the seventeenth century, the term was the equivalent of the French *chevalier servant*, a man who accompanied a married woman to the idle rituals of the aristocracy. In his study of the phenomenon, Roberto Bizzocchi has shown how common these beaus were in eighteenth-century society, particularly in Italy, creating an enduring stereotype: "The essential reason for the mythology of the institution of the *cicisbeo* was unashamedly political and consisted in a judgment, or a prejudice rather, about the negativity of Italian society, a great civilization fallen on hard times, that was unable to climb out of prostration."[37]

Outside Italy, the *cicisbeo*, devoted to a life of idleness and frivolity, was considered a symbol of decadence and immorality, an institution that threatened the proper workings of society and reflected something rotten in the Italian character. But the term had, and still has, other meanings: "a dandy, a fop, a philanderer flitting around in the presence of women in an aura of frivolity, a habitué of a society of snobs, of television chat shows and Courtly antechambers... part effeminate, part gallant, at ease in high society."[38]

Marcello is a modern *cicisbeo*. One of the in-crowd, he goes to the most fashionable places in town, concerns himself with gossip, and wanders about in the salons and parties of Rome, accompanying young and bored aristocratic ladies (Maddalena) and beautiful actresses (Sylvia), despite being married to Emma. His ways and looks are perfect for the role: the cicisbeo "pays a great deal of attention to his image, his appearance in society, clothes and manners, and dedicates a lot of time to the company of ladies."[39] Hence he is "the effeminate and idle gentleman *par excellence* and the chosen target of anti-aristocratic satire at the end of the eighteenth century, such as *Il giorno* by Giuseppe Parini."[40] In Parini's satirical poem, set in the aristocratic circles of Milan (and structured much like Fellini's film, in separate and unrelated sequences comprising the day of a young Italian nobleman), he assigns a central role to the institution of *cicisbeismo*. Through a criticism of this institution, he shows his scorn for the feebleness and decadence of specifically the Italian aristocracy but, more generally, of the Italian national character, like Carducci after him, who (in *ça ira*) attacked his fellow Italians for continuing to be a "population of monks, brigands, tourist guides, and *cicisbei*."

If Marcello succeeds in fascinating foreign filmgoers with his immoral and unscrupulous behavior, his effeminacy and idleness, he does so while embodying ancient prejudices about the Italian national character. Unsurprisingly, one of the fiercest attacks on *La dolce vita* came from the conservative right and focused precisely on the watered-down male: "Sweet life? Yes, with the sickly sweetness of the diabetic. We have always preferred and continue to prefer bitter masculinity."[41]

An Enthusiastically Fascist Country

When *Amarcord* was released in 1973, the film was given the best reception by the general public since the onset of its disaffection with the filmmaker, dating back to *8 ½*.

In *Giulietta degli spiriti*, *Toby Dammit* (part of the omnibus film *Spirits of the Dead*), *Fellini-Satyricon,* and *Roma,* the visual pyrotechnics of the unconscious seemed to have ousted the need to communicate with filmgoers. *Amarcord* was different. The story is told in fragments, in separate sequences, but this time the overall effect of the fresco was clear to everyone.

Invited to the showing of a working copy of the film before synchronization—as was customary with Fellini—the critic Valerio Riva said it was utterly unlike his previous films:

> You go to see *Amarcord* knowing everything that has been rumored about the film: it is about Romagna in the thirties seen through the eyes of a boy, it is a container for all of Fellini's memories of his childhood... so you imagine it will be one memory after another, and you feel a little skeptical: a memoir, autobiography, something personal...what's it got to do with me, the spectator? For the first few reels the question buzzes somewhere at the back of the head... then everything changes. The moment when the film shifts direction, is steered somewhere else, is when the fascist officer arrives... Instead of an anthology of memories, you get the impression that you are viewing an essentially political film, the most explicitly political film ever made by Fellini—one in which, without much personal reference, everything is said about an entire period of Italian history and perhaps not only that period.[42]

Fascism had already been handled by Fellini in *I clowns* and *Roma*, albeit in isolated episodes unrelated to the overall development of the film. And these were certainly not the only films of the time to tackle the subject. In Italy, Bertolucci's *Il conformista* (1970), based on the novel by Moravia, had caused a huge stir, but Fellini, Italy's least political filmmaker, making a film of personal and collective memory about the fascist period? That required a reappraisal of his cinema.

The film suggests an intrinsic relationship between the fascist and Italian mentalities. And it does so at a time when neofascist-inspired terrorism was creating nationwide tension and violence (the bomb in Piazza della Loggia, Brescia, exploded a few months after the release of the film). Fellini said:

> It isn't fascism seen, as in most political films today, with—what can I call it?—a judgmental approach, from the outside. Detached judgments, aesthetic diagnoses, definitive and absolute formulae always strike me as a little inhuman. The province of *Amarcord* is a place where we are all recognizable, myself above all, in the ignorance that got us all confused. Immense ignorance, massive confusion. Not that I want to play down the social and economic causes of fascism, but what interests me still today is the psychology and the emotions of being fascist. What are they? A sort of obstacle, a blockage at the adolescent stage of development.[43]

Amarcord bears less resemblance to the political films of the seventies than it does to a particular work by the performance artist Fabio Mauri. The show was called *Che cosa è il fascismo* (What is Fascism?) and was staged for the first time in the Safa Palatino Film Studios in Rome on 2

April 1971, featuring students of the Academy of Dramatic Arts. It was then included in the Venice Biennale of 1974. Mauri, too, started with autobiography: "I wanted to reconstruct what I'd seen and lived through: the 1939 Florence rally of the Italian youth Movement and Hitlerjungend. With *ludi juveniles*, athletes, intellectuals, artists, as was the syncretic and kitsch custom of the fascist and Nazi youth organizations. The two dictatorships mobilized the masses in massive theatrical sets. Undoubtedly lethal, deadly politicians, Hitler and Mussolini were first and foremost set designers with limitless budgets."[44]

What is Fascism? reproduced one of the *ludi juvenilis* with all its theatrical apparatus, the whole program. That way, the spectator was no longer outside but inside the event, "trapped halfway between reality and fiction, representation and apology, attraction and repulsion... a position that becomes increasingly uncomfortable, embarrassing, repugnant." As in *Amarcord*.

From the initial atmosphere of farce, with the arrival of the fascist officers "with running step," ushering in the Parade of 21 April, commemorating the birth of Rome, the sequence takes us to the embarrassing and repugnant scene in which we are forced to witness the humiliation of Titta's father swallowing castor oil, a mixture of acceptance and repulsion that Fellini said was part of his experience: "You feel that Italy is your country, is you, and if now you can look back on its history without pity, all the same it is a mirror. Then, all things considered, you feel that time has run out and the life you look back on pitilessly and which you would like to leave behind you, well...that is the only life you had."[45]

In a letter sent to *Il Tempo* in response to criticism and to explain his point of view, Fellini added: "... in the film there is a distance, a judgment and rejection, but that is not all, it's a little more complex that that, because all of this is accompanied by *nostalgia*. Yes, strange as it may seem, nostalgia for a world like that, because that was part of our life, and the regret is just as strong as the rejection."[46]

This is something not worked through that is relevant to all Italians, as is made clear by what many critics have remarked upon: the fact that the characters frequently look directly into the camera (the promotional posters emphasize this aspect of the film) and speak to the audience.[47]

Through his trademark poetic imagination, Fellini was describing a profound fracture in Italian society. Questioning oneself about fascism and its relationship to the national psyche, describing it as an inseparable part of Italian history, meant rejecting the temptation to expel it from the collective imagination, in order to relegate it to a mere *parenthesis* in Italian history (as Benedetto Croce famously described fascism) or to the metaphysical vagaries of "absolute evil." It would mean turning it into something foreign, extraneous to the true nature of "good folk" like the Italians, anti-fascists to a man, as many Italian films of the seventies portrayed them.

Clearly the discussion is fraught. It flared back into life following the seminal work on fascism first by Renzo De Felice and then by Emilio Gentile but continued to simmer. For many years, as De Felice wrote, "the unifying element that turned so many ordinary people into fascists"[48] was ignored. Recently, David Bidussa has written:

> Those events—which were and are a structural part of Italian history—involved Italians, their choices, their feelings, their convictions, and the advantages that fascism brought to a large number of the population. But also in play, once the regime had collapsed, was the Italian vice of immediately pushing those events away, as if fascism were something extraneous, and hence a refusal to take responsibility for what happened, for its workings, duration, and the large-scale approval it received. This is true of fascism and would be repeated for the first Republic as well.[49]

The choral fresco of *Amarcord* is the most evident example of what Calvino said of the film and of Fellini in general, that it portrayed the "symptoms of Italian hysteria."

At the same time it is one of Fellini's films with the widest appeal, appreciated and loved the world over precisely for the reasons (the nostalgia, the suffering over the past and in childhood) that made it ambiguous in Italy.[50]

At home, critics of the left and far left had numerous reservations about the film. Fellini was accused of portraying a papier-mâché fascism, historically inaccurate, glib, with no serious analysis. By showing the enthusiastic participation of the crowd in fascist parades, Fellini was failing in his duty to portray anti-fascism (in this, Fellini appears to have been of a like mind with Flaiano: "in Italy there are two types of fascist—fascists and anti-fascists").

The politics of *Amarcord* lie elsewhere, in the eternal adolescence of Italians, the childishness of the *vitelloni* and their collective rituals, which, in this film, have an ideological framing. It should be remembered that one of the initial working titles for the film was *Viva l'Italia*.

Affirming a link between the fascist mentality and the Italian national character, *Amarcord* takes up from some analyses of fascism from before the end of the war, before—that is to say—opportunism dictated the line suggested by Croce, that fascism was a sort of hiccup and Italians were essentially "good people." I am thinking of the works of Gobetti, Colamarino, Rosselli, Borgese, and, most specifically, of Fabio Cusin. *L'Italiano*, published in 1945, was one of the first studies of fascism to use psychology and psychoanalysis as part of its investigative tools. It was a hard-hitting attack on every level of Italian society and the Italian way of life, starting with the institution of the family, which was accused of being the cause of the recent ill-fated events in Italian history. Practically only Dante escapes Cusin's fierce criticism, and he is judged to have been "misunderstood by Italians, unable to look into their souls."[51] In *Amarcord*, the only icon of Italian culture and identity able to rival the Duce is Dante.

Amarcord and the "Italian Way of Seeing Things"

But *Amarcord* is also a film of the Fellini-esque, and perhaps this is what makes it so ideologically ambiguous.

The cardboard *Rex*, symbol of the megalomaniac dreams of fascist Italy, of the huge "floral" Duce who blesses the avant-garde wedding of Ciccio, the parade of fascist officers at the station which—left undisguised and recognizable—is actually the entrance to Cinecittà: in their excessive theatricality they are symbols both of the fascist idea of putting on a show and of Fellini's aesthetics.

The film's debt to caricature and comic strips has been noted by numerous commentators.[52] If *Amarcord* is the film in which "the relationship between caricature and filmic *mise-en-scène* is most organic,"[53] the same can be said of the essential spirit of fascist visual culture and the "gloomy melancholia" Mario Mafai saw in the paintings of Carrà and Scipione.[54] As though this were in itself Fellini-esque.

Caricature, as Gombrich says, "sets reality next to a deformed reproduction of it."[55] The "permanent spectacle" organized by fascism functioned similarly, in its constantly deformed transpositions of the Italian countryside, characterized by theatricality verging on the kitsch and grotesque. As Fellini said: "Since we are talking about a small town and a metaphorical closure, a lack of relations with the outside world, in this sense the film shows more evidently than before, and with greater clarity, what fascism was and what being a fascist meant in psychological and emotional terms: it meant being ignorant, domineering, exhibitionist, puerile."[56]

In *Amarcord*, the "metaphorical closure" recalls Fellini's *mise-en-scène*, his famously cloistered filmmaking in the studios of Cinecittà. "Theatrical," "baroque," "operatic"; these adjectives recur in Fellini criticism and refer not only to aesthetics but to a profound and unresolved relationship between the technology of modernity and the cultural heritage of Italian "visual civilization," investigated along with the ideological implications of an "Italian way of seeing" most lucidly by Giulio Bollati.

Via Walter Benjamin and Giacomo Leopardi, in a "draft for a possible chapter on Italian ideology dedicated to the visual and, in particular, to photography,"[57] Bollati interpreted the unique nature of Italian modernity and its crisis in terms of its relations with tradition, establishing a connection between photography and the "backwardness" of Italian society. The first figures of modernity who investigated photography (Baudelaire, Benjamin) and then the cinema (Benjamin, Kracauer) based their observations on countries (England, France, Germany) that could be unified within common paradigms, but Italy stood apart: its temporal features could not be aligned—according to Bollati—with those of other countries:[58] "The fact that Italy became an industrialized nation *so late* means that, among other things, traditional culture and a certain classical ascendancy persisted and became the most traditional and classical of any industrial country."[59]

Benjamin noted that the rapid development of photography and the impetuosity of the ideology that accompanied it had, for many years, prevented people from "looking back," but in Italy the new technology of photography was all about looking back, preserving traditional figurative culture and national aesthetics.

The lack of industry in recently unified Italy corresponded to a certain "way of seeing": "The first daguerreotypes reveal a Leopardian immobile Italy, moonlike, suspended over the abyss of the past. This image was destined to last for many years in the nineteenth century, and persists even today, where the asphalt roads of civilization by-pass deserted stretches of countryside and old collapsing villages."[60]

The weighty classical heritage, the lack of a true industrial revolution, the hostility against a true scientific culture, the primacy of "literary" expression—all of this made Italy particularly unsuited to assimilating the modernity of photographic "reality." It became a sort of process of mourning: the loss of primacy in the visual arts, the "decline of the *topos* that from the Renaissance onward considered us more skilled than other nations in the art of seeing and representing reality."[61]

In Bollati's view, this condemnation of positivism and of the "miserable cultivators of non-idealized truth" was an "ideological-fantastical nebula" that included Carducci, D'Annunzio, Pascoli, Croce, and Gentile.[62] And, we might add, Fellini.

Instead of following the implications of the modern "truth" of images, such as the loss of "aura" by the artwork, undermined, as Benjamin was to say, by its technical reproducibility, the opposite happened: between the nineteenth and twentieth centuries, Italian culture made an essentially theatrical use of photography. By this I mean the attempt to use the new medium to show the artist at work and the results of this work, following the classical rhetoric of the "beautiful," the magical afflatus of poetic creation, in forms and ways that lead—and could only have led—to a "pictorialism of the kitsch." The aesthetics of fascism are the culmination and triumph of this attitude.

Bollati's thoughts about photography show how Italy's reaction to modernity boiled down to "the illusion that its own was the only culture able to mediate between all others, in time and space, bridging East and West, *the archaic and science fiction*,"[63] (an illusion that was to find its apotheosis and defeat in fascism). Within the film world, Fellini took on a very similar role.

From *La dolce vita* on, Fellini's films are both the product of cinematographic modernity and an entirely new way of thinking about storytelling in film, and also the recovery of the most arcane forms of the spectacle, almost a revisitation by an auteur of the origins of cinema, with its papier-mâché seabeds, its uncertain syntax ("I would have liked to make films in 1920, to have been twenty years old then, at the time of the pioneers";[64] regret for an original and lost cinematic purity is another of the commonplaces of the Fellini myth).

In Fellini's hands, cinema—the symbolic form of late modernity—becomes an ancient magical ritual. Like a sort of reworking of the theatrical phantasmagoria of the seventeenth century and the cinematic synthesis of the entire Italian stage tradition. The Fellini myth, after all, is that of a Renaissance artist ("poet," "magician," "sorcerer"), plying his trade in the film industry.

At the beginning of the modern era, according to Bollati, the adjective "Italian" takes on a specific sense of backwardness and innovation, over which presides the reconciling spirit of "nostalgia."[65] It is a good description of Fellini's aesthetics. Yet *Amarcord* seems to say that the problem of Italy is not that it has lost its classical heritage and its links with a late lamented rural society, but the fact that it can never get far enough away from them.

Pinocchio, or the Allegory of Ideology

Without discussing Pinocchio, no conclusions, even of a sketchy nature, can be reached about Fellini and the Italian identity.

Although Fellini never made a film based on Collodi's character (Benigni tried and largely failed), this Italian icon circulated in his work like another archetype assimilated by Fellini's mythobiography. "He venerated *Pinocchio*," says Ermanno Cavazzoni, the author of *Poema dei lunatici*, filmed by Fellini as *La voce della luna*: "and told me it was *the* book about us

Italians, with its lying, its changes of heart, its bursting into tears, its mistakes, continuous mistakes, and the strict but forgiving Fairy Godmother. I don't think he ever thought of making a film—film adaptations of Kafka yes, I believe so—but, after all, Pinocchio is everywhere in his films."[66]

The essential traits given to Pinocchio by Collodi—the lack of discipline, the tendency to idleness, a permanent state of childhood and the wish to grow up—are features of all of Fellini's male characters.

And of Fellini himself. An integral part of the myth and legend he skillfully created about himself is that he "invented everything": "I make films because I like to tell fibs, invent fairy stories," he said, way back, at the time of *La strada*. Some titles rammed this myth-making home, such as *Fellini, Je suis un grand menteur* (a 2002 documentary by Damien Pettigrew) or *Ciò che abbiamo inventato è tutto autentico* (Everything We Invented Is Authentic), chosen for the publication of Fellini's letters to Tullio Pinelli. Or an image from *8 ½* in which Guido, sitting at a table of film critics, producers, actors, and extras working on the film he is pretending to make, dons a Pinocchio nose.

The myth of Fellini, who invented and told anecdotes about events that never actually happened, and was reluctant to be drawn into discussing the meaning of his films, has been passed on from book to book. Fellini, like Pinocchio, is childish, egocentric, the creator of the world in his own imagination. A world he manipulates, becoming its puppet master.

In a TV special filmed on the set of *La città delle donne*, featuring interviews with actresses and extras, Fellini was described as "a good man… a man who gives everyone a job…a father-figure…a big kid," but also as "a dictator, someone who treats you like a puppet, who does what he wants with you."[67] The poster for Pettigrew's documentary shows him as a giant puppet master pulling the strings of each character.

That there is something essentially Italian about Collodi's puppet is a standard reading of the text, from Benedetto Croce—who, albeit not single-handedly, rescued the book from neglect and turned it into one of the masterpieces of Italian literature—to Asor Rosa and others (leading to such a proliferation of interpretations that the term Pinocchiology was coined).[68] Its influence is still felt today. For example, the artist Maurizio Cattelan has recently acknowledged his own debt to this ghost of the Italian collective unconscious in relation to his "hanging children," part of an installation of that name in Milan.

Recent studies include Suzanne Stewart-Steinberg's *The Pinocchio Effect: On Making Italians, 1860-1920,* which provides a broader interpretation of Italian modernity. More than elsewhere, the unification of the nation forced Italians to face the void left by the traumatic separation of church and state. Partly because of this, specifically Italian subjectivity is constantly susceptible to questions about its origins and the "essence" of being Italian. These investigations operate as a counterbalance to the anxiety provoked by Italian modernity, seen as potentially destroying the previous sense of identity. According to Stewart-Steinberg, the unrelenting self-commiseration of Italians is not the sign of a lack of modernity, it is its true expression. An "anguished modernity," *always* fretting about its foundations.[69] Hence the importance of Collodi's fable. *Pinocchio* is an allegory of the fear of "being nobody" (and here we might think of Alberto, drunk, at the end of the carnival celebrations in *I vitelloni* and his: "Who are you?... You're nobody. You're all nobody!... All of you.") So what is the Pinocchio effect? It is the strange combination of anxiety about the potential emptiness of the Italian subject, his fictional and rhetorical quality, his immaturity and even inhuman, puppet nature, and yet also the profundity of Italian investigations of the social bond in a modern, post-liberal society that I have dubbed the Pinocchio Effect."[70]

The paradox of Pinocchio, a puppet that moves without strings, expresses both the need to obey power and the inner call for self-determination (independence, self-assertion).

> I put forward the hypothesis that the fable inaugurated a totally new space: a space not beyond ideology but which raises the problem of ideology itself. Pinocchio is an allegory of the functioning of ideology: he produces an ideological system and becomes its first victim. This is what struck me so powerfully about the end of this novel: when the puppet becomes a "real boy," he doesn't change from being a puppet into a boy, but becomes a double.
>
> Pinocchio leaves the puppet master behind and becomes something else. But he never quite leaves things behind, and this is fascinating. This part that remains will guide him in the future but will also follow and persecute him. It is both the father (or *maestro*) he has left behind and the trace of a pleasure he has somehow lost. Pinocchio is a dual subject, a subject lacerated by the orders of the father which tell him to renounce pleasure, but which therefore incite the pursuit of this pleasure.

If lying is the popular image most often associated with Pinocchio, often cited in connection with corrupt Italian politics and Italian duplicity, this interpretation has far wider ideological implications.

"In order to transgress," Fellini confessed, "I need a very rigid order, with many taboos, punishments wherever you turn, a moralistic order, processions, Alpine choirs. Only to be rewarded by the powers that be, the mayor, the Cardinal, as a transgressor who has acted with honor."[71] The Pinocchio running through the work of Fellini should be considered in this more complex light: as an Italian and emblem of the divided self.

It is this *divided subjectivity* and the continuous investigation of national character that fascinated Fellini about Pinocchio.

The dual ending of the fable also features in Fellini's films, in an equally ritualistic initiation. In the last scene of *I vitelloni*, Moraldo/Fellini decides to take the train to Rome and, as the critic Renzo Renzi has noted: "The final scene of the film is illuminating. It is typical, if not archetypical, of the filmmaker. Moraldo, Fellini's *alter ego*, leaves after rejecting the life and the world he has experienced until then. Yet, moments later, the young boy who comes to see him off at the station, he too is an embodiment of Fellini, returning home by the railway track, as if along a path he is obliged to follow."[72]

As Fellini confessed in a letter to the vice-chancellor of Bologna University, declining the offer of an honorary degree: "Allow me to speak confidentially, I would feel like Pinocchio decorated by the Headmaster and the Police for rioting in Toytown."

Notes

1. Page 120 of *The Dictionary of Media and Communications*, ed. M. Danesi (New York: M.E. Sharpe, 2009) defines Fellini-esque as referring to: "A film or media text that blends reality and fantasy, reminiscent of the methods of Federico Fellini, the renowned Italian motion picture director. Fellini often developed the script of the film as the film was being made. Many of his films rely heavily on the use of symbolism and imagery, creating obscure dreamlike sequences." This reflects the Anglo-Saxon view of Fellini, as an originator of film technique, and is less concerned with autobiography and references to provincial life, as generally cited in Italian dictionaries.

2. A. Arpa, *L'Arpa di Fellini*, 33 and 38.

3. E. Bernhard, *Mitobiografia* [Mythobiography] (Milan: Adelphi, 1969).

4. For Bernhard, the "Great Mediterranean Mother" is what discloses the "enigma of the Italian soul" and is not associated with a concrete mother, but acts "endopsychically" in men and women alike, creating a maternal sort of superstructure, whose main effect is the absence of objective principles. In 1962, Antonio Gambino published a purely political reading of Bernhard's theory, "La civiltà materna" [Maternal Civilization], in *Tempo presente*, no. 4–5, 328–337.

5. "Fellini al contrattacco" [Fellini Counter-Attacks], *Il Tempo*, 8 December 1965.

6. F. Cossiga (with Pasquale Chessa), *Italiani sono sempre gli altri. Controstoria d'Italia da Berlusconi a Cavour* [Italians Are Always Someone Else: Counter-History of Italy from Berlusconi to Cavour] (Milan: Mondadori, 2007). From the mid seventies on, Cossiga was one of the most influential politicians in the Christian Democrat Party. He became president of Italy in 1985 and in the nineties was the focus of the Gladio scandal, the secret stay-behind NATO organization during the Cold War.

7. G. Fofi, "Ci ha capiti e raccontati, noi italiani, come nessuno" [He Understood Us Italians and Told Our Story Like No One Else], *l'Unità,* 1 November 1993.

8. M. Tropeano, "Le tangenti? Nel nostro sangue" [Corruption? It's in Our Blood], *La Stampa,* 30 March 1993.

9. Ibid.

10. A pose that can be found in *8 ½,* too. A website providing courses in the Italian language and culture uses the image of Guido, sitting lazily at a table, his feet up, as an example of the "indefinable quality of Italian style."

11. Ennio Flaiano claimed the word was his: "The term *vitellone* was used in my day to define a young man from a modest family, perhaps a student—but one who had either already gone beyond the programmed schedule for his coursework, or one who did nothing all the time... I believe the term is a corruption of the word *vudellone,* the big intestine, or a person who eats a lot. It was a way of describing the family son who only ate but never 'produced'—like an intestine, waiting to be filled." T. Kezich, here in the translation by Minna Proctor with Viviana Mazza, *Federico Fellini: His Life and Work* (London: Tauris, 2007), 132.

12. S. Patriarca, *Italianità. La costruzione del carattere nazionale* [Italian-ness, the Construction of National Character] (Rome/Bari: Laterza, 2010), xviii.

13. M. Grande, *La commedia all'italiana* (Rome: Bulzoni, 2003), 180.

14. G. Aristarco, "*La strada,*" *Cinema Nuovo* no. 46 (10 November 1954).

15. S. Patriarca, *Italianità,* xii. My italics.

16. G.P. Brunetta, *Storia del cinema italiano. Dal neorealismo al miracolo economico,* 507.

17. Peter Bondanella, *The Cinema of Federico Fellini* (Princeton: Princeton University Press, 1992), 72–73.

18. G.P. Brunetta, *Storia del cinema italiano. Dal neorealismo al miracolo economico,* 505–506.

19. G.L. Rondi, in *Il Tempo,* 30 September 1953.

20. G.L. Rondi, *La fiera letteraria,* 11 October 1953.

21. G.L. Rondi, "I vitelloni di Fellini, film sulla nostalgia borghese" [Fellini's *I vitelloni,* a Film about Bourgeois Nostalgia], *Il Tempo,* 28 August 1953.

22. M. Gromo, "Italia e Cecoslavacchia" (comment on the film from the Venice Film Festival), *La Nuova Stampa,* 28 August 1953.

23. See C. Alvaro, *Il nostro tempo e la speranza. Saggi di vita contemporanea* [Our Era and Hope] (Milan: Bompiani, 1952) and M. D'Amelia, *La mamma* (Bologna: il Mulino, 2005).

24. Edward Banfield published his study under the title *The Moral Basis of a Backward Society,* in 1958, based on research carried out between 1954 and 1955 in Montegrano, in the province of Potenza, in southern Italy. The book was translated into Italian in 1976.

25. S. Patriarca, *Italianità,* 16.

26. P. Bondanella, *The Cinema of Federico Fellini,* 91–92. My italics.

27. P. Bondanella, *The Cinema of Federico Fellini,* 90.

28. S. Patriarca, *Italianità,* 12–13.

29. For an analysis of how the term entered the language, see for example F. Rossi, "La partita acustica della 'Dolce vita': dalle parole al rumore" [Acoustics

in *La dolce vita*: From Words to Noise], in *Fellini. Mezzo secolo di dolce vita. Atti del convegno "Mezzo secolo da La dolce vita"* [Fellini: Half a Century of *Dolce Vita*: Conference Papers, Rimini: 14–15 November 2008], ed. V. Boarini and T. Kezich (Rimini/Bologna: The Fellini Foundation, Bologna Film Library, 2010), 129–139. The first definition is from the *Grande dizionario della lingua italiana* (Turin: UTET, 1961–2003), the second from *The Oxford English Dictionary* (Oxford: Clarendon Press, 1989).

30. The manuscript is in the Lilly Library of Rare Books. The script was published in *Amarcord. Rivista di studi felliniani* no. 1–2 (October 2006).

31. L. Barzini, Jr., *The Italians* (New York: Atheneum, 1964). Fellini had a copy of the 1970 Mondadori edition in Italian. See O. Maroni and G. Ricci, eds., *I libri di casa mia. La biblioteca di Federico Fellini* [Books in My Home: The Library of Federico Fellini] (Rimini: The Fellini Foundation, 2008), 69.

32. O. Calabrese, "I segni dell'identità italiana" [Signs of Italian Identity] in *Identità italiana tra Europa e società multiculturale. Atti del convegno* [Italian Identity between Europe and a Multicultural Society, Conference Papers, Siena, 12–14 December 2008] (Fondazione Intercultura Onlus), 39. For the perception of *La dolce vita* abroad and the relationship between the film and Italian stereotypes, see D. Vogler, *La Dolce Vita: Italy and the Five Senses* (seminar on 12 July 2010 at the Laboratory for Statistics and Social and Educational Research, Florence University), http://www.strse.it/materiali/vogler/prospectus2011.pdf.

33. In "Notes on Sloth," *Granta* 109 (Winter 2009), 69–70.

34. S. Bellassai, "Mascolinità, mutamento, merce. Crisi dell'identità maschile nell'Italia del boom" [Masculinity, Change, Goods: The Crisis of the Male Identity in the Italy of the Economic Boom], in *Genere, generazione e consumi. L'Italia degli anni Sessanta* [Gender, Generation and Consumption: Italy in the Sixties], ed. P. Capuzzo (Rome: Carocci, Foundation of the Gramsci Institute, Annals, 12, 2003), 110.

35. Ibid., 125.

36. J. Reich, *Beyond the Latin Lover: Marcello Mastroianni, Masculinity and Italian Cinema* (Bloomington/Indianapolis: Indiana University Press: 2005), 47.

37. R. Bizzocchi, *Cicisbei. Morale privata e identità nazionale* [Gallants: Private Morality and National Identity] (Rome/Bari: Laterza, 2008), 340.

38. Ibid., 3

39. S. Patriarca, *Italianità*, 26.

40. Ibid.

41. A letter from Carlo Emanuele Basile, given pride of place on the front page of *Il Secolo d'Italia*, 26 February 1960.

42. V. Riva, "La balia in camicia nera" [The Black-Shirted Nanny], *L'espresso*, 7 October 1973.

43. Ibid.

44. F. Mauri, "Note tecniche comunque disorganiche sull'azione 'Che cosa è il fascism'" [Technical but Inorganic Notes on "What Fascism Is"], photocopied and handed out on the evening of 2 April 1971 on the Safa Palatino premises, Rome, in F. Mauri, *Che cosa è il fascismo*, published in full in *Der Politische Ventilator* (Milan: Achille Mauri Editore-Krachmalnicoff, 1973), 16.

45. V. Riva, "La balia in camicia nera."

46. "Fellini: la storia di un paese negli anni del fascismo" [Fellini: History of a Town During the Fascist Years], letter sent to Gian Luigi Rondi and published in *Il Tempo* on 20 December 1973.

47. Giacomo Manzoli has observed that *Amarcord* "is one of the very few works that tell the story of fascism from the inside and reach a critical understanding of the reasons that gave rise to it, irrespective of a historical judgment. The film continuously involves the viewer, both directly when the actors address the audience, and indirectly by conjuring memories and by representing the viewer on screen." See the entry on the film at: http://www.treccanni.it/enciclopedia/amarcord_(Enciclopedia_del_Cinema).

48. In 1983, almost fifteen years after the first edition of his book *Le interpretazioni del fascismo* (1969) [Interpretations of Fascism], Renzo De Felice ended the new preface with the words: "A whole series of problems remain substantially to be cleared up. What has been neglected is the cultural dimension (above all in the anthropological sense), so the unifying factors of fascism remain unknown, the cornerstone, what made so many ordinary people fascists." R. De Felice, *Le interpretazioni del fascismo* (Rome/Bari: Laterza, 2007), xxv.

49. D. Bidussa, *Fare I conti col passato* [Reckoning with the Past], http://www.linkiesta.it/blogs/storia-minima/fare-i-conti-col-passato. See S. Romano, "Oggi una mostra sul nazismo, domani forse sul fascismo" [Today an Exhibition on Nazism, Maybe Tomorrow One on Fascism], *Corriere della Sera*, 10 July 2011.

50. See P. Bondanella as well as R. Renzi, *Il fascismo involontario e altri scritti* [Involuntary Fascism and Other Writings] (Bologna: Cappelli, 1975) and P. Parshall, "Fellini's Thematic Structuring: Patterns of Fascism in *Amarcord*," *Film Criticism* no. 2 (1983) 19–30.

51. S. Patriarca, *Italianità*, 228.

52. See the thoughts of Italo Calvino in "Autobiografia di uno spettatore" [Autobiography of a Spectator], in F. Fellini, *Quattro film* [Four Films] (Turin: Einaudi, 1974), xxi–xxiii, or, more generally, P.M. Santi, ed., *I disegni di Fellini* [Fellini's Drawings] (Rome/Bari: Laterza, 1982). For Fellini's relationship with caricature, particularly in *Amarcord*, see A. Costa, "Grafica e messa in scena, I disegni di Fellini" [Graphics and *Mise-en-scène*, Fellini's Drawings], in *Il cinema e le arti visive* [Cinema and the Visual Arts] (Turin: Einaudi, 2002), 79–86. See also P. Pallottino, "Fellini e il 'Corriere dei piccoli'. Ipotesi sulla genesi, non solo iconografica, de 'La strada'" [Fellini and the 'Corriere dei piccoli': Hypothesis of the Not Only Iconographic Origins of *La strada*], in *Federico Fellini. Da Rimini a Roma 1937-1947, Atti del convegno di studi e testimonianza* (Rimini, 31 October 1997) (Rimini: Federico Fellini Foundation, 1997), 71–75.

53. A. Costa, "Grafica e messa in scena," 82.

54. M. Mafai, "Possibilità per un'arte nuova" [Opportunities for a New Art], *Rinascita*, 3 March 1945.

55. E. Kris and E.H. Gombrich, "The Psychology of Caricature," included in the Italian edition of E. Kris, *Ricerche psicoanalitche sull'arte* [Psychoanalytical Explorations in Art] (Turin: Einaudi, 1988), 170–171.

56. "Fellini: la storia di un paese negli anni del fascismo."

57. Initially published with the title "Note su fotografia e storia" [Notes on Photography and History], the essay by Giulio Bollati (with Carlo Bertelli) was the first in the Annals of the History of Italy (Turin: Einaudi, 1979) retitled *L'immagine fotografica 1845-1945* [The Photographic Image, 1845-1945]. Subsequently, the essay was amended and published as "Il modo di vedere italiano (note su fotografia e storia)" [The Italian Way of Seeing—Notes on Photography and History], in G. Bollati, *L'italiano. Il carattere nazionale come storia e invenzione* [Italians: National Character as History and Invention] (Turin: Einaudi, 1983-1996-2011). The quotations are from the 2011 edition.

58. Bollati writes: "Let's admit it, influenced by the charm of the first historians and theorists who investigated the origins of photography at the heart of bourgeois capitalist and industrial culture, we overlooked the relationship between photography and backwardness in a country such as ours; given that the origins of Italian photography at the edge of the European industrial revolution must have influenced its development and determined its character." G. Bollati, *L'italiano*, 134.

59. Ibid., 129. My italics.

60. Ibid., 133–134.

61. Ibid., xxv.

62. It could be objected that Italy was the cradle of futurism. However, Bollati read the movement within the context of national transformation, as "able to adapt the theme of mechanical modernity to drive a hyperactive, drugged, version of national aesthetics." Ibid., 168.

63. Ibid., 119.

64. Fellini, *Fare un film*, 168.

65. For the way nostalgia circulated and was handled by film and in Italian popular culture, see E. Morreale, *L'invenzione della nostalgia. Il vintage nel cinema italiano* [The Invention of Nostalgia: The Vintage in Italian Film] (Rome: Donzelli, 2009).

66. O. Maroni and G. Ricci, *I libri di casa mia*, 47.

67. See D. Zanelli, "Ecco Fellini nella 'Città delle donne'" [Fellini in "The City of Women"], *il Resto del Carlino*, 9 March 1980.

68. J. Stone, "Pinocchio and Pinocchiology," *American Imago* 51, no. 3, (Fall, 1994) 329–342.

69. S. Stewart-Steinberg, "Fare gli italiani, ossia l'effetto-Pinocchio" [Making Italians, i.e., the Pinocchio Effect], in *Identità Italiana tra Europa e società multiculturale*, 32.

70. S. Stewart-Steinberg. *The Pinocchio Effect: On Making Italians, 1960-1920* (Chicago/London: Chicago University Press, 2007), 6.

71. F. Fellini, *Intervista sul cinema*, 142.

72. R. Renzi, "Fellini che va Fellini che viene" [Fellini as You Like Him], in *Il primo Fellini* [Early Fellini] (Bologna: Cappelli, 1974), 13.

Chapter 3

La Dolce Vita and Its Relevance Today

> *I'd say that the sweetness of life exists in certain epochs for a certain category of person. Democracy doesn't afford much sweet life. Whereas absolute regimes, dictatorships, oligarchies, do.*
> —Leonardo Sciascia

> *In '65 everything will be depraved. You don't think so? Just wait! It'll be truly disgusting!*
> —La dolce vita

> *Boredom is etched on the faces of all of Rome's pleasure seekers.*
> —Giacomo Leopardi

A Glamour Brand?

The transformation of *La dolce vita* into a symbol of glamour, a synonym of elegance and frivolity, is one of the most impressive manipulations of the "signified" ever carried out in relation to a work of art. An emblem of Western anthropology and of the Italian identity, *La dolce vita* has been reduced to a fashion show striking a series of poses and exhibiting a range of clothes that, for the past fifty years, have inspired advertisers, fashion designers, and tourists. If not a deliberate manipulation, it has been, at the very least, a curious example of the social construction of meaning.

Not that Fellini wanted to make a straightforward, unambiguous film. Its fascination through the years consists precisely in the fact that it is so open to contrasting interpretations.

The scandals, excommunications, and parliamentary questions—the furor—following the release of the film are well known,[1] yet the subsequent myth has eclipsed and displaced what, at the time, was the head-on collision of the film with society.

Fellini experts were quick to come to the aid of the film and to smooth things over. Kezich, for example, spoke of *La dolce vita* as the manifesto of the "second liberation," a film whose explosive liberating force could be identified within an "anti-metaphysical tradition that would later be called *weak thought*."[2] Except that weak thought, in its literal sense, was used to transform the film into a picture postcard, with Mastroianni and Anita Ekberg in the Trevi Fountain indistinguishable from Gregory Peck and Audrey Hepburn on the back of a Vespa in *Vacanze romane*. In the face of such an intense and consolidated imaginary version of the film, critical commentary and analysis can do very little.

However much Via Veneto, the party-going, the scene in the Trevi Fountain—seen on our screens again and again, and quoted in umpteen films—might justifiably prompt nostalgia for an era in which Italy was admired and not just for how it dictated the rules of fashion, an era that came and went and will never be repeated, today someone watching *La dolce vita* for the first time might be perplexed. Assuming she manages to get through the three hours of the film, she will certainly be struck by the "emptiness" that all this beauty brings. An emptiness that is not only strangely relevant today, but is perhaps more evident now than in 1960.

When the film was first shown on Italian television, on 24 September 1975, the newspapers recalled somewhat nostalgically the petty squabbles it provoked on its release, the scandals and divisions, for and against. A priest, don Ernesto Pisoni, wrote: "After the flood of erotic films which has submerged us in recent years, to think of *La dolce vita* as scandalous seems rather pathetic."[3] The television consecration of the film, broadcast at peak viewing time, was the first step in the process of rendering it harmless, of reducing it to the description of a bygone era. Stripped of its provocative nature, *La dolce vita* entered the collective memory as a hymn to the euphoric years of the economic boom.

Shortly afterward, when two young actors, Christian De Sica and Dalila Di Lazzaro, reproduced the scene in the Trevi Fountain for the TV show *Odeon,* the newspapers wrote: "Do you remember the scene? What had seemed practically indecent is now broadcast on television without the least embarrassment… what can be seen of Dalila wouldn't make even a schoolgirl blush."[4] Of course not. True, the exuberant sensuality of Anita Ekberg and the lasciviousness of the parties Marcello stumbles into provoked the indignation of sticks-in-the-mud, but the film wasn't just an unending series of scandalous scenes that only a few years later even the harshest censor would have found innocuous.

When released, many understood that the film didn't only fly in the face of public decency, but held up a huge deforming mirror to society and its rapidly changing values. The process was taking place under everyone's nose, but what distinguishes Fellini from other commentators is his ability to show the transformation in one powerful image after another. The ruins of Italy displayed in neorealist films had been cleared away during the postwar reconstruction; now, Fellini displayed the spiritual ruins left behind by the Italian economic boom.

The fiftieth anniversary of the film was the perfect opportunity to investigate its relationship with Italian society, starting with how its original sense had been jettisoned and replaced by "the exact opposite of what Fellini was saying about the future of society."[5] Significantly, the film has recently prompted a series of books investigating the politics of postwar Italy.[6]

Rather than return to the well-known themes of *La dolce vita*—the loss of values, modernization, the crisis of the sacred, the advent of the society of the spectacle, and the vacuity of intellectuals—or investigate its style (as already done elsewhere),[7] today it is perhaps more useful to show the effects and symbolic attainments of the film in a variety of fields. One viewer understood these effects at the time. In February 1960, at the height of the furor, an anonymous reader of the newspaper *La voce del popolo* wrote: "What I liked about the film was its scandal. A scandal that is finally clear, after so many that have ended up utterly nullifying [the real]. Here we know who the killer is (Fellini) and who the victims are (the characters)… It is a perfect document for anyone who, tomorrow, looking back, wishes to study its contents as they deserve."[8]

The World Everyone Wants to Belong To

> There is no doubt that a film by Fellini was a genuine cultural event influencing the way his contemporaries thought and felt or, rather, capturing the essence, sometimes ahead of the developments that were later to emerge, on the basis of the sort of general survey of a given situation, at least in terms of Western civilization, of late capitalist society and consumerism, … a debate into which he crept almost surreptitiously, with no intention of doing so, asking disquieting questions.[9]

Thus, the cinema historian Gianni Rondolino commented on the film at a conference on the fiftieth anniversary of *La dolce vita*. A little later, the film director Paolo Sorrentino gave a precise idea of what these "disquieting questions" were:

Camouflaged behind the great beauty of the sweet life, Fellini actually was probing the greatest of all fears: the inability to find any sense in life. The vehicle is disturbing, because the miasma of nihilism is always disturbing, and is the true scandal of *La dolce vita*... It is one of the reasons Fellini's masterpiece will never become old. It touches the ground we are standing on and says, with the candor of the maestro's soft, childlike voice, that actually we are walking on quicksand. It's just a matter of time before we sink. To bring out these atrocious doubts, Fellini doesn't choose contextual rhetorical short-cuts, he doesn't place Marcello in a world of material deprivation, but renders life more complex by giving him a world of luxury and ease, apparently without a care, seemingly one of amusement. The world everyone wants to belong to.[10]

It is no accident that Sorrentino took part in a discussion on the current relevance of *La dolce vita*: "Life is rendered more complex by placing the protagonist in a world of luxury." At the time of the interview there were rumors of a film Sorrentino was thinking of making, based on *Cafonal*, a book of photography by Umberto Pizzi, a paparazzo in today's Rome and a habitual contributor to the gossip blog *Dagospia*. "*Cafonal* is the dolce vita of today in its utmost degeneration," Sorrentino said in various interviews. "Cafonal" is a difficult term to translate: in the Italian imagination it indicates the senseless and tasteless garishness of a host of manifestations of public, political, artistic, and cultural life, above all in Rome. Hence, on the blog, the section headed "Cafonal" has become a regular feature.

On the rear cover of the book, Roberto D'Agostino (director and creator of the blog) comments: "Every day, 'Cafonal' celebrates the rituals of loutish Italy. Which stuffs its face, dances, makes itself over, throwing itself into parties in Rome's most elegant buildings, generally the property of an aristocrat of the Papacy or a member of the nouveau riche, someone working on public tenders and speculative housing developments."

As many have said, "Cafonal" is also an anthropological treatise that is fundamental to the understanding of Italy today.

The comparison between *La dolce vita* and *Cafonal* gave the general public a new idea of the myth of the dolce vita. Reworking Christopher Lasch's idea of narcissism, the writer Marco Belpoliti has developed the parallelism on the basis of the extinction of the classical concept of "shame," replaced in postmodern society by a so-called amoral shame.

A surface shame, without a trace of guilt, shame based on a model of conduct in which *everything is possible*; and "not being there," not managing to get noticed among the anonymous mass, is the supreme fear: "The result is the replacement of Oedipus, symbol of patriarchal society and the bourgeois sense of guilt, with the figure of Narcissus: society as a mirror, success as confirmation or negation of one's own status. Narcissus carries with him the gift of freedom, but also of increasing emptiness and the ghost of impotence."[11]

And this is precisely the dramatic situation of Marcello in *La dolce vita*, an impotent and aimless wanderer within a city as it celebrates itself in bored rituals. It is no accident that photography, the quintessential instrument of mass narcissism, is central to Fellini's film and Belpoliti's thinking.

Fellini said of *La dolce vita*: "It should be shown all at once in one gigantic shot, with the characters in the fresco moving, undressing, attacking each other ferociously, dancing, drinking as if they were waiting for something. What are they waiting for? Who knows?"

A fresco that Umberto Pizzi's photographs create in all their banal atrocity. These photographs show the monstrous, grotesque, and deformed, which, in *La dolce vita*, are hidden behind the glamour of a stylized beauty.

Moravia saw the sea monster washed ashore at the end of the film as "the part of reality that cannot be turned into spectacle, i.e., consumption, because it is, precisely, authentic."[12] In other words, the return of the repressed in the inauthenticity of the "generalized spectacle" portrayed in *La dolce vita*.

In *Cafonal*, on the other hand, there is no reality to counteract fiction. The veil of elegance behind which the character and poses of *La dolce vita* hide has been removed, revealing flabby faces, smudged makeup, the monstrosity of a masked ball that Fellini had evoked with both fascination and repulsion.

There is an exemplary sequence in which Marcello and his father, visiting Rome, go to a nightclub. The choreography of the dancing girls flirting with Marcello and his father, in a retro and old-fashioned atmosphere that is nonetheless one of entertainment and frivolity, is followed by the act of the elderly clown Polidor. The devastating sound of his trumpet is heard, striking an immediate echo of melancholia, then Marcello and the clown, standing nearby, exchange glances: unmistakably it is a pained look of mutual understanding.

As usual in Fellini, illusion and disillusionment go hand in hand. And in this scene what we see is the solitude and human sadness that is held in check beneath the euphoria of the "dolce vita."

Giuseppe Siri, Archbishop of Genoa—one of the most severe critics of Vatican Council reform and a staunch defender of the film—wrote in a note: "The film is truthful; and it is so because it strikes so horribly at the heart of many lives, so much so that some have reacted against it in the press: they saw themselves in the film and were frightened by what they saw."[13]

Yet Fellini in *La dolce vita* does not pass judgments. He makes Stendhal's motto his own: "Je ne blâme, ni n'approuve, j'observe." Similarly, in Pizzi's photographs there is no sounding of a warning, no indignation.

The lack of shame in the people he portrays in his photographs: "... is not a sort of criticism of their behavior or attitudes, their evident immorality; nor, on the contrary, is there any approval of their shamelessness. *Cafonal* creates a sort of no-man's land that is both visual and moral, a world of *shame without the sense of shame*."[14]

Many years earlier, Fellini had occupied this no-man's-land with *La dolce vita*. He showed how the relationship between truth and fiction needed to be radically rethought not only in art, but as the "anthropological structures of the imaginary."[15]

The work in which the echo of *La dolce vita* is most persistent is that of Andy Warhol, with its interminable, repetitive gallery of famous faces immortalized in Polaroid, or in films comprising a single shot, as Fellini wanted for *La dolce vita*. This echo is symbolized in *La dolce vita* by the presence of Nico, who was about to become an icon of the Factory.

Warhol and Fellini can equally be associated with a political position, the overcoming and annulment of antagonism through the creation of a world in one's own likeness and image: "The cold war never took place! Everything in Andy Warhol's work tells us that with reference to the culture and values on which it is based, this conflict was merely a fiction, the paranoid ghost of two worlds that justified their existences by inventing opposite images of themselves."[16]

Both artists were fascinating in the mythopoetic dimension of popular culture; omnipresent in the media and newspapers, Warhol and Fellini transformed themselves into art. The work of Warhol and *La dolce vita* are "profoundly superficial," to use the oxymoron of the American himself. Like *La dolce vita*, in the eyes of the general public, the Factory was the emblem of artistic effervescence and the *indie* glamour of New York. Few saw its solitude and despair. Both Warhol's Factory and Fellini's *La dolce vita* became famous based on this ambivalence.

In 1960, *La dolce vita* caused a scandal because of its interclass mixture of aristocracy, the world of entertainment, the bourgeoisie, and subproletariat; all appeared together, with no distinction, in a cynical and amoral circus. Yet it is only now that Fellini's extraordinary vision can be fully appreciated. As many howled their indignation and wanted the film to be boycotted, a few noticed how Fellini, ahead of his time, had exposed a nerve. In other words, "the general public of *La dolce vita* may show itself as scandalized by the pleasures of this little world, but in fact in the provinces and outskirts, they are envious and long for that world: for them it is a dream world."[17]

Returning to the parallelism between Fellini's *café society* and the world portrayed in the pages of *Cafonal*, the differences between the two are also of interest.

We could wonder, for example, why Pizzi's photographs are so far from the mythical world Fellini managed to create. Is it only a question of the "dissemination of bad taste," as many would like to think? A change of fashion? I don't think so. At the time, the world of *La dolce vita* was seen as vulgar and repugnant. Evidently, the point lies elsewhere.

As is well known, Baudelaire defined *modernity* in art as a mixture of the transitory and the eternal. "The beautiful," he wrote in 1863, "has an eternal, invariable element, the quantity of which is extremely difficult to determine, and a relative, occasional element, which is, if you will, from time to time or at the same time, the era, fashion, morals, passion."[18] According to Baudelaire, without the second element—the transitory— nothing absolute or eternal could be shown to spectators of "modern life."

In Umberto Pizzi's photographs we find today's *dolce vita* crushed into an absolute present. Everything is transitory and ephemeral, nothing is invariable or aspires in any form to the eternal.

This phenomenon brings with it the inevitable inversion of the strong and weak sides of the imaginary in the worlds of film and television: "There is practically no cinema in Pizzi's snapshots, which are dominated by politics, finance, TV. And the intermediate landscape of micro powers. Fellini's Italy was true because it was recreated in the studio. The world of *Cafonal* looks like it was recreated in the studio but is real life."[19]

La dolce vita foreshadowed many of the phenomena of life today. Some years after the release of the film, the political importance of the film was noted clearly by Moravia: "Through Marcello, the person and his profession, Fellini avoids the fate of crepuscular artists that consists mainly in a sort of derisory and resigned sentimental education; and freezes in his film the historic moment of transition of Italian society from the reality of provincial life to the unreality of myths, from the traditional scale of values to the values of the spectacle, from an economy in which people save to one in which people spend. Marcello's job shows that everything can be consumed, even disappointment."[20]

"I'd Like to Portray in Images the Inauthenticity of This World"

The inspiration for *La dolce vita* was the world of illustrated magazines and the scandals reported in them at the height of the period known as Hollywood on the Tiber. Cinecittà was frenetically busy. At the beginning of the fifties, taking advantage of low costs (granted by a law of 1949 promoted principally by the future Prime Minister Giulio Andreotti, at the time under-secretary for entertainment),[21] numerous American productions had transferred to Rome, bringing with them famous actors and actresses, a godsend for the gossip columns and glossy magazines. Specifically, Fellini's film drew from the Roman summer of 1958, famous for its celebrity quarrels and film stars pursued up and down Via Veneto and elsewhere by journalists and photographers on the trail of a scoop.[22]

These magazines inspired the form rather than the content of the film, which imitated their rhapsodic structure, with individual episodes arranged in fragments, sketches, the embryos of potential stories that reached no conclusion. As noted by many critics, this structure gave the film its extraordinary modernity and compositional freedom.

However, Fellini didn't simply transfer the narrative form onto the screen. What attracted him was the production of images from other images. In other words, he saw in the glossy magazines and gossip columns something that related to mythology and archetypes. *La dolce vita* transforms social documents into monuments of the imagination:

> In *Tempo*, on 14 October 1958, Stelio Marini wrote an article under the heading 'Fellini explores the Rome of the wealthy': the walls [of Fellini's study] are covered with color photos from glossy magazines; scantily dressed actresses; men made up to look as beautiful as women; of all these photographs one is particularly important and attracts Fellini's insistent gaze. It is a photomontage of Via Veneto at night, showing the customers in the cafes as *plaster cast busts*.[23]

Statues of a new mythology *La dolce vita* was to make famous the world over. As Fellini himself confirmed: "I think the film was nourished by the life of the glossy magazines, including in the creation of images ... *L'Europeo, Oggi*... they reflected the features of a disturbing society forever celebrating itself, representing itself, giving itself awards."[24]

Although some critics have posited a connection between *La dolce vita* and *Le nozze di Figaro*, both works that portray the end of an era and the death throes of the aristocracy, Fellini's film gives us the harrowing dawn of a new world knocking at the door.[25] Far in advance of other films, *La dolce vita* revealed the idea of *mise-en-scène* behind the poses, the stripteases and quarrels in Via Veneto, photographed and splashed over the covers of the magazines. It portrayed the start of the era we live in today, in which emptiness and nullity are turned into drama and spectacle.

Not that the film didn't capture the events of the time. *La dolce vita* was, above all, an instant movie:

Calling *La dolce vita* a film-cum glossy magazine, emphasis was placed on its origin and the postwar relationship between cinema and what we could call the "cultural form" of the glossy magazine. In actual fact, the phenomenon began between the two World Wars and I don't think it's accidental that the producer of *La dolce vita* was Angelo Rizzoli, the publisher who had begun to produce films in the thirties, with *La signora di tutti* [directed by Max Ophuls], with a production setup that included films and publishing in close correlation, in a decidedly multi-media strategy.[26]

The success of the film was in no small measure due to the continuous echo provided by newspapers, which artfully magnified its scandalous aspects and reinforced its explosive impact on Italian society. In addition to standing behind the camera, Fellini also drove the complex publicity machine, playing a game of hide-and-seek with the newspapers, in which he partly revealed and partly concealed the direct sources of the film.

For example, as the first unconfirmed reports were filtering through about *La dolce vita*, he denied in the strongest possible terms that there was any reference to Aïché Nanà's famous striptease at the restaurant *Il Rugantino*, an episode that was just then going through the courts. In an interview in December 1958 (before shooting began), he said:

> Through the news, often inaccurate or deliberately distorted in daily newspapers and weekly magazines, it can be understood that one of the things I want to do with *La dolce vita* is describe a certain milieu, a certain world. Directly or indirectly, we all know it, don't we? The world of Via Veneto and Cinecittà, the big international hotels and aristocratic salons (blood or money, old money or new, it doesn't matter); the world that gave rise, just to be clear, to the *striptease* at the Rugantino. I would like to portray in images the *inauthenticity of this world, its disintegration and, above all, its fundamental anxiety.*[27]

Rather than simply denouncing a way of life, the inauthenticity is rendered through a formidable play of mirrors between reality, events reported in the news, and fiction.[28] For example, Via Veneto was reconstructed in Cinecittà by the set designer Piero Gherardi. As Fellini wrote in *L'Europeo* two years after the release of the film:

> I invented a new Via Veneto that doesn't really exist, expanding it and deforming it with the freedom of the imagination and turning it into a giant allegorical fresco... the fact is that because of *La dolce vita*, Via Veneto has changed and has made every effort to become what I showed in the film. There are photographers at every corner of the street, brawls every day, starlets looking for publicity wander down the street in their nightgowns or enter cafés on horseback. The film was being shown in the outskirts of the city and I had to open the newspaper every morning, my heart beat-

ing fast, with an absurd sense of regret. Who knows what they got up to last night in Via Veneto to satisfy nostalgics of the film?[29]

The film is circular: "the newspapers are the main source of *La dolce vita*, representing and interpreting the Sweet Life. In turn, the film transforms that life into rhetoric, in other words it is a commentary on the Sweet Life and the main source of stories for the newspapers."[30]

It is a principle the sociologist Baudrillard was to describe some time later, in apocalyptic terms, as the "disappearance of reality," destroyed by the media and swallowed up by a world of simulations. After all the brouhaha over the film and episodes of life imitating art after the film's release, Via Veneto became the favorite spot of tourists wanting to rub shoulders with the famous and glamorous. "But there was nothing there. They went away disappointed. The film came out when the *dolce vita* of Rome was really coming to an end. Its cycle coincided with the economic boom of the fifties."[31]

Pseudo-Events

"Events are replaced by pseudo-events: sacred objects by fetishes, facts by factoids, fake facts. We look around, read the newspapers, switch on the TV, and notice that we are surrounded by falsifications, surrogates."[32]

Perfect for *La dolce vita*, this comment actually comes from a book by the art critic Gilles Dorfles, published for the first time at the end of the nineties, in relation to the endless counterfeiting and fictionalizations of contemporary life, pseudo-events and factoids.

The Oxford English Dictionary defines factoid as "an item of unreliable information that is reported and repeated so often that it becomes accepted as fact." What overcomes the false/true opposition in the rituals of the contemporary imagination is a mechanism of repetition and of magnification through the media. The term "pseudo-event" was coined by the American historian Daniel J. Boorstin in a pioneering study published at the beginning of the sixties. Although the book has not been translated into Italian and isn't mentioned by Dorfles, he does borrow its vocabulary and, strikingly, the dates for the release of *La dolce vita* and the publication of *The Image: A Guide to Pseudo-Events in America* coincide. Many of the episodes that prompted the film (the photographic session with Anita Ekberg, the "miracle" of the Madonna di Terni, etc.) are pseudo-events extended imaginatively by Fellini in the film.

From what was already a postmodern viewpoint in America in the later fifties, Boorstin investigated the staging of facts, news, and events in a variety of ritual contexts: television, press conferences, debates, and political conventions. Boorstin said that what they had in common was the lack of spontaneity, the simulated nature of the facts presented according to the means of communication. One scene from *La dolce vita* springs immediately to mind: the diva played by Anita Ekberg steps off the airplane and is met by a throng of waiting photographers and journalists. As soon as she takes her first steps down toward the runway, they ask her to go back and do it again, to simulate her arrival, so they can get a better shot. She complies. The shots are better when they're faked.

The sense of photographers being just as important as the people photographed, and the decision to make them a key part of the film, was what made Fellini's film so new.[33] "The transformation of reality into spectacle" Moravia wrote, "is the result of the indiscriminate greed of the photographers who make no great distinction between the image of a miracle and the arrival of Anita Ekberg."[34]

Boorstin too suggested that what really interested the general public was to see how the illusions and pseudo-events ("the news behind the news") were constructed. *La dolce vita* reveals just this, showing the mechanisms behind the creation of gossip and fame in the Rome film world. It was Boorstin who defined a celebrity as "a person who is known for his well-known-ness." *La dolce vita* and Andy Warhol are reflections on Boorstin's tautology.

However, Fellini's film didn't stop at the media and gossip; it investigated spectacle as the symbolic form of modernity.

In Fellini's film, as has been noted, the updating of the popular imagination via gossip about the film stars in Via Veneto was accompanied by the echo of an event from 1953 that had had a huge impact on Italian society: the so-called "Montesi case," the first example of a news event and political scandal that became part of the collective imagination through its treatment in the press.

In *The Montesi Scandal*, Karen Pinkus argues that *La dolce vita* makes disguised yet clear reference to the case, presenting it in a number of metaphorical guises.[35] Pinkus suggests, for example, that the fish Marcello and his companions find on the beach at dawn is a clear allusion to the body of Wilma Montesi, found on the beach of Tor Vajanica, near Rome. The case itself had a series of elements that were to become all too familiar in subsequent years: prostitution, drugs, the involvement of high-ranking politicians, the shady presence of the secret services, shoddy police work, fame-hunters, legal blunders. It was the archetypal mystery of the new Italian Republic, with the truth always one step away, ungraspable, indemonstrable.

The Montesi case sparked off the spectacular relations between the media and the law courts, backed up by the creation of micro-celebrities, people who would later be "well-known for being well-known." In his diary, Flaiano noted: "If we could take the TV cameras into the court hearing the Montesi case, we would double the sale of television sets. You realize that, don't you?"

A great deal about the case was new. The witnesses included Anna Maria Moneta Caglio who gave regular press conferences at the Hotel Plaza. One of the judges, Raffaello Sepe, played to the crowd, agreeing to be interviewed, something unthinkable only a few years earlier. In a trice, the relations between politics and information had radically changed. Newspapers no longer had any reverential fear of the powers that be: on the contrary, they lent a hand in dismantling one system of power and building another.[36]

There are numerous analogies between the case and *La dolce vita*. The historian Francesco Malgeri, estimating the importance of the event in relation to the so-called "season of centrism," wrote: "Above all those stories revealed pockets of affluence in society that were hitherto unknown, a wealth leading to behavior that was far from the traditional standards of morality. A few years later, in *La dolce vita*, Federico Fellini realistically portrayed what was in effect a dramatic change in the behavior of the emerging, wealthy and anxiety-ridden bourgeoisie."[37]

The echo of the Montesi case, with its unmasking of the hypocrisies of Italian society, reached *La dolce vita*: "In the Capital of Christianity, an abyss of corruption and decadence was revealed. Instead of censoring film posters and variety shows, Rome was the city of perdition, teeming with ministers claiming to be practicing Catholics."[38]

The Montesi murder case snowballed into a political scandal and that is how it was discussed in relation to *La dolce vita*.

Mario Melloni, then director of *Paese Sera*, defended the film, reminding his readers of the absurd official version of the death of the girl, who was supposed to have died from a footbath:

> I don't think *La dolce vita* is an educational film; *but I do think it is a political film*, which is much more interesting. You have to distinguish between those who didn't like the film and those who wanted it to be censored or even banned. I have nothing to say to the former; but to the second group I would say that they come from the same milieu and are the same people who yesterday defended the Bishop of Prato [for calling a couple who did not marry in Church but in a Registry Office concubines and public sinners], today attack the traffic-warden Melone [for giving his boss a ticket], and previously believed that Wilma Montesi drowned in a footbath.[39]

The Village of Miracles

It is too early to say whether Maratta Alta, a small group of cottages about five miles from Terni, will become a second Fatima or Lourdes. But judging by the number of pilgrims, the sick driven by the hope of being miraculously healed, and simply the inquisitive hurrying to the spot on Thursday 3 July—the third anniversary of the sighting of the Virgin Mary by two farmers, Gino Amadori and Paola Piazza, it seems likely.

These are the first lines of an article in the weekly magazine *Settimo Giorno*, published in July 1958, narrating the anniversary of the events that Fellini was to use for the fake miracle sequence in *La dolce vita*, one of the most important scenes in the film. The invocation of the divine in its most popular forms, bordering on superstition, had already been narrated by Fellini in *Le notti di Cabiria*. In *La dolce vita*, however, it is taken one step further.

The initial neorealist elements of the scene are transformed into their opposite, prompting a reflection on forms of fakery and simulation perpetrated by the media. Fellini imagines that the miraculous event is awaited with bated breath by television crews and photographers, flash bulbs at the ready, while journalists (including Marcello) prepare to tell the world about the miracle. The scene of the "appearance" of the Virgin Mary thus becomes a huge film set. A set that, as evening begins to fall, evokes the apocalyptic scenarios of a science fiction film.

Photographers, reporters, the faithful, the sick hoping to be healed, the curious, policemen sent to keep the public order, mingle amid the scaffolding set up for the spotlights as if in a circus or a spectacle of mass hysteria: "The atmosphere is one of a fairground, an Amusement Park, with the chaotic voices of the workmen."[40]

When he arrives, Paparazzo immediately starts looking for shots of commercial value, while Marcello, accompanied by Emma, interviews those present, taking notes. Fellini shows us the cynicism of the journalists and contrasts it with the genuine wonder of Emma, disturbed by so much chaos. But what interests him most is to show us the mechanics of the spectacle (tests before the camera, posing for the benefit of the photographers, interviews which are more or less scripted, simulations) that inform and give the event meaning. It all ends with the absurd pursuit of the children who playfully point to the image of the Virgin Mary.

As Buzzati wrote in one of his story-reports collected in *I misteri d'Italia* [The Mysteries of Italy], describing the frenzy in the village of San Damiano Piacentino following the sighting of the Virgin Mary: "At the fork, crosswise, there is a wooden pole painted white, holding two microphones connected to two tape recorders. A third tape recorder is further along. *For the first time in history, the words of the Virgin Mary are recorded on tape.*"[41]

An echo of the "ethnographic truth" of the sequence, as recorded by Ernesto De Martino (see chapter 1), can be found in another episode of recent Italian history.

It is 10 June 1981. In Vermicino, an anonymous clearing in the countryside near Rome (some houses built unlawfully, dirt roads, nothing more), Ferdinando and Franca Rampi are looking for their six-year-old son Alfredo who hasn't come home. The boy had been playing nearby, but then had just disappeared, swallowed by the darkness. A few hours later, the description becomes eerily literal. Alfredo had fallen down a workman's manhole, 80 meters deep, and just 30 centimeters across. He is alive, but stuck at a depth of about 36 meters. He is shouting, calling for help, appealing to his mother. When they find him, he has been there for five hours. He dies three days later, after falling a further 30 meters, covered in mud. Vermicino, a nowhere, becomes the focus of national interest and anxiety, as the story is told to the nation.

The story of Alfredino (the name that was quickly adopted) contains at least two tragedies. The atrocious reality witnessed by a crowd of twenty thousand that gathered to watch the fruitless attempts to rescue the boy. And the surreal representation of the event, on television, night and day, as every rescue effort was relayed into people's homes on live TV, three days of uninterrupted coverage, the longest "outside broadcast" in the history of Italian television.

As in *La dolce vita*, TV crews set up on location in order to tell a story (of the successful rescue of the boy) that didn't happen. So much energy was put into the television coverage because of the conviction of the imminent happy ending. When the television crews arrived, Vermicino became a circus. Rescuers, journalists and bystanders mingled; improvised sandwich makers and all kinds of peddlers swooped in to make some fast money. Dwarves, contortionists, clairvoyants offered their services, even trained monkeys were suggested as rescuers. There they were seen in front of the manhole, which nobody had thought to cordon off, under the spotlights, seeking a moment's glory and fame.

Not surprisingly, some journalists called it "a Fellini film set." The speaker in the miracle sequence of *La dolce vita* had described an almost identical scene: "A huge crowd has come to this spot, once deserted and unknown. Many of them are believers, many are simply inquisitive. And, of course, the inquisitive include journalists, photographers, and correspondents from various news agencies from throughout the world. All piled one on top of the other, an endless procession of cars."

Today, looking at the news coverage of Alfredino's tragic death is like looking at a mixture of a neorealist film, the moon landing, and a remake of a film by Fellini. The hypnotic fascination of the macabre images was made unwittingly stronger by the decision of the state broadcaster to use just one camera, so the event was filmed from a single point of view: a fixed shot focusing for eighteen hours a day on the area around the manhole and the voice of the boy coming from the shaft, practically unfiltered, without comment (the journalists had soon run out of things to say): amateurish, makeshift, mesmerizing.

Like a film by Andy Warhol, a man sleeping on the top of the Empire State Building filmed by an unmoving camera, an extreme experience of vision.

A "Fellini-esque Set"
(Postscript on the Death of Federico Fellini)

During the days of Alfredino, Leonardo Sciascia wrote: "It was like the night of the moon landing: then the triumph of technology, now its tragic defeat, in Vermicino. We can go to the moon, but we can't save a small boy who has fallen into a well."[42] At the end of the interminable outside broadcast, the journalist Giancarlo Santalmassi observed: "We will soon wonder, lengthily, what all this was for...what we have wanted to forget and what we should remember."[43] But remember how?

In Fellini's last film, *La voce della luna*, Ivo Salvini, the bizarre character played by Roberto Benigni, believes he hears voices coming from wells; together with Judge Gonnella (Paolo Villaggio), he rambles about the imaginary Po Valley, reconstructed by the filmmaker, until the moon is captured by farmers and brought down to earth. Television crews arrive to record the event. Noise, dancing, shouts, collective end-of-the-world hysteria, prompting Salvini to utter the final words of the film, an affirmation that seems to echo Fellini's latter-day pessimism in relation to a chaotic world that had become incomprehensible: "If we could all just shut up for a moment, maybe we could understand."

In an interview during the making of the film, Fellini said it was about "the suspicion that everything is a huge *mise-en-scène*, a spectacle."[44] Although the film is an adaptation of *Poema dei lunatici* [The Poem of Lunatics] by Ermanno Cavazzoni, it seems to be a reprocessing of the trauma of Vermicino, which in the intervening years had become the dark allegory of humanity crushed by television.

The tragedy was forgotten almost immediately after Alfredino's funeral: "A veil of forgetting will be drawn over this sad and pitiful story.

The national psychodrama that has shaken the whole of Italy for days will become only private memory, doubtless stark and indelible like a brand burnt into the skin."[45]

Paradoxically, or rather out of some obscure retaliation, the next time Vermicino was mentioned in the press was on the occasion of Fellini's death.

On 9 October 1993, Fellini was admitted to the Umberto I General Hospital. Within a week he had fallen into irreversible coma. He died on 31 October. From the moment of his admission, television crews had set up around the hospital grounds. As the filmmaker's conditions deteriorated, the hospital became a film set, in which the rival crews of the state broadcaster and Silvio Berlusconi's private network vied for the scoop: Fellini's death.

As an article with a telling heading, "Assalto al policlinico" [Assault on the General Hospital], put it:

> On Wednesday, the coach of the Channel 5 crew managed to get into the hospital grounds, parking right in front of the Center for Reanimation. Yesterday, the competition responded, using every available means to obtain permits and permission to use technical equipment and telephone lines, making the life of the RAI journalists a little easier. And there are old ladies with rosaries, plants and flowers in the hospital wards, gifts from the elderly fans of the filmmaker, mediums, professional liars... Giuliano Ferrara criticized what he called the "dismal circus of Fellini's death throes, staged in recent days by journalists at the death bed of the great filmmaker." He went on: "Is it right to fight for information, to inform public opinion minute by minute, on live television, *as if we were watching a repeat of the tragedy of Vermicino?*"[46]

In the hospital, Igor Mann interviewed one of the peddlers of Vermicino, who told the journalists about the big bucks they had made at the time of Alfredino's death.[47] But what makes the most dreadful impression of all is the "stolen photo," a dark counterpoint to the paparazzi of *La dolce vita*. It is a photo of Fellini, with a breathing tube, helpless in his hospital bed, probably taken by an unscrupulous nurse and sold (the newspapers say) for a million lire.[48] On 22 October, Fellini's doctor declared: "That stolen photo of Fellini in a coma is an outrage which thankfully many newspapers will not wish to reward. I am grateful to those who refuse to publish it." The newspaper *La Repubblica* published an official statement:

> The ANSA Press Agency yesterday distributed to the newspapers a photograph of Federico Fellini, dying in his hospital bed, alone, surrounded by the medical technology that can help in the last moments of desperate resistance. It is a sad photo, and is painful to look at. It is a pointless photo

that adds nothing to what readers already know of the dramatic moment of Fellini. Therefore, La Repubblica has decided not to publish it. This decision also reflects the criticism voiced by our readers about the publication of another sad photo, showing the filmmaker on a gurney, as he was admitted to hospital after he was taken ill."[49]

Fellini's wife, Giulietta Masina, publicly thanked the newspapers that did not publish the photo, although it did appear abroad, in France's L'Humanité and Spain's El País. It was also shown on Channel 5 News at 8:45 P.M. on Thursday 21 October. "It was a decision taken by Mentana and by myself—said Lamberto Sposini, deputy director of the news program—perhaps superficially because we had very little time to think... but this moralistic campaign on behalf of Fellini strikes me as in rather bad faith, because every day television shows people sick or dying in hospital wards as well as the war dead."[50]

A disconsolate Marcello Mastroianni said: "There is all the vulgarity of our country in this death sold off as if in a TV show."[51]

Fellini had told the story of the invasiveness of reporters and photographers, he had invented the name Paparazzo, which was to become universal, and he had warned us against the cynicism of the information industry and ridiculed the rituals of television, but he could not prevent himself from becoming the object of another media circus, the unwitting protagonist of another, macabre "Fellini film set."

Like Steiner's wife in La dolce vita, who finds hoards of journalists and photographers desperate for a scoop about her husband's suicide, Giulietta Masini was informed of her husband's death by television. Fellini's masterpiece here completes its prophetic parabola. He complained that he could not shrug off the weight of La dolce vita, and lived the consequences of that inability to the bitter end.

Notes

1. For an overview, see for example P.M. De Santi, La dolce vita. Scandalo a Roma, Palma d'oro a Cannes [La dolce vita, Scandal in Rome, Palme d'or in Cannes] (Pisa: Ets, 2004) and D. Monetti and G. Ricci, La dolce vita raccontata dagli Archivi Rizzoli [The Story of La dolce vita from the Rizzoli Archives] (Fellini Foundation and CSC, the National Film Library, 2010).

2. T. Kezich, Fellini (Milan: Camunia, 1987), 290.

3. Quoted in F. Zamponi, Una diva nella fontana [Diva in the Fountain], 3 November 1977.

4. Ibid.

5. M. Cicala, "La dolce vita compie cinquant'anni" [La dolce vita Turns Fifty], Il Venerdì di Repubblica, 17 April 2009.

6. See S. Greggio, *Dolce vita 1959-1979* (Paris: Stock, 2011); S. Gundle, *Death and the Dolce Vita: The Dark Side of Rome in the 1950s* (Edinburgh: Canongate, 2011).

7. See V. Zagarrio, "Fellini dal moderno al postmoderno," in *Storia del cinema italiano, vol. 10, 1960/1964*, ed. G. De Vincenti (Venice: Marsilio, 2001), 82–96; M. Waller, "Whose 'Dolce vita' Is This Anyway? The Language of Fellini's Cinema," in *Federico Fellini, Contemporary Perspectives*, ed. F. Burke and M.B. Waller (Toronto/Buffalo/London: Toronto University Press, 2002), 107; A. Costa, *La dolce vita*, 201.

8. Letter to the director of *La voce del popolo*, 21 February 1960.

9. G. Rondolino, "La dolce vita e il cinema degli anni Sessanta" [*La dolce vita* and Sixties Cinema], in *Fellini. Mezzo secolo di dolce vita* [Fellini: Half a Century after *La dolce vita*], ed. V. Boarini and T. Kezich, (Rimini: Teatro degli Atti, 2010), 49.

10. P. Sorrentino, "Quel ritratto di una vita dorata svelava che la vita non ha senso" [The Portrayal of a Life of Luxury Demonstrated that Life Has No Sense], *Il Venerdì di Repubblica*, 17 April 2009.

11. M. Belpoliti, *Senza vergogna* [Without Shame] (Rome: Guanda, 2010), 22.

12. A. Moravia, "Roma mille film orsono" [Rome, A Thousand Films Ago], *L'Espresso*, 12 October 1975.

13. The historian Paolo Gheda has reconstructed the conflict over *La dolce vita* in letters between Siri and Montini, who sought "a certain uniformity of judgment from our side." Se A. Carioti, "E Siri difese La dolce vita dopo le censure di Montini" [Siri Defends *La dolce vita* after the Criticism of Montini], *Corriere della Sera*, 9 September 2008.

14. M. Belpoliti, *Senza vergogna*, 212.

15. The reference is to G. Durand, *Les structures anthropologiques de l'imaginaire* (Paris: PUF, 1962).

16. D. Ottinger, "Le communisme esthétique d'Andy Warhol," in *Le grande monde d'Andy Warhol* (Paris: RMN Editions, 2009), Exhibition catalogue, 39.

17. V. Pandolfi, "Cinema italiano '59-'60" [Italian Cinema '59-'60], in V. Spinazzola, *Film 1961* (Milan: Feltrinelli, 1961), 10.

18. C. Baudelaire, "Il bello, la moda, la felicità," [The Beautiful, Fashion, Happiness] in Baudelaire, *Scritti sull'arte*, ed. Einaudi (Torino, 1992), 280.

19. M. Cicala, "La dolce vita compie cinquant'anni."

20. Ibid.

21. So-called "Law 1949" allowed American producers to use the facilities of Cinecittà and to exploit the low cost of labor, on the condition that they reinvested their profits in Italy, creating a virtuous circle for Rome and the Italian film industry.

22. "Fellini had already noticed the comings and goings, the tailings, the real or faked arguments, but in summer 1958 some specific episodes caught his imagination: the photo-reporting of a miracle in the countryside of Terni, an argument between Steel and Ekberg in which they slapped each other in the street, some photos by Secchiaroli, a night-time dip into the Trevi Fountain, Anita Ekberg again, photographed by Pierluigi Praturlon, and dozens of small episodes, rumors, and long tedious nights that the glossy magazines reported in detail, with names and locations." G. Bertelli, *Divi e paparazzi: La dolce vita di Fellini* (Genoa: Le Mani, 2009), 34.

23. Ibid.

24. F. Fellini, *Intervista sul cinema*, 110.

25. M. Cabona, "A cinquant'anni *La dolce vita* non è ancora finita" [At Fifty, *La dolce vita* Is Still Not Over], *Il Giornale*, 30 January 2010.

26. A. Costa, *La dolce vita*, 90–91.

27. "Il sacco di Fellini" [Fellini's Bag], interview in *Schermi*, December 1958.

28. As Kezich recalls, "The idea that *La dolce vita* was a sort of instant film and semi-documentary on the goings on in and around Via Veneto is so deeply rooted that when, on the night of 21 June, a fire broke out in the Ambasciatori Hotel and four cloakroom attendants trapped by the flames threw themselves from the windows giving onto Via Liguria, some newspapers said Fellini had decided to add the episode to the film." T. Kezich, *Federico Fellini*, 198.

29. See *L'Europeo* (July 1962, cited in E. Grippa and A. Magistà, "Dalla Dolce vita alla 'Dolce vita': un sistema circolare" [From the Sweet Life to *La dolce vita*: A Circular System], in F. Muzzarelli, *Gossip. Moda e modi del voyeurismo contemporaneo* [Gossip: Fashion and Customs of Contemporary Voyeurism] (Bologna: BUP, 2010), 65.

30. Ibid., 64–65.

31. V. Ciuffa, "Notte per notte ho raccontato la dolce vita" [Night after Night, I've Narrated *La dolce vita*], *Informazioni*, 2 September 1975. See also *La dolce vita minuto per minuto. Tutta la verità su un fenomeno falsato* [*La dolce vita* Minute by Minute: The Truth about a Falsified Phenomenon] (Rome: Ciuffa Editore, 2010).

32. G. Dorfles, *Fatti e fattoidi. Gli pseudoeventi nell'arte e nella società* [Facts and Factoids: Pseudo-Events in Art and Society] (Rome: Castelvecchi, 2009), 27.

33. "Fellini didn't want to confine himself to the news being reported; he said the protagonists were no longer those who were photographed, but the photographers themselves. So, one evening, he decided to meet them; he invited them to the restaurant Gigetto il pescatore and arrived with a bundle of magazines under his arm, anxious to hear what they had to say, and as a result of this he created one of the most important characters in the film, the aggressive photographer." G. Bertelli, *Divi e paparazzi*, 34.

34. A. Moravia, "Roma mille film orsono."

35. See K. Pinkus, *The Montesi Scandal: The Death of Wilma Montesi and the Birth of the Paparazzi in Fellini's Rome* (Chicago: Chicago University Press, 2003).

36. See E. Grignetti, *Il caso Montesi. Sesso, potere e morte nell'Italia degli anni '50* [The Montesi Case: Sex, Power and Death in Fifties Italy] (Venice: Marsilio, 2006).

37. F. Malgeri, *La stagione del centrismo. Politica e società nell'Italia del secondo dopoguerra (1945-1960)* [The Centrist Season: Politics and Society in Postwar Italy (1945–1960)] (Soveria Mannelli: Rubbettino, 2002), 316.

38. Ibid., 70.

39. "Gli inventori del pediluvio oggi aggrediscono il film di Fellini" [The Inventors of the Footbath Today Attack Fellini's Film], *L'Unità*, 27 February 1960. My italics.

40. P.M. De Santi, *La dolce vita*, 140.

41. D. Buzzati, *I misteri d'Italia*, 128. My italics.

42. L. Sciascia in *Epoca*, 27 June 1981, cited in M. Gamba, *Vermicino. L'Italia nel pozzo* [Vermicino: Italy Down the Well] (Rome: Sperling & Kupfer, 2007), 169.

43. Ibid., 159.

44. L. Tornabuoni, "Fellini: 'Il mondo che non c'è'" [Fellini: The World that Doesn't Exist], *La Stampa*, 14 April 1989.

45. M. Gamba, *Vermicino*, 240.

46. E.G. Polidori, "Assalto al Policlinico" [Hospital Taken by Storm], *il Resto del Carlino*, 22 October 1993.

47. I. Mann, "Quel cast all'ospedale" [The Hospital Film Cast], *La Stampa*, 24 October 1993.

48. M. Corbi, Fellini, agonia di polemiche [Fellini, Agony of Polemics, *La Stampa*, 22 October 1993.

49. M. Garbesi, *In fotografia il coma di Fellini* [Fellini Photographed in a Coma], *la Repubblica*, 22 October 1993.

50. G. Giovannetti, "Fellini, dolore e rabbia" [Fellini, Suffering and Rage], *Il Messaggero*, 23 October 1993.

51. G. Grassi, "No al circo intorno a Federico" [No Circus around Federico Please], *Corriere della Sera*, 27 October 1993.

Chapter 4

Fellini, Mussolini, and the Complex of Rome

> *Only in Rome could you seriously and continuously think of ancient phantoms, which elsewhere would rapidly have lost their force and efficacy... Now, the political class to which the destiny of unified Italy had been entrusted was about to be transferred definitively to this place of ancient stones.*
> —Federico Chabod

> *Rome became my home the moment I set eyes on it. That's when I was born. That day is my real birthday. If I remembered the date, I'd honor it.*
> —Federico Fellini

> *"In his journey to Rome, did he feel like an artist setting out on a career, or like a prophet following his calling?*
> —Emil Ludwig, Conversations with Mussolini

Fellini and the "Parliamentary Novel"

In October 1972, prompted by Fellini's latest film, *Roma, Corriere della Sera* invited the writer Goffredo Parise and the filmmaker to discuss the age-old topic of the opposition between Rome, the capital, and Milan, the business heart of Italy. During their conversation Fellini said:

> I remember a phrase that struck me when I first came to Rome and was living in furnished digs. My landlady and her son repeated it quite often. In the evening, her son would say to his mother and his wife: "Let's go out

to see Rome." They lived near Santa Maria Maggiore. They had the idea of strolling through Rome, as if going to a show. I don't think people in Milan say, "Let's go out to see Milan."

"Perhaps," Parise replied, "they say: Let's go to see Rome."[1]

The anecdote shows why Fellini was fascinated by Rome: for him, first and foremost it was a form of spectacle, and only secondarily a city. And—as an "idea" that lives off the tension between what it had been, what it should be and what it is—Rome could hardly have failed to fire up Fellini's imagination.

As every tourist standing in front of the Trevi Fountain knows, Fellini's imaginings of Rome are now an integral part of the city; at times, his film sets and the actual city seem to change places or blend one into the other. Wandering through Rome, Nick Hornby has recently noted, "you are inside the myth that began with the Emperors and continued until Fellini."[2] Immediately after his death, an article appeared in which the question was posed as to "whether Rome, without Fellini, would continue to exist."[3]

A great deal has been written about this strong association.[4] Rome does not only provide important scenery for his films—"an open-air film set" as he used to call it (only to reproduce much of it in Cinecittà)—but is actually itself like Fellini's films, with the "excess, stratification, splendor, theatricality, disintegration"[5] characteristic of Fellini's imagination.

For Fellini, Rome was polyphonic, fragmentary, a palimpsest continuously being written over anew. More than a place, it was a "world opus" in the sense given to this term by Franco Moretti,[6] discussing the form of the epic.

Certainly, like a great deal of Italian cinema, Fellini showed a changing Rome: from the semi-deserted city of the fifties to the traffic-paralyzed and rubbish-strewn streets of the eighties, bombarded with advertising, in *Ginger e Fred*. But this is not what matters most here.

If Rome establishes the identity of Italian filmmaking, in Fellini what can be seen is an investigation of the myth of Rome and its place in Italian identity. In addition to being an allegory of cinema and "semi-pagan, theatrical" Catholicism, Fellini's Rome is the symbolic space for aspects of Italian modernity, its contradictions and traumas.

Fellini's mythology of Rome can be seen in relation to the myth constructed by Mussolini about the nature of Rome and Italian identity. This does not simply involve looking at a parody of fascism, but reflects two different forms of identification with the Eternal City, in Fellini's case recreating it in Studio 5 in Cinecittà, and in Mussolini's rebuilding it in the name of a new Empire. Fellini's set designs and the choreography and architecture of fascism are both transformations of Rome and, by extension, of the whole of Italy, on a massive stage.

The mirroring between Fellini and Mussolini is not confined only to their fascination with the myth of Rome. It involves a similar conception of the artist and of the "leader," as *absolute creator,* where creation, for both, indicates simultaneously rootedness in the ancient past and impetus toward the future. This explains, perhaps, the numerous references to fascism and the myth of Mussolini in Fellini's films, starting from *I clowns.* In some cases, the message is almost subliminal, as in the night scene in *La città delle donne.* As Snaporaz/Mastroianni is pursued by bands of feminists in their cars, suddenly, for a few seconds, without rhyme or reason, we see the word "Dux" on the tarmac, unrelated to the sequence or to the film in general (later, in *Ginger e Fred,* there is a similar moment, as a bronze bust of Mussolini is shown in the lobby of a hotel).

In the history of Italian cinema, Rome has had a mythical and poetic function, and has been a continual inspiration in all eras of filmmaking. It was reconstructed in the studio for *Quo vadis* (E. Guazzoni, 1913) and *Nerone e Agrippina* (M. Caserini, 1914), and used for propaganda purposes, for example in the famous film *Scipione l'Africano* (C. Gallone, 1937). It was exhumed in the fifties at the time of Hollywood on the Tiber for a new series of American blockbusters and then for Italy's own sword-and-sandal Peplum films. Between these two periods, starting in the early forties, the city was increasingly filmed in outdoor locations. In Luce newsreels during the fascist period, it became more or less a backdrop, reinforcing the idea of the regeneration of the myth of empire proclaimed by Mussolini: a city for military parades not unlike filmed costume dramas. Things changed with the decline of fascism and the Second World War.

In the films of the popular duo Aldo Fabrizi and Anna Magnani, such as *Campo de fiori* (M. Bonnard, 1943), *L'ultima carrozzella* (M. Mattoli, 1943)—made a few days before the Allied bombing of Rome—and, above all, *Roma città aperta* (R. Rossellini, 1945), Rome became the capital of neorealism.[7] At its epicenter, Rome began to be used to describe the reality of the country as a whole, until the creative force of neorealism ran out and the city was then portrayed in all its contradictions by the new genre of Italian-style comedy.

Rome as, on the one hand, a mythical evocation and, on the other, as the symbol of neorealism: this apparent opposition runs through Italian cinema and was only resolved in the imaginative filmmaking of Fellini.

Fellini's Rome is *his,* in the sense that he produces a synthesis of these two great forms of representation in a cinematic continuum, bringing together the Rome of myth with the Rome of popular film, decisive in defining the relations between the myth-making machinery of Fellini's films and Italian identity.

A fairly widespread literary genre of postunification Italy was the so-called parliamentary novel, which examined the new political setup in the unified country, through the leitmotif of a young parliamentarian from the provinces taking up his seat in Rome. The stories were all pretty similar: "he attempts to make a career for himself but fails to become a true representative of the nation by falling foul of his passions for women or for politics, or for both."[8]

Generally the woman the young man could not win over stood for Rome.

Fellini's Rome shared the elegiac nature of this literary genre that had contributed so much to the sense of Italian identity. In his treatment of the city, national and personal memories blend, producing a kaleidoscopic effect in which the city becomes fantastical. Rome as the projection of the ambitions of a young man from Rimini and of the illusions of the nation as a whole, against the baroque backdrop of the Church of Rome: from the promise of the Risorgimento to make Rome, as Quintino Sella[9] put it, "the capital of science" to the megalomaniac dreams of fascism.

Let us now look at how Rome became part of the advertising machine for *La dolce vita* and how it got involved in the polemics that followed the release of the film.

Capital Vices, Deadly Sins

"The real woman in *La dolce vita*, dirty, seductive, repulsive, attractive, with a thousand faces and a thousand years old, is the city."[10] So said Fellini, talking about the chief subject of the film.

In April 1959, the film was announced as a "work that will show some aspects of Rome by night,"[11] as a "Roman cocktail,"[12] or as a "fascinating but desolate, luxurious but spiritually miserable picture of *a certain Roman ambiance*."[13] For the press, it was a fresco of a "Babylonian," "pagan," "nocturnal," and "amoral" Rome. It was Fellini himself who had encouraged this comparison between pagan and Christian Rome, the mythical and modern-day city, making a film of snapshots evoking the mythology of the city. The presence of Anita Ekberg, for example, would immediately have reminded contemporary audiences of the film *Nel segno di Roma* (G. Brignone, 1958), a sword-and-sandal affair in which the actress played Zenobia, Queen of Palmira, who challenges the Roman army under Emperor Aurelian. And it is for this reason, too, that Totalscope was used for *La dolce vita*, the format made famous for Hollywood's historical blockbusters in the fifties; and the black-and-white photography was made rather silvery to exalt the almost sculptural dimension of the images.[14]

The relationship between Rome and *La dolce vita* was constructed on the basis of the relationship between mythology and modernity. As the sets were readied for outdoor shooting the film was superimposed on the city, becoming a sort of "happening." The nighttime scenes of *La dolce vita* were a regular appointment for the gatherings of Rome society people during the spring and summer of 1959. As *l'Europeo* saw it: "… toward one in the morning, half of high society in Rome decides to go and see 'Federico filming': one day the Trevi Fountain, the next the Baths of Caracalla, then the alleyways beneath the Quirinale Presidential Palace… in Rome, these outdoor sets are quite common, but in relation to *La dolce vita* the curiosity is heightened: it is a film that has a great deal to say about Rome itself."[15]

When the film was released, its identification with Rome became an important part of the debate.

Parodying the censors of *La dolce vita* in *Le tentazioni del Dottor Antonio* (Fellini's contribution to the omnibus film *Boccaccio '70* made immediately afterward), the protagonist Antonio Mazzuolo (played by Peppino De Filippo)—a moralist obsessed by the advertising hoarding beneath his window with a gigantic Anita Ekberg—spends his time disturbing loving couples in the parks of the city, shouting, "We are in Rome, the cradle of civilization. And you are turning it into a brothel!" Inspired by an episode involving Oscar Luigi Scalfaro, the future president of the Republic,[16] the film played on one of the most persistent criticisms of *La dolce vita*, i.e., that it presented the Eternal City with "the nauseating image of rotting suburbs and vice-ridden districts."[17]

The geography of the reactions to the film reproduced the age-old rivalry between Rome and Milan. The response to the Milan preview (5 February) was particularly significant. Unlike in Rome, two days earlier, the film was jeered, and Fellini was insulted, called a "Communist!" with a hail of spit. As Lo Duca wrote in *La douceur de vivre,* published in France in the same year as the film's release: "The blind and foolish indignation of bourgeois courtiers in Rome and the nouveau riche in Milan is a marvel to behold. In Milan, they fear that if Fellini's film is true the Cossacks, or maybe the Chinese, will soon be at the door, while in Rome the film has made the city sacred once again, as if it has been newly declared an open city, as in wartime."[18]

Perhaps to distance itself from the decadence of Rome, the magazine *Epoca* turned to the elegant prose of Camilla Cederna to launch an investigation—*is there a Milanese dolce vita?*—which soon revealed that, unlike in decadent revel-rousing Rome, in Milan, the "moral capital" of Italy, people were "safely tucked up in bed at midnight." In the same issue a reader reported that the film had been shown in Turin, without causing any fuss, despite the fact that "we are far less worldly-wise than the Milanese." He wondered: "Should I conclude that members of high society and the frequenters of coffee-shops in Milan saw themselves rather too much in their Roman cousins, so pitilessly portrayed in the film, and that they were far from amused?"[19]

Milan, capital of the economic miracle, rejected the emptiness behind the glittering surface of the boom shown unambiguously in *La dolce vita*. The film reinforced the difference between the two cities as symbols: Milan was the city of "work, factories, frenetic movement, wealth"[20] and Rome the city of filmmaking and the high life (during the eighties, Milan duly took its revenge, becoming the capital of the advertising industry and private television channels).

A Brescia newspaper insisted on the decadence and parasitism of a portion of society, "especially in Rome": "Fellini's film is a timely and courageous denunciation of undisturbed privilege, parasitism, prima donnas, the moral decadence and economic satiety of some social groups, whose corruption is an outrage to working Italy."[21]

In a letter published by *l'Unità,* a Milanese factory worker wrote: "Anyone who lives by the sweat of his brow can only marvel at the manner in which some people fritter their time away. No doubt, it could happen elsewhere and perhaps it would surprise me less; *but in Rome, supposed to be the city of prayer, it is just astonishing.* These people would have no time to waste if they had to get up every morning at six o'clock to go to work."[22]

The Rome magazine *La Settimana Incom illustrata* hit back with an investigation it called *True Stories of La dolce vita,* announcing, "Not only in Rome are parts of society corrupt, bored, perpetually on the lookout for new amusements. Here, we reveal an even sadder and more desolate picture of what goes on in the provinces."[23]

The provinces were dragged in to universalize the shabbiness on display in the film: "*La dolce vita* has come to the peaceful town of Ancona, where the excesses of part of Rome society are [so] disconcerting."[24]

An article in *Il Resto del Carlino* summed it all up: "Rome, a Prohibited Paradise Only for Dreamers from Afar." The article analyzed the "regional character" of Fellini, which, presumably, was also Mussolini's, since the two men came from the same area: "In the eyes of people in the provinces, Rome has become a Paradise lost... The provinces dream exactly as Fellini dreams. The filmmaker has an utterly provincial sensibility (he is from Romagna and therefore a dreamer and sentimentalist, like everyone from there, despite the apparent vigor, even violence)."[25]

In 1960 Italians were about to celebrate the hundredth anniversary of unification, and Rome was hosting the Olympic Games, so there was a wish to have a certain image of Rome spread throughout the world, not the kind that was on offer in Fellini's film. The defense of Rome was part and parcel of the furor over *La dolce vita*.

In response to three parliamentary questions from members of his own party, the Christian Democrat Domenico Magrì, under-secretary of state for entertainment, spoke of certain events "which should not occur, above all, in Rome," absolving the film at the end of his speech, with the following wish: "Luckily, in the main, Italians and their ruling class are working people… we hope that putting on display certain filthy episodes that are unworthy of Rome and our civilization will serve as a reminder to everyone that there are limits that need to be respected…"[26]

These words, rejecting a parliamentary motion to have the film confiscated, show how little the anthropological revolution taking place in Italian society at the beginning of the sixties was understood, and this included the failure to realize that Rome was no longer the immaculate symbol of national unity and identity.

In relation to the festivities in 1961 for the hundredth anniversary of the unification of Italy, Emilio Gentile notes that actually during these ceremonies "it became obvious that the idea of the nation was disappearing from the consciousness and civil life of Italians, and with it a love for the nation and trust in the State."[27]

With *La dolce vita*, the myth of Rome—first during the Risorgimento, then during fascism—showed itself to be anachronistic, unreal, and empty, however much it was alive and kicking in the minds of many.

The Complex of Rome

Rome, as symbolic motif, coveted destination, and theater of broken dreams and shattered illusions, runs through Fellini's films from the very beginning. In *Lo sceicco bianco*, Wanda (Brunella Bovo), the young newlywed, pursues the hero of her magazine fictions only to discover the squalor behind their glossy images, while her husband Ivan (Leopoldo Trieste) is spellbound by Rome, its institutional grandeur, its glories, the moral authority of the Church. In both cases, Rome is more imaginary than real.

Talking about the inspiration behind *Satyricon*, Fellini said that reading Petronius he had been particularly struck by what was missing between the episodes: "Back in school, when we studied writers before Pindar, I tried to imagine what might have filled the gaps… the fragmentary made a great impression on me."[28]

The emptiness between one fragment and another presented Fellini with the opportunity to use his imagination. But it also indicated the huge gap between the idea and the reality of Rome.

Fellini's attraction to the fragments of ancient Rome, strewn about higgledy-piggledy, is not just evidence of a Romantic attachment to the force of the imagination, or an explanation of the emotions aroused by the sight of the ruins of Rome during the Grand Tour. Above all, Fellini saw the discrepancy between the modest real force of the city and its symbolic force and impetus, the imagination the city could inspire, and its supposed role in forging Italian identity and nationhood: the whole Rome "complex."

> Italy was unified with a Rome complex. The celebration of Rome was the great subject of the literary figures of the part of Italy that industrialized late, most prominently Giosuè Carducci, who kept alive the myth of Great Italy amid the prosaic political goings-on of the new State... Nonetheless, despite celebrating the myth of Rome, the governors of Unified Italy had no wish to exalt the Rome of the Caesars or the Popes; they wanted to create a Third Rome, an Italian Rome, not inferior to the previous embodiments of Rome in terms of power and ability to spread civilization far and wide... This new Rome attracted to itself a new rhetoric of power, no longer humanistic but modernistic, not literary but scientific, and above all, anti-clerical.[29]

How suited was this new modernistic rhetoric to Rome? Following the military campaign that finally annexed Rome to Italy, Edmondo De Amicis wrote a series of articles in which he celebrated the historic moment and illustrated to his readers the need to conquer Rome and make it the country's capital and the unchallenged heart of the nation.

De Amicis thought of these articles as the first step in educating Italians and inspiring them to civic virtue, work he was to continue in his famous novel *Cuore*. A convinced patriot, whose rhetoric was mitigated by a solid positivist culture and by his didactic intentions, he had to jump through hoops to prettify his first actual meeting with Rome, which took place on 20 September 1870. More than his readers, he tried to convince himself that Rome was a great European metropolis, the capital of this Third Italy, secular, liberal, free of the history of ancient times and papal theocracy: "They told us Rome is a museum, Rome is a city of antiquities, that the quality of life is poor, that it has nothing of the great city to satisfy its inhabitants. Rot! Rome is everywhere and in every way one of the most beautiful and pleasing cities in Italy, nay, it is potentially a great European capital. Mark my words, wait and see."[30]

In 1870, Rome had 160,000 inhabitants and its ancient ruins were decrepit, hardly the makings of a great European capital. Compared by many contemporary visitors to a dirty monumental cemetery, the city was not the automatic choice to forge the new, vibrant, secular, modern identity of the nation.

Yet the imaginative literary leaps De Amicis went through to turn a crumbling town into a magnificent example of modernity and development were nothing compared to the historical falsifications perpetrated by fascism.

Promoted at every opportunity by Mussolini, everywhere he went, the myth of the new Rome had rapidly supplanted the original distaste of fascism for the miserable, picturesque city, a symbol of vice and parliamentary corruption in the feeble Italy of Giolitti. Following the anti-Roman tradition of the Risorgimento, fascism hated the city until Mussolini "decided to inject into its nascent ideology the myth of Rome."[31]

Not that the way the city was gutted and rebuilt by fascism indicated a great affection for it. The facelift essentially symbolized the regeneration of the Italian character that fascism took to be one of its main vocations.[32] As the art historian and consultant to the Duce, Antonio Muňoz, put it: "not only is the sacred land used to build new roads, and solid stone used to build the new city, but *the soul of the inhabitants is shaped with solid intentions.*"[33]

The myth of Rome, of course, was not based on philology. Nor, on the other hand, on nostalgia. The Rome of the past, revisited as poetic myth, was the story fascism told Italy, "an inexhaustible source of ideals and energy."[34] In the creation of complex rituals, the repetition of ceremonies and military parades in the squares of Rome, Mussolini summoned the full persuasive force of fascism and, in the words of Eric Hobsbawm, invented a tradition.[35] The invention of a Rome that "was no more faithful to ancient Rome than the ancient Rome imagined by Hollywood directors."[36]

In line with the familiar literary *topos* (the disillusionment of the young man from the provinces who comes to Rome), Fellini too expressed a certain distaste for the city as it was, unable to match the myth created by fascism and the cinema: "I thought of Rome as Imperial, Fascist, Papal. But when I got there in 1938 on a steam train, I realized that none of it was true. The fact was that Rome was an African city. It had a Middle-Eastern climate, sprawling, slovenly, hot, thousands of kids playing in the streets, people with eyes averted, black, their voices hoarse, speaking dialect."[37]

Mythological Machines

Despite the influence of models broadly investigated by critics (cartoons, caricature, the circus, variety shows), an analysis of Fellini's *mise-en-scène* should not overlook the syncretic, run-down, theatrical nature of fascist Rome during Fellini's youth.

It was a permanent spectacle organized by the regime into a sparkling "phantasmagoria of rituals and symbols."[38] Superimposed signs which, as early as 1933, Bataille read as a form of *unproductive waste,* in the logic of excess encapsulated in the concept of *dépense,* developed by Bataille at that time,[39] an extremely fruitful notion in relation to Fellini's art.

On 10 June 1985, invited by the film society to New York's Lincoln Center for a gala evening in his honor, Fellini spoke of his first encounter with American cinema: "I grew up in a small town... my life was school, Church on Sundays and military parades; *they were trying to convince us that we were the descendents of the Roman Empire.* But there was another lifestyle available, cinema, American films."[40]

The Rome Fellini came to in 1938 was at the height of its transformation by fascism. In September 1938, a huge exhibition celebrating two thousand years since the birth of Augustus Caesar had come to an end, after its inauguration at the Palace of Exhibitions on 23 September 1937. The aim of the exhibition was to keep the myth of ancient Rome alive. Historians of fascism consider it (alongside the obvious Universal Exposition of Rome) to be an excellent illustration of Mussolini's policy for Rome and his overall attitude toward history. As the apotheosis of the myth of Rome, as intended, it had a great impact on public opinion.

Not surprisingly, during the event, the Exhibition of the Fascist Revolution was dusted off and repeated after its initial success in 1932. This show gave a clear idea of the relationship between modernism, the avantgarde, and monumental classicism in the visual culture of fascism.[41]

The symbiosis of modernity and myth, ancient and fascist Rome, told as one uninterrupted story, is the clearest indication of the workings of Mussolini's imagination. Anything that might have disturbed the smooth narrative—such as the disemboweling of Via dei Fori Imperiali less for archaeological purposes than to add theatricality and create an imposing scene—was omitted. And, in addition, the vision required Catholicism and fascism to become a single faith: "Fascism is the third Italic blossoming of the concept of *order, measure* and *balance, discipline* and *authority*...these concepts were born in ancient Rome and flourished again during the course of history, with a different form, in the guise of the Catholic Church in Rome."[42]

In his article "Riscoprire la romanità" (Rediscovering the Nature of Rome), in the journal *Carattere,* Julius Evola said that some Roman characteristics, such as sobriety, should be imitated, not others. In other words, "he raised the question of *which* Rome should be taken as a model. The origins of Rome and Republican Rome were perfectly suitable; not so 'decadent' Rome, with its mixed ethnicity, abhorred by the fascists."[43]

This is one of the reasons Fellini's attraction to pagan Rome and his film *Satyricon* had an anti-fascist slant: "The idea of making a film on paganism, of studying what a man must have been like before the advent of Christianity, of investigating the psychology of someone with no sense of the meaning of life or of his own actions is very stimulating; it fascinates me... I have been intending to make *Satyricon* for some time. In 1939, when I hadn't yet started working in films and was working for *Marc'Aurelio* I thought about adapting Petronius for the theater, in order to make *an anti-fascist parody*, insofar as that would have been possible."[44]

And, in fact, in *Satyricon*, Mussolini's Rome undergoes a sort of sinking process into a primordial obscurity. Fellini's imagination led him to use the ruins of the city quite differently from how fascism used them.

Studying the symbolism of Italy's ruins, Carolyn Springer noted that instead of entering into a Romantic reverie about the past, as Byron and Goethe did, ruins can also be seen as a powerful *presence*, the sign that legitimizes and fortifies the present. Indeed, this is how they were used both by popes and by the rhetorical strategies of Italian nationalism.[45] Faced with modern rationalism and fascist aesthetics, ruins became a present that signified the relevance of the past.

In *Satyricon* the opposite occurs: ruins and fragments become emblematic of a discontinuous and incomplete narrative technique. They also give visual form to a film that invents another kind of relationship between modernist rationalism and imagining ancient civilization. As Fellini said, "Pompei is contaminated with the psychedelic, Byzantine and pop art, Mondrian, Klee, and Barbaric art."[46]

In the fascist aesthetic of massive monuments, the spirit of the ruins was supposed to express an "incitement to work for a new grandiose affirmation of a country reborn,"[47] and a struggle that was intended to represent "the most sublime and direct victory of the spirit over nature."[48] Fellini's aesthetics, on the other hand, follow the theories of Georg Simmel in relation to the idea of ruins. According to Simmel, ruins inspire not a melancholy reevocation of the past but the emergence of new forces antagonistic to the spiritual values once embodied in the monuments: "buildings reached up towards the sky through the force of human will, but what determines their current aspect is the *mechanical force of nature*, a corrosive and destructive force downwards."[49]

This "mechanical force of nature" involves a non-linear conception of time and memory, important aspects of Fellini's films as the critics have often remarked.

The "form of ruin" identified by Simmel nurtures the visionary and dreamlike qualities of Fellini's ancient Rome. The sliding slums, the face of Encolpio (Michael Potter), which at the end of the film is transformed into a fresco amid the ruins, indicate the enormous distance between us and the ancient world, a distance that can only be filled by phantoms, sounds, and incomprehensible figures. As Fellini said: "What interests me, is the attempt to evoke—as an artist always does—an unknown world, the world of two thousand years ago, a world that no longer exists. The attempt to put it back together, I mean, through a figurative and narrative structure, rather as in archaeology."[50]

The final transformation of the face of Encolpio into ruins is interesting in light of one of the motifs of Mussolini's Rome, the gradual *petrifaction* of the face of the Duce after the founding of the Empire. This denoted the wish to become a monument among monuments, it was "as if Mussolini's ambition to make fascism and his own fame eternal, by rendering them immortal in stone, had taken over his own person, turning him into a living statue."[51]

Such is the dual significance of the form of ruin: on the one hand its retreat into mystery to reevoke the state of nature, as at the end of *Satyricon,* on the other hand its petrifaction into mythical status as in the image of the Duce in the mock LUCE newsreel in *Roma,* or the floral Duce in *Amarcord.*

The Ruins of Modernity

So Fellini, like Mussolini, uses Rome to read the present. Take the promotional strategy used for *Fellini-Satyricon*. As Raffaele De Berti[52] has shown, Fellini focused on the nude scenes and the scandals that the film was likely to provoke, insisting on an analogy with the libertarian culture of 1968. In other words, *Satyricon* was part of a "much broader battle for sexual liberation and civil rights, such as the divorce law. The latter was at the center of the political and cultural debate in Italy in the second half of the sixties."[53]

Where Mussolini's austere and disciplined Rome was intended to be the model for the new Empire, picking up the threads of an interrupted history, Fellini's chaotic Rome is the symbol of the disorientation of today's world.

More than a parody of Mussolini's Rome, what we have—as some of the reviews of the film indicated—is a play of mirrors: *Rome as obsession; Rome doesn't exist, it has to be invented; From Vitellone to the son of the shewolf; Fellini disembowels Rome;* the last of these was an explicit reference to Mussolini's Rome.[54]

The monumental falsification of Rome staged by Mussolini is mirrored in Fellini's falsification of the city in the studios of Cinecittà: a copy of part of Via Veneto in *La dolce vita,* a long stretch of the Orbital Road reconstructed for *Roma* and, for the same film, the rebuilding of a subway station in a quarry in Cinecittà.

For both Mussolini and Fellini, Rome is a symbolic space over which to exercise absolute control, to project and sculpt one's ego permanently: "Via Veneto reconstructed by Gherardi was exact, right down to the finest details... working on the set my disaffection for the real street grew and now I think I will never get over it... I also have the irresistible temptation to control the real street in the same despotic manner as I did the fictional one. A complicated situation, I should talk about it to someone who understands psychoanalysis."[55]

In the EUR district of Rome, created for the Universal Exposition of 1942, the play of mirrors greets the naked eye.

Designed to be the nucleus of Mussolini's new Rome, the project was interrupted in 1941 due to the intensification of the war. The building sites were abandoned, leaving tons and cubic meters of stone in the form of colossal buildings. The accumulated materials, the statues left off their plinths, looked like "a gigantic, spectral ruin, before even having been alive."[56]

A majestic reevocation of the past, improbably blending modern rationalism, metaphysical painting, and fascist monumentalism, the EUR has the fascination of an unrealized utopia, a sci-fi and archaic modernity. As such it has a leading role in Fellini's cinema. It was perhaps the only part of Rome able to compete in Fellini's imagination with the studio reconstructions of Cinecittà.

He shot a number of scenes there, from *La dolce vita* onward, including the parodies of silent films about ancient Rome (as in the fake sword-and-sandal scene shot in the colonnade of the Museum of Roman Civilization in a sequence of *A Director's Notebook*).

In *Fellini e l'EUR*, a documentary produced by RAI state television in 1973,[57] the filmmaker is shown strolling through the buildings in the district, trying to explain what it is that fascinates him about the place. He says that to his eyes the entire district is a massive film studio; the buildings have the same provisional and illusory nature as film scenery. "It's a district that both is and isn't there." He continued, making an implicit comparison with a film set: "The EUR was meant to be a certain thing... Mussolini wanted to celebrate victory alongside Hitler, so it also has the fascination of a sort of folly, a mad dream that changed into something else. I am fascinated by the provisional nature of the place; it's like living among the stands of a Trade Exhibition, say in Milan, you get the feeling you might wake up and find they've taken everything down and carried it all off."

The architects appointed to design E42 received a brief that included magical effect. They were told to build a huge complex of buildings and sculptures "with great visual impact," "able to strike and inspire the imagination of onlookers," impressing itself on the "memory of visitors by means of fantasy."[58] These aspects were all incorporated into Fellini's cinematic *mise-en-scène* and literally filmed in the one work of his shot entirely in the EUR, *Le tentazioni del dottor Antonio*. A giant Anita Ekberg coming to life on a massive billboard denotes not only an erotic obsession but "magical realism on a scale never seen before," in the highfalutin words of a contemporary article on the design of the EUR.[59]

The colossal architecture of this district that both "is and isn't there" expresses the emptiness on which the myth of Rome was based and into which it would sink. It is a mixture of the spectacular and the funereal, a sort of monumental cemetery, the essence of fascist visual culture. Such is the *"horror vacui* of modernist urban space" as evoked by Fellini in the scenes of *La dolce vita* shot in the EUR district, for example the episode of Steiner's suicide.[60]

As Gentile says, "The monumentality of the EUR was a new example of symbolic syncretism between fascism and Catholicism in the myth of Rome."[61] In other words it was a space in which to reconcile the irreconcilable tropes of progress and myth, rationalism and mysticism, that Fellini rendered with his characteristic anguished theatricality.

The Mole

The first rumors of a film to be made about Rome date back to the time of shooting *La dolce vita*. An article in *La Stampa* dated 5 September 1959 (*Fellini Works for Television after* La dolce vita) informed readers that Fellini was planning to make twenty-four documentaries about Italy and, above all, Rome. "My job," said Fellini, "will be to introduce Rome to Romans and Italy to Italians." The synoptic vision of the city Fellini presents in *Roma* is reminiscent of a project for a film on Mussolini's Rome, half investigation, half epic narrative, put forward in 1936 by the journal *Cinema*:

> [Imagine] in a few years time, walking through new districts, huge arteries for the flow of traffic, between the buildings and monuments that recall centuries and millennia of greatness, and standing in huge squares, parks, gardens, to wonder: what was Rome like before Mussolini? We can barely remember it and have difficulty—*so warm and perfect is the blend between the ancient and modern*—in recognizing the work done. What document could possibly testify to the titanic undertaking? Some photographs perhaps, writings, articles, tomes; but it will be difficult to show that *complex vision* which only cinema could afford, capturing the impressiveness, the vivacity, the dynamism of its life! A fantastic ride through three mil-

lennia of greatness, glory, and Italian history; an admirable cinematic vision which we could have enjoyed in years to come, speaking of a series of works, affording *impressive comparisons* and almost *dramatic visions*.[62]

Under the guise of an investigation and alternating memories, current affairs and imagination, Fellini's film on Rome manages to reproduce—in a whirl—all the previous images of the city presented in his films: Rome dreamed of from the provinces as in *Lo sceicco bianco*, the dilapidated popular Rome of *Il bidone* and *Le notti di Cabiria*, society Rome as in *La dolce vita*, and the ancient, mysterious Rome of *Satyricon* and *A Director's Notebook*.[63]

In addition to this, the film includes the falsification of his memories: the mythical city seen in films or imagined in fascist school books, the city that Fellini arrived in shortly before the war. And the city of the here and now, at the beginning of the seventies, that Fellini is pretending to be making a documentary about: a chaotic area invaded by traffic, where priests and hippies mix, like fragments in a colossal spectacle indifferent to time, fashion, and ideas.

Fellini is intent on showing a "complex vision" able to conjure different time periods: impressive comparisons, dramatic visions, as the article written in 1938 had called for. A homage to Rome as palimpsest, imitating—as Freud wrote during his stay in the city—the form of the unconscious itself.[64]

This function as the unconscious of Italian modernity is seen in one of the best-known sequences of the film, the excavation for the construction of the subway.

Work on the Rome subway system had begun in the thirties, during fascism, but the first line was completed only in 1955. After complications and delays, work resumed in 1969, using a machine called a "mole." This new method of digging tunnels soon ran into problems due to the discovery of numerous archaeological remains, which caused (and still cause) long stops in the progress of the work.[65] The film shows the initial use of the digger mole.

Looking for locations, Fellini and his co-scriptwriter Bernardini Zapponi visited the building site for the subway station in San Giovanni. After talking to the foreman who had just yet again been ordered to down tools by the City Authority, Zapponi commented: "Sure, the engineer loves the Mole. He has built dams in Africa, oil pipelines in Iran, he has made engineering a religion with machines for totems... but here in the city of the Pontiff, he can do nothing against other jealous divinities, who do not want schismatic machinery and heretical progress."[66]

The sequence begins with the words of the engineer. "Below ground, in Rome, you never know what to expect. Every hundred meters there are remains." The film crew, which is pretending to be shooting a documentary on Rome, enters the site and the engineer continues: "We were trying to fix a simple city traffic problem, with a subway as in Munich or Dublin, but here there are eight layers of buildings underground, we have to become archaeologists, even speleologists. They've been talking about a Rome subway since 1871, exactly a hundred years ago. Bureaucracy is even stranger than what we find underground… the correspondence between ourselves and the City Authority runs the whole length of the tunnel."

The images of the underground excavation work alternates with shots of piles of papers stacked up in corridors of choked offices. There is a tracking shot of these dingy premises, mirroring the tracking shots of the film crew and workmen in the tunnel.

When the engineer tells us that we are under the San Giovanni district of the city, we are shown a shot of the surface, where a man and woman, in the bedroom, are surprised and frightened by land slippage caused by the excavation work. This scene was inspired by real complaints of cracks appearing in houses due to the vibrations of the burrowing mole. The engineer then points to an underground river running through the city and emerging at the Cessati Spiriti, a street in a working-class area to the south. The same street had been used in *La dolce vita* for the scene in which Marcello and Maddalena take home the prostitute they had picked up at the beginning of the film only to find the house completely flooded.

The transmitters indicate a void on the other side of the wall and the mole has to be shut down. A milling machine is fitted to test the terrain. The workmen discover a Roman *domus,* dating back two thousand years. They go in, carrying torches. Everything looks intact, statues, frescoes on the walls, portraits. Then, the paint begins to corrode and the frescoes disappear: "It is the air outside, it's destroying the frescoes! Look at this disaster! Do something!" But nothing can be done; even the statues begin to flake and split under our very eyes and in the room no trace of the past remains.

"Rome is the Sum of All Our Errors"

The past cannot be recovered, only dreamt, imagined, and evoked, as Genius—Fellini's medium friend—attempts in *A Director's Notebook* at the tomb of Cecilia Metella on the old Appian way, with the strange experiment in "parapsychological stratography."[67]

In *Roma,* the subway sequence picks up from Fellini's previous film/documentary, in which Fellini and an archaeologist travel on the Rome subway and see through the windows of the train the sudden appearance of ancient Romans standing among the waiting passengers in the station. Fellini says, "in a way we are travelling in time, not space."

The initial shots of the piles of documents in the dark corridors mentioned by the engineer were filmed in the State Archives. Although barely glimpsed, the frames have a precise purpose. As Zapponi wrote in his diary of the filmmaking process:

> This huge building, new but with long black lines already on the radiators, holds all the documents about the country, particularly its political life: data sheets filled in by the OVRA with lists of people sent into internal exile by fascism, documents relating to the life of the Court, the decrees of the censor. Fellini is enthralled by the dossiers and the details of the dinners of the House of Savoy...endless rooms, perfect for the *anguished tracking shot he has planned*... in a civilized country paper should be disposed of rapidly: be written on, read and destroyed, returned to the paper mill. But here, undigested paper piles up, becomes heavy, gives you liver trouble as can be seen in the yellow faces of the employees. They are the result of accumulating information for centuries and include secret reports, anonymous letters, applications, pleas, letters of introduction... the literary illusions of millions of crazy schoolteachers and the verdicts of thousands of policemen, they all end up here in the silent temple of the State Archives.[68]

In light of these observations, the scene has additional significance. The idea of oneiric nostalgia is expressed both by the "national memory" (State Archives) and "mythical memory" (underground Rome). The tunnels twisting and turning through the belly of the city recall the 110 kilometers of documents in the Archives, twice the distance covered by the underground railway.

The "fatal voice of Rome," Giulio Bollati writes, carries with it the rhetoric and ideals that have functioned over time as a "fundamental reservation about modernity."[69] In the conflict between antiquity and progress, in the form of a palimpsest, what can be seen is the traumatic background of Italian modernity, a modernity that fails to expunge anti-modernity because—as we know only too well—it is "unable to leave the past behind or resolve its problems, but simply superimposes itself over antiquity and mixes with it, producing only incongruities and inefficiencies."[70]

The infinite political vicissitudes of the Rome subway are a good example of the anomalies of the failure of Italy to modernize and the archaic inheritance against which it has to measure itself. Nonetheless, Fellini's Roman elegy is not simply anti-modern. Using Rome as the idea of a dream that cannot be turned into reality, Fellini's reconstructed city serves as a representation of the entire dystopian nation. In this representation, the rhetorical strategies used to attempt to define the Italian identity take form and, at the same time, disappear: Rome as a mixture of antiquity and modernity, Catholicism and the secular, North and South.

Treated like a character in a film, Fellini's Rome reflected his concern with infantilism and the inability to achieve a true maturity. In Rome, he said, "there are no neurotics, but there are no adults either. It's a city of indolent children, skeptical, badly behaved, psychically a little deformed, because to prevent growth is unnatural."[71]

Chronically immature, ignorant, grievous, superficial, badly behaved, these are the characteristics of Rome Fellini returns to again and again in the book *Fare un Film* (Making a Film), a collection of his writings and interviews. What emerges from those pages is his fascination with the city, which does not cancel out his irritation with its intrinsic nature. In this, he was not unlike Mussolini, who was equally attracted to mythical Rome and repelled by the actual city before his eyes.

In a short sequence cut from *Roma*, Alberto Sordi—a sort of personification of Rome—is given this monologue: "Why am I happy to live in Rome? It's a question of habit. I am a creature of habit. But it's not as if people here are all that pleasant. Actually... I don't even like the dialect. When I first went to Milan... I was fourteen... I realized that the dialect in Rome is ugly... course, guttural... like belching. Today, of course, everyone understands it... because of films... People know that to say a certain thing... to be funny in a certain way... the violence of Roman dialect is needed... but it's still ugly... and I don't even much like Rome."[72]

And yet, Fellini is considered to be someone who was able to express "the soul of Rome," its virtues and its vices, who, in *La dolce vita*, had given the city a new lease of life, based on tourism. This was the spirit of the Romarcord exhibition organized by Vincenzo Mollica and Alessandro Nicosia in 2003, to commemorate the tenth anniversary of Fellini's death.

On that occasion the then mayor of Rome, Walter Veltroni, said: "Fellini invented a new way to tell the story of Rome and the capital is everywhere in his films. He was in love with the city. The film *Roma* reveals its most hidden aspects."[73]

Far from loving the city, you could wonder whether Fellini even liked it. Indeed, reviewing *Roma*, Oreste del Buono did just that.[74] Fellini's attitude to the city he rebuilt in the studios of Cinecittà was at best ambivalent. It was, for him, an eternal fiction and allegory of emptiness, a void on which the idea of national identity was based.

Moravia remarked that Fellini had placed Rome "outside history, in the immobile and inert area of aestheticism"[75] and this does not seem wide of the mark. In another scene shot in the Trastevere district but cut from the film, a Christian Democrat minister is seated at an open-air table, with the look of a facetious cynic. He is given the following words: "What can I say? Rome is the sum total of all errors. I could even add: it is the topographical expression of our mistakes. A center that doesn't work, where you can't turn left. Endless roadworks."[76]

As for Mussolini, so for Fellini: Rome was not only a symbolic place but also the ghost of art and one's "mission" (which, for Mussolini, was both political and artistic). As Fellini has the novelist Gore Vidal say, Rome is the "seat of the Church, the government and cinema: *all things that produce illusions.*"

Notes

1. A. Spinosa, "Roma e Milano, faccia a faccia" [Rome and Milan, Face to Face], *Corriere della Sera*, 15 October 1972.

2. F. Giuliani, "Le mie passioni di ragazzo dentro una Roma che è un 'mito'" [My Boyhood Passions in a "Mythical" Rome], *la Repubblica*, 5 June 2008.

3. G. Russo, "Il maestro e la capitale" [The Maestro and the Capital], *Corriere della Sera*, 2 November 1993, now in G. Russo, *Con Flaiano e Fellini a via Veneto* (Soveria Mannelli: Rubbettino, 2005), 139–141.

4. See for example M. Bertozzi, "La città necessaria. Roma nella poetica felliniana" [The Necessary City: Rome in Fellini's Poetics], in *Roma nel cinema* [Rome in Film], ed. A. Sbardella (Rome: Semar, 2000), 15–25; the volume edited by Bernardino Zapponi, *Roma di Federico Fellini* (Bologna: Cappelli, 1972); F. Di Biagi, *La Roma di Fellini* (Genoa: Le Mani, 2008); see also Fellini, *Fare un film,* especially 144–150.

5. M. Bertozzi, "La città necessaria," 23.

6. F. Moretti, *Opera mondo. Saggio sulla forma epica dal 'Faust' a 'Cent'anni di solitudine'* [The World Opus: Essay on the Epic Form, from *Faust* to *One Hundred Years of Solitude*] (Turin: Einaudi, 2003).

7. Fellini was a co-scriptwriter on all three films.

8. S. Stewart-Steinberg, "Fare gli italiani, ossia l'effetto-Pinocchio" [Making Italians, i.e., the Pinocchio Effect], in *Identità Italiana tra Europa e società multiculturale,* 31. Stewart-Steinberg sets out her thoughts on the novel by Matilde Serao, *La conquista di Roma* [The Conquest of Rome], one of the most famous of parliamentary novels. See also G. Caltagirone, *Dietroscena. L'Italia post-unitaria nei romanzi di ambiente parlamentare* [Behind the Scenes: Unified Italy in the Parliamentary Novel] (Rome: Bulzoni, 1993).

9. Minister of finance (1862–1876) and an important politician in the Kingdom of Italy.

10. From a lengthy interview published in France by *Express* on 7 July 1959, and quoted in J. Gili, "L'accoglienza della 'dolce vita' a Parigi, Stampa, censura, pubblico" [The Reaction to *La dolce vita* in Paris: Press, Censorship, and the Public], in *Federico Fellini. Mezzo secolo di dolce vita* [Federico Fellini: Half a Century of *La dolce vita*], ed. V. Boarini and T. Kezich, 161.

11. "Più viva che mai Anita di notte" [Anita by Night, Livelier than Ever], *Annabella*, 5 April 1959.

12. See *La Notte*, 25 May 1959.

13. G. Sandrelli, "Arrivano i Festivals" [Here Come the Festivals], *Gazzettino Sera*.

14. Various aspects of the film are reminiscent of the atmosphere of mythological films, including the opening music by Nino Rota, as the credits roll. Fellini described it as "a tune that suggests the sumptuously oriental and decadent: sort of Chinese-sounding" (quoted by P.M. De Santi, *La dolce vita*, 93). Fellini added, "the clothes are costumes because, after all, my film is a costume drama."

15. N. Minuzzo, "La città quasi nuda" [The Almost Naked City], *L'Europeo*, 19 April 1959. In one photo Silvana Mangano can be seen, with the caption "the actress joins with others, watching Fellini shooting. It is 2 o'clock in the morning. Today it is fashionable to come out of the theaters and watch Fellini at work."

16. One of the most absurd and exemplary events in the bigoted Italy of the fifties: in a hot Rome restaurant Edith Mingoni took off her jumper and the parliamentarian and future president of Italy Oscar Luigi Scalfaro walked the length of the room to upbraid her for her inappropriate dress. The episode ended up at the police station, after a complaint from Mingoni, a supporter of the right-wing Movimento Sociale. The newspapers embroidered the facts, inventing a slap between the contending parties. First the woman's father, a retired Air Force general, then her husband, publicly challenged Scalfaro to a duel, turned down because such a thing, according to the recipient of the challenges, was "contrary to Catholic morality." At this point the comic Totò weighed in, with an open letter published in *L'Avanti* accusing Scalfaro of cowardice and baseness.

17. "È questa la dolce vita?," *La voce dei Berici*, 21 February 1960.

18. J. Gili, "L'accoglienza della 'dolce vita'," 163.

19. Letter to the director of *Epoca*, 21 February 1960.

20. J. Foot, *Milan Since the Miracle: City, Culture and Identity* (London: Bloomsbury, 2001), in which Milan is called a non-cinematic city.

21. "Può la politica incidere sul costume?" [Can Politics Influence Customs?], *Il Cittadino*, 21 February 1960.

22. Letter to the director of *L'Unità*, 24 February 1969. My italics.

23. C. Stampa, "Le storie vere della Dolce vita" [True Stories of *La dolce vita*], *La settimana Incom*, 25 February 1960.

24. From *Il Gazzettino di Venezia*, 27 February 1960. In *Divorzio all'italiana* (1961) Germi has Baron Cefalù (Marcello Mastroianni) say: "Preceded by a great clamor, scandal, polemics that had barely died down, protests, soul-searching and praise up to the skies, a sensational film had come to town. The San Firmino parish priest hurled his lightning bolts against the film, warning sons and daughters against it, and told the faithful not to go, but without much success... There are orgies worthy of Tiberius, wife-swapping, striptease shows.... Let's go lads."

25. C. Marabini, "Roma è un paradiso proibito soltanto per chi sogna da lontano," *Il Resto del Carlino*, 26 February 1960.

26. J. Gili, "L'accoglienza della 'dolce vita'," 165.

27. E. Gentile, *La grande Italia. Il mito della nazione nel XX secolo* [The Greatness

of Italy: The Myth of the Nation in the Twentieth Century] (Rome/Bari: Laterza, 2009), 407.

28. F. Fellini, *Intervista sul cinema*, 136–137.

29. E. Gentile, *La grande Italia*, 47–49.

30. E. De Amicis, "La città di Roma," 26 September 1870, in E. De Amicis, *Impressioni di Roma*, ed. Gabriella Romana (Venice: Marsilio, 2010), 65–66.

31. E. Gentile, *Fascismo di pietra* [Fascism of Stone] (Rome/Bari: Laterza, 2007), vii–viii.

32. As Gentile wrote: "The pick became the symbol of the frenetic energy with which Mussolini wanted personally to destroy the old picturesque quarters of Rome. Under fascism, newspapers and newsreels highlighted the Duce, sometimes in uniform, sometimes in plain clothes, on the roof of a house wielding a pick." *Fascismo di pietra*, 74.

33. A. Muñoz, *Roma di Mussolini* (Milan: Treves, 1935), xii.

34. J. Nelis, "Constructing Fascist Identity: Benito Mussolini and the Myth of Romanità," in *Classic World* 100, no. 4 (2007), 409.

35. E. Hobsbawm and T. Ranger, eds., *The Invention of Tradition* (Oxford: Oxford University Press, 1992).

36. E. Gentile, *Fascismo di pietra*, 258.

37. Fellini, interviewed by Lietta Tornabuoni in *La Stampa* on 21 March 1971, repeated the phrase of Francesco Saverio Nitti (also copied by Flaiano): "Rome is the only southern city without a *European* quarter."

38. S. Falasca-Zamponi, *Fascist Spectacle: The Aesthetics of Power in Mussolini's Italy* (Berkeley: University of California Press, 1997).

39. G. Bataille, "La structure psychologique du fascisme," *La Critique sociale*, 11 March 1934. For the use of the notion of *dépense* in the interpretation of Fellini's cinema, see A. Minuz, "La seduzione permanente o l'elogio attrazionale del cinema" [Permanent Seduction or the Attractive Acclaim of the Cinema], in *Studi (e testi) Italiani* no. 29 (Rome: Bulzoni, 2007), 85–102.

40. E. Franceschini, "Gran festa a New York per Federico Fellini" [New York Celebrates Fellini], *la Repubblica*, 12 June 1985.

41. See J. Schnapp, *Anno x. La Mostra della Rivoluzione fascista del 1932; genesi—sviluppo—contesto culturale-storico—ricezione* [Year X. Exhibition of the Fascist Revolution of 1932; Genesis—Development—Cultural-Historical Context] (Rome/Pisa: Istituti editoriali e poligrafici internazionali, 2003).

42. O. Di Giambernardino, *Il fascismo e gli ideali di Roma* [Fascism and the Ideals of Rome] (Florence: Vallecchi, 1931). My italics.

43. S. Patriarca, *Italianità*, 157.

44. Statement by Federico Fellini to *Il Popolo*, 24 July 1968.

45. C. Springer, *The Marble Wilderness: Ruins and Representation in Italian Romanticism, 1775-1850* (Cambridge: Cambridge University Press, 1987). A huge number of books have been written on ruins, particularly the ruins of Rome; see for example V. De Caprio, ed., *Poesia e poetica delle rovine di Roma* [Poetry and Poetics of the Ruins of Rome] (Rome: Istituto Nazionale di Studi Romani, 1987).

46. F. Fellini in D. Zanelli, ed., *Fellini-Satyricon* (Bologna: Cappelli, 1969), 71. For *Fellini-Satyricon* see the multidisciplinary study edited by R. De Berti, E. Gaggetti,

and F. Slavazzi, *Fellini-Satyricon. L'immaginario dell'antico* [Fellini-Satyricon: Imagining Antiquity] (Milan: Cisalpino, 2009).

47. A. Chiappelli, "Il fascismo e la suggestione delle rovine" [Fascism and the Splendor of Ruins] in *Educazione fascista*, 20 April 1931, quoted in E. Gentile, *Il culto del littorio. La sacralizzazione della politica nell'Italia fascista* [The Cult of the Lictor: Rendering Politics Sacred in Fascist Italy] (Rome/Bari: Laterza, 2009), 211.

48. Ibid.

49. G. Simmel, "The Ruin," *Hudson Review* 11, no. 3 (Autumn 1958).

50. F. Fellini in D. Zanelli, *Fellini-Satyricon*, 21.

51. E. Gentile, *Fascismo di pietra*, 131.

52. R. De Berti, "Riflessi di 'Fellini-Satyricon' nella stampa periodica" [Reflections of *Fellini-Satyricon* in the Press], in *Fellini-Satyricon. L'immaginario dell'antico*, R. De Berti, E. Gaggetti, and F. Slavazzi, 254.

53. Ibid., 263–269. In this sense, the imaginary created for *Fellini-Satyricon* functions as a "continuous contamination at multiple levels between the ancient, modern and ethnic, a contamination that operates not only at the level of costume, make-up and hair styling, but also, as the film makes very evident, at the level of music and dialogue." E. Gaggetti, "La percezione dell'antico. I Romani di 'Fellini-Satyricon' tra musei capitolini e 'Harper's Bazaar'" [The Perception of Antiquity: The Romans of *Fellini-Satyricon*, Part Rome's Museums, Part 'Harper's Bazaar'], in *Fellini-Satyricon*, ed. R. De Berti, E. Gaggetti, and F. Slavazzi, 173.

54. Respectively, U. Casiraghi in *l'Unità*, 17 March 1972; G. Grazzini in *Corriere della Sera*, 17 March 1972; L. Cavicchioli in *Domenica del Corriere*, 8 June 1971; A. Scagnetti in *Paese Sera*, 17 March 1972.

55. F. Fellini in *L'Europeo*, 8 July 1962, in *Dalla dolce vita alla 'Dolce vita', un sistema circolare* [From the Sweet Life to "La dolce vita," a Circular System], ed. E. Grippa and A. Magistà, 64.

56. I. Insolera, *Roma moderna. Un secolo di storia urbanistica 1870-1970* [Modern Rome: A Century of Urban History 1870-1970] (Turin: Einaudi, 2001), 168.

57. The film, directed by Luciano Emmer, was part of a series of documentaries entitled *Io e...* [Me and...]. Each film showed an artist talking about his relationship with a certain work of art. Fellini chose the EUR; Pasolini chose the city of Orte.

58. E. Gentile, *Il culto del littorio*, 228.

59. G. Ponti, "Olimpiade della civiltà. L'E42 città favolosa" [The Olympics of Civilization: The E42, Fabulous City], in *Corriere della Sera*, 4 May 1938, in E. Gentile, *Il culto del littorio*, 229.

60. See A. Ricciardi, "The Spleen of Rome: Mourning Modernisim in Fellini's 'La dolce vita'," *Modernism/Modernity* 7, no. 2 (2000), 212. Also relevant is the famous ending to Antonioni's *L'eclisse* [Eclipse], part of the omnibus film *Boccaccio '70* (1962).

61. E. Gentile, *Il culto del littorio*, 231.

62. "Proposta per un film. Documentare la rinascita di Roma" [Proposal for a Film: Documenting the Rebirth of Rome], *Cinema* 1, no. 8 (25 October 1936), 304.

63. Fellini cited among the sources of the film Aldo Palazzeschi's novel *Roma*, adopted for the stage. Probably he used it for the episode of the bombing of San

Lorenzo. Other sources include the drawings of Giacchino Colizzi, aka Attalo. From the twenties on, Attalo was one of Italy's most accomplished satirical cartoonists, famous for his sketches of street life in Rome. Fellini met him while working for *Marc'Aurelio*, where Attalo was revered. His drawings were not openly anti-fascist satires but the Roman life he portrayed was light-years away from the version of it propounded by fascism. Guglielmo Guasta, the director of the magazine *Il Travaso*, said of him: "Attalo's cartoons have a historical value, like the watercolors of Roesler Franz. They show the streets, the squares, the buildings of a 'disappeared Rome'; they are drawings of interiors, not exteriors, of the intimacy that had gone from Rome." (G. Guasta, "La Roma di Attalo," in Attalo, *Il Gagà che aveva detto agli amici* [What Gagà Told His Friends] [Rome: Lara, 1968], 5). These interiors showed not the compact and disciplined Rome Mussolini would have wanted, but a lazy lower bourgeoisie of "untidy kitchenettes, cats, potties, foot-baths on the balconies, serving wenches with big bottoms and bushy armpits, libertine granddads and miserable fops; a host of office workers and shopkeepers, Rome's sad multitudes." B. Zapponi, *Roma*, 38.

64. In *Civilization and its Discontents*. Also relevant—as Fellini criticism has pointed out—is the essay on Jensen's novella *Gravida* (drawn to Freud's attention by Jung).

65. Recent findings include, in 2009, Hadrian's Athenaeum, built in A.D. 113 for poets, philosophers, and scientists. It was discovered during the excavations for the C Line of the Rome Subway, in piazza Venezia, in front of the Altare della Patria.

66. B. Zapponi, *Roma*, 17.

67. Elisabetta Gaggetti notes that in the film Fellini's imagination is drawn to the extrasensory and intuitive, unmediated by philology or archaeology. E. Gaggetti, "La percezione dell'antico. I Romani di 'Fellini-Satyricon' tra musei capitolini e 'Harper's Bazaar'," in R. De Berti, E. Gaggetti, and F. Slavazzi, *Fellini-Satyricon*, 181–190.

68. B. Zapponi, *Roma*, 45. OVRA was the fascist secret police.

69. G. Bollati, *L'italiano*, 117.

70. E. Galli Della Loggia, *L'identità italiana*, 139.

71. F. Fellini, *Fare un film*, 145.

72. B. Zapponi, *Roma*, 192.

73. In his pamphlet, *Controfellini*, Pietro Angelini suggested that Fellini's Rome was accurate and colorful but by no means unknown: "Behind him, in support, Fellini has a long tradition and repertoire of rhetorical commonplaces, hard to get rid of, if this centuries-old image of the easy-going goddess with a vocation for unending death is the one that continues to fascinate tourists." 115.

74. O. Del Buono, "Roma 1972 D.F. (Dopo Fellini)" [Rome 1972 A.F.—After Fellini], *L'Europeo*, 23 March 1972.

75. A. Moravia, "Un défilé col cardinale," *L'espresso*, 26 March 1972.

76. B. Zapponi, *Roma*, 192.

Photos

From *La dolce vita*: the image of Christ transported by helicopter over the Parco degli acquedotti in Rome, 1960 (still)

From *The Great Beauty*: the artistic performance—Parco degli acquedotti, Rome, 2014 (still)

Alberto in *I vitelloni*, 1953 (still)

OGGI, 13 November 1958 ("Via Veneto will act for Fellini" — article on the making of *La dolce vita*)

Le Ore (13 February 1960—"Milan's millions accusing Rome's wealthy," article on the infighting between Milan and Rome after the Milan release of *La dolce vita*.)

"Avanti!" 11 February 1960 (Fascists and *azione cattolica* against *La dolce vita*)

"What would Garibaldi say?" — *Paese Sera,* 24 September 1975
(on the TV broadcast of *La dolce vita*)

Umanità, 14 January 1974, 23 (article by Giulio Cesare Castello:
"Fellini's used memories" on *Amarcord*). Text:
"A historical/prophetic photo that explains *Amarcord*. A young Fellini from the Provinces (right) observes the face of fascism, in an early form but already with its essential features: the Duce, the clergy, generals, society ladies. The boy observing the scene was to live through twenty years of the regime and to become obsessed with memories of the period, which he has now put into a grotesque film, *Amarcord,* or 'I remember'. It is not his fault if what was grotesque was reality and not his film."

Amarcord ("Famiglia Cristiana," 29 July 1973—article on the film)

Amarcord ("Famiglia Cristiana," 29 July 1973—from the same article)

"STOP," 11 November 1964, Divorce according to Fellini (Text: "Giulietta Masina returns to the cinema with a film in color all for her. "It's the story of the breakdown of a marriage, a couple that separates" says Federico.)

"We're always arguing, but we'll grow old together"—GENTE, 15 October 1964 (Text: "Federico Fellini and Giulietta Masina tell us about their life together—"My wife is full of talent, but doesn't know how to make the best of her clownish personality"—"My husband is a genius but he expects too much of me.")

"Novità," January 1965: on the set of *Giulietta degli spiriti*

Fellini's harem, *Paese Sera*, 24 April 1978 (on *La città delle donne*)

La Repubblica, 23 February 1979—on *Prova d'orchestra*

Prova d'orchestra (still)

Photos

Prova d'orchestra, the dead harpist is pulled out of the rubble (still)

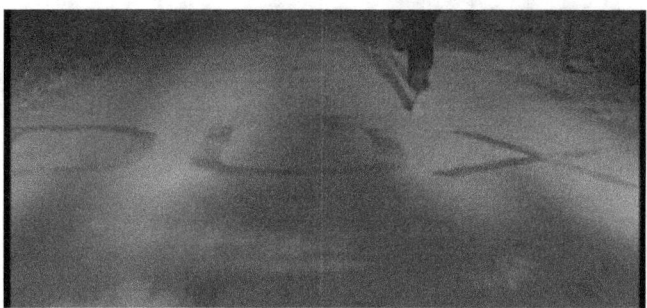

La città delle donne (still)

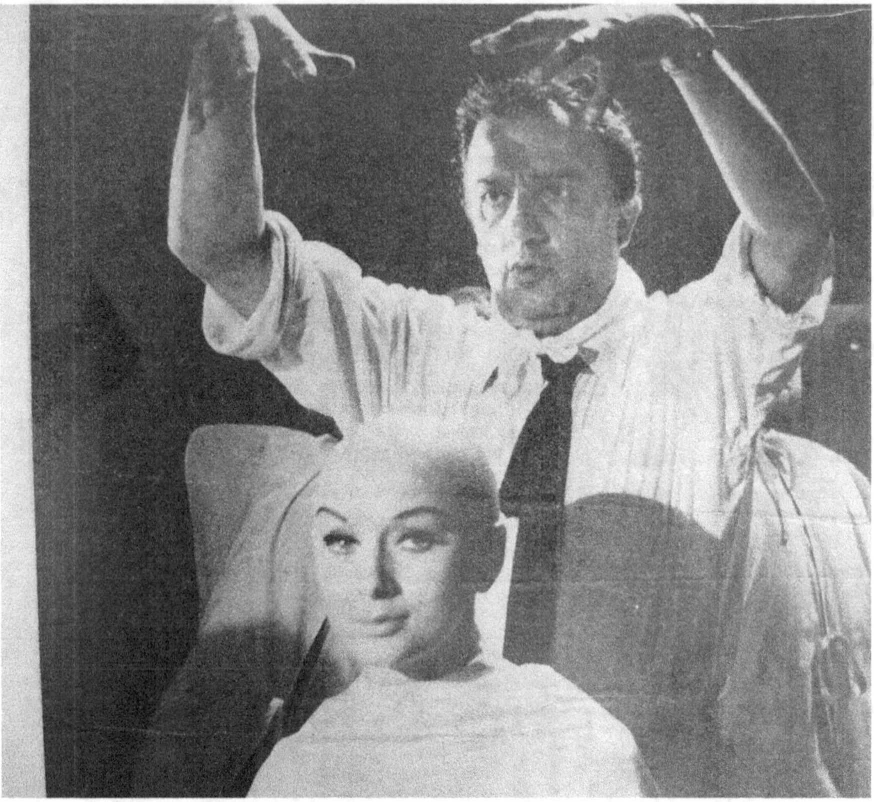

"Vie Nuove," 31 December 1964: on the set of *Giulietta degli spiriti*

Ginger e Fred, 1985 (still)

Chapter 5

Fellini and Feminism

> *Cinema, irresistibly seductive, is essentially feminine.*
> —Federico Fellini

> *When revolution, philosophy, art, religion, no longer gained our complete trust, we confronted the central—the sexual—element of our inner worlds.*
> —Carla Lonzi

> *The creators of religion, philosophers, saints, inventors, all belonged to the female gender; but men, to steal their glory, falsified the ancient records, incorporating into themselves those glorious women.*
> —Vicente Blasco Ibáñez, *The Paradise of Women*

A Conservative Feminist

From *La strada* to *La città delle donne*—a trajectory that includes *Le notti di Cabiria, Giulietta degli spiriti,* and *Casanova*—the political dimension of Fellini's imagination, in relation to women, becomes increasingly explicit. At the end of the seventies, Fellini invited people to take another look at *La strada,* this time to see it as a "feminist" film. Naturally, he did so during the filming of *La città delle donne* in order to show that the new film was merely the last episode in a linear progression, actually—in the case of Gelsomina—predating the claims of feminism. Talking to the journalist Eugenio Scalfari, on the set, Fellini said: "In *La strada* the female protagonist was a doll, treated by the man as a doll, an object, an animal; but when she dies, he loses his mind. In *Giulietta* it is more or less the opposite, but the sense is the same. Those films were made over twenty years ago but they were two feminist films. Not many realized it, but I can assure you that they were."[1]

In his biography of Fellini, Kezich says that feminist movements had opposed the film right from the start (a troubled start back in 1975). He mumbles something about "criticism wide of the mark," "futile attacks," and "polemics based on hearsay," all symptoms of the difficulty of understanding Fellini's relations with "planet woman" (as Kezich calls it):

> The film could have provided a platform for a deeper and more complex discussion of Fellini and the world of women, but such potential is spoiled by numerous misunderstandings and fed by a feminist literature that will continue to label Fellini as a champion of sexism, ignoring the fact that he is behind some of the most extraordinary female icons in modern cinema (Gelsomina, Cabiria); and that the harem dream in 8 ½, La Saraghina and the repeated appearances of the megamatrons are nothing more than inventions, repetitions and embellishments that have to be taken in a self-ironizing light.[2]

In addition to the iconic female figures (Gelsomina and Cabiria), Fellini also evokes controversial and popular figures from the male imagination. "It's true," Kezich goes on, "that in Fellini's fantasies, men and women are never equal, but that's because the woman is almost always on a higher plane, shrouded in mystery."[3] So much a higher plane, indeed, that women are placed altogether outside history, in the unreality of an existence guaranteed by the rhetoric of "feminine mystique."

The fragility of Gelsomina, the insecurities of Giulietta, the superbuxom Saraghina, the greedy sexuality of Volpina and so on, come straight from Fellini's imagination. The elements of male chauvinism and sexist vulgarity in Fellini's drawings are generally interpreted as autoironic and comic caricature.[4] Fellini himself repeatedly encouraged these interpretations, explaining that women in his films were grotesque caricatures of male frustration, like "a poor man when he thinks of money, he dreams not of thousands, but of millions, billions."[5]

Yet, the so-called "mystery of woman" should be seen within the wider context of an investigation of Italian identity, in which "the Fellini woman" (the expression is his) plays a significant part. There is a clear discrepancy between the progressive views Fellini the show-biz personality professed to in interviews and the way women are portrayed in his films, which is anything but progressive. Fellini talked a good game but the women in his film are persistently marginalized.

In an interview with *Panorama* in 1974, Fellini expresses his ("strictly apolitical") approval and support for the feminist position, all the more valid, he says, in an archaic context such as Italy:

How long will it take until profound changes begin to take their effect on the Italian male psyche, before he tries to accept in good faith that his carnivorous sexual behavior—encouraged by certain morals and a certain upbringing—needs to change? Things are still more or less like this in Italy, despite the debates, the roundtable discussions, demonstrations in the streets, women's magazines, and all the other initiatives for the liberation of women from ancestral prejudices... It is impossible not to agree with this political struggle, which moves in the direction of the evolution of society. I admire the women of the movement and often find myself envying them. But I am not the kind of person to turn into political struggle, or dress up as political struggle, a discourse that should be psychological or artistic. So, if what is called feminism is a women's rights movement in all fields, to affirm the personality and qualities of women, which are so often misunderstood or ignored, I'm a feminist. If, on the other hand, it is a pseudo-revolution in which women who are unable to be women want to pass off their incapacity as some kind of virtue, I don't think this feminism has much to offer... Quite right, this rebellion. Absolutely right that they demand equal rights. And inevitable, understandable, that there are moments of hysteria. The real problem lies elsewhere. In the difficulty women have in inventing a new relationship with men, a complete reshaping of that relationship.[6]

The woman interviewing Fellini pointed out that his films portray traditional models of women and "illustrate the exact opposite of what you are saying." Fellini defended himself: "It depends on how you look at these films. Let me say, for the sake of setting the record straight, that the male protagonist of my films, episodes of whose life are being portrayed, is almost always a chronically immature Italian, someone who falsifies reality, confused, a liar, a scoundrel, a loser."[7]

Here too, Fellini cites Italian immaturity and infantilism as the dominant motifs of his films, inviting us to take a fresh look at them from the point of view of gender. The metaphoric density of his films, however, suggests a political dimension, not only in relation to feminism, as in *La città delle donne,* but in relation to recent Italian history, from the battle over divorce to ongoing issues.

Camille Paglia has spoken of "Silvio Berlusconi as Mastroianni in *8 ½,*" a man who "ends up creating a Utopian world in which he can be absolute master of a harem inhabited only by adoring acolytes."[8]

If Italy has become Fellini-esque—here meaning not poetic, but grotesque—it is most evident in its treatment and representation of women: Fellini lurks behind the inauguration in Porto Cesareo, Salento, of a statue of the showgirl Manuela Arcuri, portraying the buxom actress as a "symbol of beauty and prosperity" (as the plaque under the statue recites), as dutifully reported in the newspapers: "A cumly village fête, with a band and fireworks, was the occasion for the unveiling of a statue of Manuela Arcuri on the seafront of the small Salento town. Italy's favorite policewoman was there herself, pleased with the statue. 'It is a great joy to have a statue made of me, living. I am only twenty-five,' said Manuela."[9]

"What's surprising," says Lea Melandri, an important figure in the history of Italian feminism, writing today, "is that the obstacles women leaders encounter in the economic sphere, in politics, in culture, have all been brought to light, but there is no debate about the increasing and exclusive representation of women's bodies as an *erotic* and a *maternal body*."[10] And that, of course, is how Fellini represented the female body, as erotic, maternal, disturbing. In the seventies the body was absent from political discourse altogether. Now, it is everywhere, in the Fellini-esque form of the grotesque and caricature.

Giulietta

Like Kezich, Bondanella sees *Giulietta degli spiriti* as "the affirmation of woman's right to a free expression of her individuality, a topic that Fellini was one of the first directors to introduce into European cinema."[11] Both follow Fellini's own indications, aimed at fending off criticism after the practically worldwide success of *8 ½* and the relative failure of *Giulietta*.

Today, many regard *Giulietta* as one of the best examples of the workings of Fellini's imagination, important for any analysis of the influence of Jungian psychoanalysis on his *mise-en-scène*. It is a rococo fantasy with a succession of inventions that must rate as one of the high points in visual experimentation in auteur cinema in the sixties. In 1965—particularly in Italy—it was this visual impact that was criticized most and the main reason the film was panned. From then on, like a dog with a bone, critics would not let go of the notion that Fellini equaled baroque, a formula in which the baroque was considered, in Croce's famous remark, a "nonstyle" or "delirious ornamentation"[12] of the surface, hiding the true subject of the film or—worse still—masking the absence of a true subject.

Aware of the ideological shortsightedness of Italian film criticism always on the lookout for sociopolitical comment, Fellini tried to direct the attention of critics to the battle for divorce, which was just beginning in Italy and was later to be given the decisive support of the Radical Party.

In 1965 the debate was entering the mainstream thanks largely to a pioneering campaign carried out by the popular glossy magazine *Abc*: "They managed to get the debate out of the conference halls and the pages of specialist journals and into the squares by addressing a new subject of fundamental importance: ordinary people... In the summer of 1965, *Abc* began to run a series called *Letters from the Separated,* featuring a series of complaints about marriage law, an idea evidently inspired by the 1963 film of the Taviani brothers *I fuorilegge del matrimonio* [Marriage Outlaws]. The series changed its name when the divorce movement picked up speed, to *Letters by Advocates of Divorce.*"[13]

In 1965, not many people were talking openly about divorce law, but the film (released in Italy on 23 October 1965) was able to take advantage of a certain groundswell.

In women's magazines a radical change was taking place in terms of the image of women, where the question of independence was presented in the form of a new culture of consumption, fashion, household design, magazine features targeting women. This "moderate mass feminism"[14] was championed, among others, by *Amica, Gioia, Grazia,* and *Annabella.*[15]

As is well known, *Giulietta degli spiriti* is a sort of female version of *8 ½*: where Guido fought the ghosts of creativity, Giulietta fights the ghosts unleashed by a battle in her marriage. Her husband's indifference and betrayals prompt a self-analysis in which Giulietta confronts her fears and repressed aspirations, just as Guido's creative crisis leads him to rethink his life.

Comparing the reactions to the film in America (where it was appreciated) and Italy (where it wasn't), Fellini said: "I thought that in the United States, where divorce is allowed, Giulietta's anxieties would not be of much interest, and would not be so readily understandable. But in New York they understood the picture better than in Italy. Few people in Italy saw that the film is a fierce criticism of some deformities caused by a Catholic upbringing. Of the politically committed directors who say they want to show us the ills of society, which of them has shown the burden of lies, errors, compromises afflicting the individual?"[16]

In a perpetual seesaw, after momentary reconciliation over *8 ½*, Fellini once more lost the support of the Church. The Catholic Center for Cinematography called *Giulietta degli spiriti* "confused and unpleasant": this time, the criticism of a Catholic upbringing, which in *8 ½* was part of a generally positive view of religion, was considered "unjust."

Compared to *8 ½,* the verdict of the Catholic world confirmed the radically different view of the Church about a film based this time on the existential crisis of a woman and wife. Fellini expected to be understood by the women in the audience:

> The negative reactions to the film come mostly from the men who do not want to admit that a woman's lack of satisfaction may explode and would

prefer women to remain in a sort of silent and supine resignation. In America women are independent but not emancipated from men. There too being a woman means having a relationship with a man. And men, in America, are as immature as they are here. There are many males, but few men. Men are very selective and reduce the range of women they find attractive to just a few stereotypes, if not one alone. Mature men tend to be monogamous. The Italian Don Giovanni is unable to love one woman, he has the indifference toward her of an adolescent.[17]

Nonetheless, in *Giulietta degli spiriti,* this impetus toward independence and the invitation to a woman to rid herself of her ghosts lead to self-understanding through the acceptance rather than the *transformation* of the existing situation. Bondanella highlights the point: "…Giulietta recognizes that even Giorgio has added something positive to her life, since his behavior has triggered her search for a stronger sense of self… this development comes about as the result of self-acceptance, not because of any ideological consciousness-raising."[18]

For all its visual impact, its talk of inner revolution, the clash between Catholic submissiveness and sexual liberation, the intercessions of "grace" and the *Kama Sutra*—mixed up in a pastiche of oriental philosophy and pop art—there isn't much in the film that is feminist. And Giulietta Masina was hardly suitable for the role of the bourgeois housewife, Catholic, frustrated by her husband's unfaithfulness, which inevitably drew the filmgoer's attention to the mirror play between the fiction of the film and the real married life of the actress and the director (as in the sequence of the private investigator).

The message of an inner acceptance was altogether ambiguous, more useful to Fellini's marriage, one might think, than to women's liberation. In 1994, after her death, one tribute to the actress stated: "Masina is a star, but above all she is an ordinary woman, a faithful wife who goes shopping, makes dinner and tries not to contradict her husband: a difficult husband, Fellini, who puts her through arduous trials, but their marriage proved extraordinary precisely for this reason, and able to overcome all forms of adversity."[19]

It sounds like the most conventional portrait that could be imagined from a popular magazine of the fifties and it makes quite an impression to think that a faithful wife who goes shopping and makes dinner, etc., could still be held up as a model of marital happiness for a woman in 1994. In Masina's case, the image of the devoted wife living alongside the creative genius of her famous husband was a media favorite.

During the shooting of *Ginger e Fred,* women's magazines pushed this image still further, highlighting certain comments by the actress, such as:

"I do not dominate Federico, I only love him,"[20] and "when I work with him I'm careful not to contradict him, Federico is always right."[21]

Similarly, when she died, the newspapers said she died of sorrow after losing her husband, to whom she had been devoted throughout her life. As if the tumor she had been fighting against for years had nothing to do with it.

Casanova, Fascist *Vitellone*

> It is a ritual that takes place at night on the Grand Canal, from which the gigantic, black head of a woman must emerge. A sort of lagoon goddess, mother Mediterranean, the mysterious female we all have inside of us.[22]

This excerpt from a letter to the poet Andrea Zanzotto, in which Fellini asked for help with the Venetian dialect for *Il Casanova*, describes the sequence that is "the ideological metaphor for the entire film."[23]

An immersion into feminine mystique, *Il Casanova* became another of Fellini's attempts to come to terms with Italian identity in the portrayal of a still current Italian stereotype. "Who really is Casanova?" Fellini wondered: "A product of the Counter-Reformation, someone who desperately, instinctively, with healthy animal instinct, is trying to escape the collective psychological effects of a Catholic-based upbringing."[24]

The time of the Latin lover as in *La dolce vita* had come and gone, and Casanova served Fellini as the symbol of a mechanical/mortuary model of sexuality and the means for putting the Italian identity on trial: "presumptuous yet servile, superficially passionate, deeply sensual, mellifluous, empty, with skin-deep affections, a deceiver: Casanova is a concrete example of all of this, the quintessential Italian, yesterday, today, tomorrow."[25]

In other words, a decomposing national phallus: "Fellini continues his work of purging memory with an allegory of the present, in the guise of a plastic eighteenth century, and unleashes his lightning bolts against the vices of Italy in the seventies, sexist and still populated with *vitelloni*. Our greatest puppet master pillories the archetype of the Latin male, showing him to be the product of misogyny and sex phobia, as administered artfully by the Catholic Church… a man whose (above all moral) maturity has been prevented by a paralyzing hankering after women, built up over centuries."[26]

In this respect, the documentary made by Fellini's collaborators, Liliana Betti and Gianfranco Angelucci, during the shooting of the film (*Is this Fellini's Casanova?*) does not only bear witness to the preparatory work (interviews about masculinity with famous actors, writers, and scholars) that went into *Casanova*, but is itself an interpretation of the film. The idea is to show a direct line of exhibitionism and immaturity, the cult of the ephemeral and of misogyny, from Casanova to the present day, in the shape of the seventies playboy Gianfranco Piacentini, interviewed by Olimpia Carlisi.

In this, *Il Casanova* mirrored the crisis of Italian masculinity that popular erotic/comic films had been focusing on since the beginning of the seventies. Mixing the exhibition of the female body with the frustration of male desire, these films had only one real subject: the obsession and chronic immaturity of Italian men, their essential impotence masquerading as barrack room virility, which the new figure of women in the seventies was rendering more and more pathetic.[27]

The female bodies put on show in the films of the seventies function as bait for the imagination:

> Like it or not, women were the protagonists of the films made between 1970 and 1976, but it is as if the cinema had abolished them only to evoke their phantom, without showing their metamorphosis. The screen was filled with docile buxom lasses satisfying a far from simple voyeurism: what was being shown was not so much the extraordinary physicality of women as uncontrollable male desire. The successes of erotic cinema with Edwige Fenech, Barbara Bouchet, Laura Antonelli and Gloria Guida lending themselves to a rather tired theater of desire, are a sort of tragicomic counterpoint to the feminist struggle.[28]

Horror movies and thrillers also dealt symbolically with the crisis of masculinity, this time ripping the female body to shreds in a sadistic and purely misogynist spectacle, a sort of relief valve (or release).

Fellini seized on this to write a new chapter in the history of the nation, encouraging political interpretations of the film by suggesting that Casanova was part *vitellone*, part fascist, "that orgy of decisive action, the parading up and down... the worst aspects of adolescence, overbearing, vigorous, fanatically idealistic, hypocritical. Fascism is a protracted adolescence long past its sell-by date."[29] And fascism is displayed in the film quite deliberately, in the Bohemian Castle—Dux—where Casanova lives, old and forgotten, and through the choice of Donald Sutherland, recently "Attila," the ferocious bloodthirsty fascist in Bertolucci's *Novecento* (1976).

The fundamental inexistence of women, an inevitable consequence of Italian masculinity, is shown in *Casanova* in an almost countless series of metaphors and rituals: *Great Mother* and "Great Vagina," the latter being a halfway house between Pinocchio's whale and Plato's cave and an explicit allusion to the myth, the cinematic seduction and sexuality of women:

> On the trail of a giantess who has spellbound him, Casanova comes into the presence of the whale queen. Entering her belly, there are end-

less metaphors for the vagina (spider's web, oven, heart of all flowers, mouth of God...)... The journey into metaphor ends with a magic lantern projecting a series of symbolic vaginas drawn by the artist Roland Torpor. Amid the pubic hair there is, in order: a huge gash toward which a miniaturized man is moving, a girl on her haunches enveloped on the banks of giant thighs, a third leg, a beckoning but frightful abyss, a fleshy maelstrom sucking in three men, the eyes and fanged jaws of a monster. After this vision, Giacomo runs into Egard, a drunken, wise English Lord, who tells him that all his journeys into the female body have brought him nowhere.[30]

The metaphor, over-literal although intriguing in the way the set designed by Danilo Donati manages to evoke Pinocchio, is the Fellini take on female mystery and the familiar chain of associations: woman-uterus-cave-dream.[31]

The analogy between women and the cinema was at that time the focus of feminist thought. It was the subject of Laura Mulvey's famous essay "Visual Pleasure and Narrative Cinema,"[32] influenced by psychoanalytic theory put to political use in the identification of the cinematic gaze with the male gender. At that stage in her thinking, cinematic language was structurally based on male pleasure, assigning to women a passive role and to men the domination of the gaze (via an analysis of point of view and image in classic Hollywood films). Unlike this, the Fellini allegory seems to give free rein to the primal force of female sexuality, unapproachable except via a form of disorientation. It is a seduction that cannot be reduced to classic cinema rhetoric, to linear narration and conventional filmic language, but offers itself as the semblance of a pure force, an anxiety. Where Mulvey's attention is on narrative codes, Fellini shifts the emphasis to the rituality of the movie theater where the female image becomes a metaphor for the force of all images. Clearly this position is open to a number of criticisms.

In a roundtable discussion on the "representation of sex" in Fellini's *Casanova*, organized immediately after the release of the film, the women invited (Susanna Agnelli, Emma Bonino, Biancamaria Frabotta)[33] noted the ambiguity of the film: "*Casanova* is an anti-feminist film, but it is also against male chauvinism, above all it is a film against life, full of death," Susanna Agnelli commented, adding:

> *Casanova* is the film of an elderly man, who sees eroticism from a certain distance. But the dance with the mannequin at the end of the film, in my opinion, is more important, it shows that Fellini too has woken up to the fact that women are treated as objects. And he is clever enough to finish his film with Casanova becoming a mannequin himself.

Emma Bonino:

With *Casanova* Fellini gives us a conventional version of male sexuality, which women have begun to question and undermine: the mechanical act of penetration which, as we have seen, gives less pleasure.[34]

The verdict of Germaine Greer (a key figure in feminism during this period) was implacable:

After ten years of New Feminism, Fellini dares to show us an image of women which is more alienated and fetishistic than the most pornographic of pornographic films. In the panoply of Venetian decadence, he creates female forms that are increasingly grotesque, a phantasmagoria of winks and lascivious gazes, monumental breasts, massive asses, and in the final analysis not a single woman in the film is human.[35]

La città delle donne and Italian Feminism

What is *La città delle donne*? The tangle of a "delicious and at the same time tormenting ordeal,"[36] in the words of the poet Zanzotto, the epitome of Fellini's primal imagination or, to put it more prosaically, a coming to grips with his obsession with the feminine in light of the new woman of the seventies.

In any case, it is a dark and obscure film, among the least liked and least understood in Fellini's career, despite the reservoir of visions and fantasies that Fellini draws from uninterruptedly, as if in some kind of unending Kafkian dreamscape. Perhaps because of the sense of sinking into an abyss, of all of Fellini's films, this is the one that most evidently and explicitly recalls Dante and in which there is the strongest echo of the unmade film, *the Journey of G. Mastorna*,[37] and its investigation of the hereafter.

Together with *Ciao maschio* (1978) by Marco Ferreri, *La città delle donne* is a rarity in Italian filmmaking in the seventies, and one of the few films to use the symbolic/visionary plane to directly represent feminism, otherwise entirely absent in the so-called social and engaged cinema of the period. Of all the political subjects dealt with in the films of the seventies, the "female question" was the only one to be shown allegorically, using the matrix of genre films and comedy. As Barbara Grespi wrote (mentioning as an exception Alberto Grifi's *Anna*): "alone in its failure to become a genre or achieve even the background rhetoric of social and civil engagement, the feminist battle is something that is referred to with surprising reserve, extraneous to a cinema which elsewhere intervenes without a trace of shyness, boldly asserting its point of view."[38]

La città delle donne perfectly exemplifies the logic of Fellini's filmmaking, "[in which the] searing heat of current events, projected against a science-fiction background, is continuously placed in an attritional relationship with archetypical data, emblematic characters (whether male or female) of ancient origin and ascendancy."[39]

The poet Zanzotto provided an excellent summary of the film, which he regarded as a typical Fellini project exploring the collective unconscious and the heated politics of the day. According to Zanzotto, *La città delle donne*: "touches on a theme that is so vast that it terrifies anyone who tries to deal with it, even someone with the artistic stature of Fellini: the world of Mothers, the Eternal Feminine, Eros as a primal force opposed to death, threatening and seductive throughout the film. But this subject is addressed necessarily in terms of current issues, aspects of the legitimate feminist revolt including some of its almost crazy extravagances."[40]

In 1973, as *Amarcord* was receiving almost universal praise, the newly created magazine *Effe* voted Fellini *anti-feminist of the month.* The citation was entrusted to Adele Cambria, one of the magazine's founders. While international criticism was paying ritual homage to Fellini, she wrote, the sexist dialogue and scenes in *Amarcord* confirmed the nature of Fellini's stereotypes and the reduction of the female universe to "trite and melancholy stereotypes: the prosperous, buxom wench, pinched, touched up, explored (if slim, as in very rare cases, utterly voracious); the long-suffering mother/wife, and the 'pure' young girl, the maiden to be deflowered by all (matrimonial) means available."[41]

This strict verdict is later expanded: "Wading into the bog of four stereotypes, mother, wife, fiancé, whore, Fellini shows himself to be out-of-date and culturally backward."[42] In relation to Guido's wishful thinking in the harem scene of *8 ½* (in which women over the age of twenty-five are obliged to "go upstairs"), Cambria glosses: "Male, past his best, maybe he should start to worry about his own future upstairs. Nor can Gelsomina help: a woman is not a clown but—simply and unequivocally—a person."[43]

The criticism, not without a streak of personal animosity, was fairly typical of the harsh and intransigent terms of the argument raging at the time and of "the first feminist magazine in Italy, created to cover current affairs and cultural events related to the movement," as *Effe* described itself.

The award put Fellini into good company. Subsequent centerfolds for *anti-feminist of the month* were Pope Paul VI, Kissinger, Fanfani, Roberto Rossellini, and Pier Paolo Pasolini (presciently, the first issue chose Muammar al-Gaddafi). The almost certainly unexpected result was that for the filming of *La città delle donne* Fellini asked Cambria (who he had met on the set of *La strada*) to write "two pages on the music of the vagina." In her recent memoirs, she tells the story, beginning with Fellini imploring her on the phone:

> The winner of 3 Oscars wants me to write the music of the vagina for a film, *La città delle donne,* as it turned out. I am dumfounded. What barefaced cheek, baiting a notoriously unrepentant feminist in this way! The soft musical voice insists on the phone: "Don't American feminists in their self-help groups teach women to listen to the music of the vagina, to be proud of their sex, no longer dominated by men?" Son of a....gun. The Great Filmmaker! He'd heard about Luce Irigary's *Speculum of the Other Woman,* had maybe read one or two issues of *Effe,* knew that in 1973 a self-help group had come from America to La Maddalena feminist theater, headed up by a brilliant young woman originally from Puglia, Anselma Dell'Olio (ten years later the wife of Giuliano Ferrara, after a change of heart)... "Federico—I reply—I have no idea what you are talking about. All I can do for you, if you really want, is write a satire on an over-the-hill Latin lover trying to stay young..." "Yes, yes, write it, Adelina, we'll pay you know..." I wrote nine pages, they paid me, and of course there isn't the slightest trace of it in *La città delle donne.* (Or maybe there is.)[44]

The account is interesting because it shows how Fellini habitually went about his business. Not so much the result of study and research, his screenplays are based on echoes, references, appropriations, intuitions. Everything is then catalyzed and assimilated, and reality transformed through the visionary and imaginative reinvention of Fellini's initial sketches.[45] This figuration draws from the events of the moment and from their signs, magnifying them, deforming them in what must necessarily appear to be a grotesque criticism of the present day, accompanied by the usual sinking into archetypes of the collective unconscious.[46]

During the lengthy gestation of *La città delle donne* (1975–1980), with numerous stops and starts, a complex transformation of Italian feminism occurred. The gradual distance taken by the Radical Party, to which the Women's Liberation Movement was initially federated, relations with the PCI and the left generally, the intensification of the armed struggle and its turning point in 1977–1978, all led to changes in the various currents of Italian feminism.

On 2 October 1976, a free radio-supported occupation in Rome (in Via del Governo Vecchio) of a former district court led to a self-managed Women's Home, providing hospitality to women of all walks of life. Fellini tried to visit the Home for research purposes but was turned away.

1976 is considered a watershed in the history of Italian feminism, the year of its greatest expansion and public support, and the beginning of its decline. "The arrival on the scene of the second generation of feminists from groups on the extra-Parliamentary left shifted the center of gravity of the movement toward social and political action, to street demonstrations, but its origins lay elsewhere and its political culture was different."[47]

The death of the student Giorgiana Masi during a demonstration in Rome on 12 May 1977 and the kidnapping and murder of Prime Minister Aldo Moro in 1978 were decisive events in the gradual transformation of feminism in Italy, away from political action and toward a theory-based movement in the eighties, i.e., toward less antagonistic positions. In the account of A. Rossi-Doria: "Life and thought, which had been so closely linked in the political feminism of the seventies, divided once again in the cultural feminism of the eighties and nineties: inevitably the price had been too high… the movement was still in mourning, trying to understand the external reasons for the crisis of feminism in the seventies, including its relations with the Seventy-Seven Movement in Rome and Bologna. In my opinion, what can only be regarded as the guilty silence of feminists in relation to terrorism played a major role."[48]

The armed struggle was the most dangerous terrain for the unity of the movement. After episodes of female violence (for example the shooting in the legs of a guard at the New Prison in Turin on 5 February 1979, by a group of commandos comprising women only), public opinion turned against the movement for "biological" reasons, the conviction that violence in women was "against nature."

In relation to this episode, *Corriere della Sera* declared its alarm at the "gradual destruction of the mammal code," which it considered one of the most disastrous features of modernity. Violence simply *could not* be female: "by virtue of looking after children, in our species women are the primary source of tenderness, empathy, love, generosity, and altruism."[49]

As the neutrality of the movement in relation to the armed struggle came under fierce scrutiny, so did the women in the movement in relation to their allegiances and beliefs. As *Effe* wrote in relation to the press coverage of the armed struggle by women: "… this type of discrimination seems to us not only to be turned against all women but specifically against women who refuse to consider their identities as biologically determined and believe the personal to be political, hence seek a living space for themselves individually and independently."[50]

Although utterly unlike Fellini's usual concerns, this discrimination is an essential part of *La città delle donne*. By then, of course, Fellini was presenting the film as a "piece of tomfoolery, the opening act of a vaudeville show,"[51] but this definition, the caricature of a caricature, cannot be taken seriously.

In the film, after the convivial gathering of the feminists in the Hotel Miramare, things get decidedly dark. Some sequences—such as Marcello's nighttime car journey with a group of drugged girls—are symptomatic of the doom and gloom of the time, the mindless and inhuman violence of the period that feminism was being obliged to rethink.

At the end of the film, balaclava-clad women read the accusations to Snaporaz/Mastroianni; the similarly sinisterly masked Donatella, who had previously helped him to escape, is given the task of shooting down the woman/ balloon in which Snaporaz is fleeing, with a rapid burst of machine-gun fire.

In the final trial scene Kezich saw an allegorical reference to the kidnapping and interrogation in the "people's prison" of Aldo Moro: "The convulsions of the visual images are all-too-lively and make the film congested, the metaphor of woman is pressed into service as a vision of the present day: the violence about to be unleashed in the scene of the girls in the car and the moral torture of the prisoner, a very personal meditation on the fate of Aldo Moro."[52]

The Harem-Set

Shooting *La città delle donne,* a film about feminism, Fellini found himself in the studios of Cinecittà enacting the harem sequence of *8 ½,* giving orders to and "taming" the women and extras on the set.

His rather uneven declarations to the press were strategically intended to soften the general public up in relation to what was about to be revealed as his "feminism." In the red-hot atmosphere of summer 1977, Fellini appeared to some as almost Maoist, declaring his solidarity with the more extreme positions of feminism, "the only true revolution that is taking place in Italy. Like all revolutions, it has its extremisms, its excesses, hysteria, sure. But these aspects are also necessary, because it is natural for a revolution to step over the line. Revolutions aren't made of peace and quiet."[53]

In other words, they aren't polite social events. A few months later, he was saying that his intention in *La città delle donne* (now a "circus" and a piece of "flippant clowning") was "to make a conciliatory film, declare an armistice, to reconcile the sexes."[54] Then, when the project was resumed after a break over the first few months of 1978, he came up with another version, this one actually close to what the film was to become:

> A city with a museum containing all of his projections of women from his first films, in the form of statues. Masturbatory projections softened to the level of *dolce stil novo,* sublimated, devilish. A crowd of female figures, schematically fixed into cliché and simulacra, lifeless, mummified. A part of the city with which he had lived and which is now rebelling against

him. The protagonist—an Italian, a caliph—realizes that there is a new kind of woman, femininity has become something he doesn't understand, something terrible. Previously, one way or another, the relationship of conditioning and subjection, the fear, had been pacified, some kind of mutual toleration had been reached. But with these new faceless women, the relationship can no longer be the same; he needs to change it but he knows no other way, nothing has prepared him for this, there is no gradual transition, no learning curve.[55]

The set began to take shape in the spring of 1979. When Fellini was working in the studios of Cinecittà, it became an almost hallowed place; there was a constant stream of famous visitors curious about how the Maestro went about his work. All the more for *La città delle donne* with its unusual cast of extras.

The newspapers reported that many feminists from via Governo Vecchio in Rome were on the set; Fellini's press office said he had asked for more than 2,600 extras, a number they handed out with the pomp of an organization seeking to make a point: this is a film to rival the biggest Hollywood productions, a massive blowup of the harem scene in *8 ½* in which Guido/Fellini surrounds himself with women and whips them into obedience.

Quotidiano Donna dedicated a lengthy article to the film, accusing Fellini of selling out feminism and using women as "trained monkeys." The metaphor is reinforced with a picture of Fellini, whip in hand (the famous pose on the set of *8 ½* that Fellini wanted Mastroianni to adopt for the harem sequence), as though Fellini were now putting into practice the harem dream by paying dozens of women to dance under the lash.[56]

Arguments that had broken out within the movement about whether or not it was acceptable to work with Fellini didn't die down even after the film's release. Some, like Ippolita Avalli (a consultant on the film), took a conciliatory position: "I can't bring myself to criticize someone who is being honest with himself; you have to remember he is sixty years old."[57]

Playboy and *Playmen* joined in, publishing photos taken on the set (Donatella Damiani, a young and unknown actress, was playmate of the month). On 15 March 1980, just after the film's release, RAI state television broadcast a documentary by Ferruccio Castronovo on the making of the film, produced by Lisa Caracciolo. The documentary is a record of the show within a show that every Fellini set had become and portrayed the filmmaker/demiurge controlling and directing a chaos of extravagant extras, stagehands, and set designers. It was a homage to the great showman Fellini embodied to perfection and was to contribute to the myth of Fellini, shown bossing hundreds of women about.

Interviewed on the set, Mastroianni declared: "Of course I've changed since the days of *8 ½*! We've all changed, the world has changed... I play a man who is disoriented by the changes in women... the protagonist of *8 ½* understands that the time of the whip is over."

Meanwhile, one minute Fellini was claiming the film was political, and the next saying it wasn't. As soon as it came out, he confessed his utter ignorance of feminism. "It's not a film about feminism, it's a film about the female."[58] Or: "I can't make a feminist film, I can only represent the fantasies of someone like me, a man of my generation, in relation to this new and disturbing world of women, which feminism represents."[59] He continued, focusing on the preparations for the film, almost as if to distance himself from its political limitations: "I've met a large number of feminist writers, including Germaine Greer, the author of *The Female Eunuch*. Sadly and as if giving her blessing, like a retired Pope, she kept on saying: 'But Federico, what on earth do you know about women?' Some even wrote a few pages for me. I listened to what they had to say, to songs, to passionate feminist discussions. I tried to get into the feminist headquarters in Rome, in via Governo Vecchio, but they threw me out. I asked a lot of feminists to take part in the film and they agreed."[60]

In *La città delle donne*, the discrepancy between Fellini the progressive in politics, the sympathizer with feminism mocking masculinity, and Fellini the conservative, smugly showing the traditional image of women, became the distance between the two "spectacles," on the one hand the film, on the other, the film set.

The distasteful but effective promotional poster of Fellini brandishing a whip to dominate feminists was seized on by the press and media. Fellini's relations with Germaine Greer were symptomatic. The disarming woman in the train at the beginning of the film, trailed by Snaporaz to what turns out to be feminist convention, is reminiscent if not actually a representation of the Australian writer and symbol of Anglo-Saxon feminism.

Invited by *Effe* as the spokeswoman of the sexual revolution and the author of the one of the sacred texts of feminism, she first visited Italy in 1973. Later, Fellini wanted her for a role in *Casanova*. Much later, in an article in *The Guardian* (11 April 2010), she broke cover and described her tryst with Fellini, concluding, "Sexual athletes are tuppence a dozen. Fellini was a many-sided genius. I do not hope to meet his like again."[61]

The idea of the *anti-feminist of the month* in bed with the symbol of international feminism was probably part of the circuitry of Fellini's cinema-life machinery, which nonetheless nourished his work and inventiveness.

The Same Old Male

The narrative frame of the film, the dreamwork, is paradoxical: the film begins with Snaporaz in a train not falling asleep but waking suddenly out of sleep.

Similarly paradoxical is the location of the feminist convention, the Hotel Miramare. It looks like something Fellini had remembered from long ago. In fact, the set for the hotel was created by Dante Ferretti from sketches by Fellini and is clearly modeled on the large luxury hotels of seaside resorts in the thirties.

Hence it was another "sign of memory," the characteristic of Fellini's films since *8 ½* if not before. It is based on "the need to identify certain formal leitmotifs as direct intermediaries with what in Fellini's vision of things was the age of memory, i.e., the creative season of childhood."[62]

There are also references to certain utopian universes imagined by so-called fantasy feminism, with its worlds governed entirely by women (as in *Satyricon*, created less by thinking of Ancient Rome as *Flash Gordon*).[63]

In the script, Fellini and Bernardino Zapponi include a host of criticisms of Fellini's art along the lines of the Aristarco-style hatchet jobs put into the mouth of the intellectual critic in *8 ½* by Pinelli and Flaiano. Memorable is the monologue of the woman Snaporaz tries to have sex with in the toilet of the train, now speaking at the convention:

> Once more we have been deceived. Underhandedly, as is his wont. We were generous, welcoming, motherly. We spoke, discussed, hang it all, even showed him our rites. Even the most naïve of them, unreservedly, without feminine modesty, in the absurd hope of getting him to understand—someone incapable of understanding, someone who has no wish to understand—just how much freedom, authenticity, how much love and life has been denied us. Sisters, it has all been to no avail. The eyes of the man who has sneaked in here, with a phony look of respect on his face, who says he wants to gather information and to get to know us better, because it is only by knowing us better that he can change his relationship with us…. Of all his false and hypocritical self-justifications, this is the most ignoble. *The eyes of this man, as I was saying, are the eyes of the same old male,* which deform everything they see in the mirror of scorn and mockery. He is no less a scoundrel than before. We women are merely a pretext, enabling him once more to trot out the animals in his zoo, his circus, his neurotic curtain-raiser. And us the clowns… This gloomy, dark, tired old caliph should realize once and for all that we are not Martians, that we want to live on earth, on *this* earth, but not as fertilizer as has been the case for four thousand years.

Fellini acknowledges and shows his limits in a way that is itself mocking. Yet this is the confession of a man who grew up under fascism, in the shadow of monolithic female models, on the one hand the glorification of the Mother, on the other brothel performers. How can such a man, Fellini seems to be asking, cope with today's women, above all with *these* women? Who seem to have no need for a man like him, who wear balaclavas and have taken up arms.

When the film was released, Adele Cambria—who has recently reaffirmed her negative opinion—wrote what is probably the harshest review of a Fellini film ever penned. It was given pride of place on the front page of *Il Giorno* and summarized Fellini's philosophy thus:

> 1) The world is a female ass that I call (this partial object) woman. 2) The last human being with a human face is me: male, of course, over fifty but so what? ("Actually I'm fifty but I'm still up for it," trills Mastroianni), a lecherous pig but basically a good man. 3) The generations after mine are monstrous and, as chance would have it, the monsters are all women. 4) Feminists? Lesbians, worse, dykes. Or delirious about the phallus. Or both. And drug addicts. Fascists and Nazis. 5) Yesterday's women were also monstrous: except that I liked that monstrosity—anatomical deformity, big tits, huge thighs, etc.—and what I particularly liked was how they became available at the drop of a hat. It's not my fault if these propositions, which are actually philosophical, seem rather crude and backward, like the boasts of boys in the bar at the Sports Club (with the greatest respect for Sports Clubs, since now that feminists are all haggish old dykes, I fear that they no longer dare to have such conversations even in eminently men-only locations).[64]

Cambria goes on to specify what she regards as Fellini's most offensive allusion:

> Right from the start in his thinking about this film, Fellini had in mind Germaine Greer, the author of the first theoretical works of feminism (*The Female Eunuch*). Germaine, whom I and many others in the feminist movement know personally (not only Fellini knows her, I mean), is a great Australian, full of courage and energy, who, especially at the time of the initial explosion and rupture of feminism (in the Anglo-Saxon world), forced her essential shyness and her Victorian upbringing into an ironic and aggressive stance in relation to men. Fellini turns her into a nymphomaniac slut with voracious lips shaped like a gimlet, laddered black stockings (which, who knows why, elderly Italian men find so sexy).[65]

The article, far from tender, can be understood only in the context of the atmosphere of the time. It rounded off the attitude of *Effe* to Fellini after his election to *anti-feminist of the month*. But not all feminists agreed.

Apart from less severe judgments by Fernanda Pivano and Natalia Ginzburg, the weekly magazine *Noi Donne,* which took a less radical feminist position than *Effe* or *Differenze* (another Roman feminist magazine created at the time), disagreed with Cambria's view. In an open letter to the reviewer, Patrizia Carrano said the press had seized on the article and turned what was Cambia's personal opinion into an "official" representation of the feminist position. The rebuttal has the feel of a retreat from the attempt by feminism to create a monolithic movement and the opening up of more nuanced and individual positions:

> Admittedly, these are the problems one encounters writing for the "male" press. The same problems you complained about in your review in relation to the women who decided to work with Fellini, without necessarily sharing his views. And while we're on the subject, why criticize someone who at least has the courage to say—and say so sublimely—how men have always seen us? Yes, true, for many men a woman is just an ass, a big round ass walking with swaying hips and a swish of buttocks, driving them to a frenzy. But that is hardly Fellini's fault, he is the messenger, is he not? And as for the grotesque representation of women, you surely aren't saying that Katzone is not equally grotesque, are you? All of Fellini's films are mocking.[66]

Katzone, the trivial and performative version of Snaporaz, who fails to make any female "conquests" (like Marcello in *La dolce vita*) isn't mentioned by Cambria or any other of the negative feminist reviews.

Epoca, on the other hand, dedicated a great deal of attention to him. The articles showed how structurally rooted in Italian anthropology certain grotesque positions were and how little feminism had managed to weed them out.

The writer of the screenplay, Bernardino Zapponi, said that the idea for the scene in which Snaporaz/Mastroianni wanders through the deathly "museum of women" bedded by Katzone came partly from the actor/playboy Maurizio Arena himself. He had been made famous by Dino Risi in *Poveri ma belli* (1956) but now at the age of forty-five (in 1979) he was a forgotten actor fallen on hard times. Zapponi says the actor had hundreds of tapes, all neatly ordered on a shelf, on which he had recorded the orgasms of his sexual partners. When a guest came to see him, the first thing he did was to take him to what he called the Womanary and ask him to choose a tape. "He was vegetating surrounded by erotic relics: black satin bed sheets, dildos, snapshots of a crowd of female trophies, fighting against time. He kept a photo of his erection in a drawer. When he was depressed he showed it proudly to friends."[67]

A contemporary playboy (Gianfranco Piacentini), unfailingly interviewed in relation to the figure of Katzone, said that times had changed:

"Perhaps today Katzone is a woman, a woman of the latest generation. Who chooses you, fucks you, smokes a cigarette and when you look for a moment of tenderness gets dressed, is busy."[68] For the psychoanalyst Ignazio Majore: "Katzone is no longer the old collector of female prey, he has become something more complex. He is a man who has been exposed to feminism in the wrong way. You want to be free because you're all whores? Fine, then I'll use you like before, worse than before."[69]

But Bernardino Zapponi saw in this phenomenon something broader in Italian culture:

> [Katzone] is the scurrilous version of dreamy Mastroianni; the vulgarity he rejects ... the sinister Candlewick of a childishly sexual Pinocchio... He represents failed machismo, fascist aggression, the stupidity of programmed eroticism; basically a melancholy and anachronistic figure, rightly confined to a dilapidated forties villa... It would be wrong, however, to confine Katzone to the banal ghetto of playboys, seducers for the gutter press. Certainly he is greedy, lustful, vain like hunters with their collections of trophies; but his attitude is more complicated and threatening, and his approach to women is transferred onto politics, where he is loutish, and finance, where he does crooked deals. Katzone is not so much a nightclub seducer as one of the Caltagirone brothers, a mobster, a Mr. Fix-it... In the film he is shown as an imitator of Air Marshall Italo Balbo, a Blackshirt, thuggish, like a fascist officer carrying out orgies in a villa built illegally from the proceeds of some building speculation. Despite the outmoded setting, he isn't a thing of the past, just open any newspaper and you'll find him.[70]

With hindsight, looking at Italy today, it seems that this outmoded setting has absorbed and metabolized the rebellious demands of the seventies. If *La città delle donne* is the portrayal of a particular time, and of feminism at that time, if *these* women are not exactly today's women, the world of men, immature and trivial, is hauntingly unchanged.

The fantasies of Fellini's male are more the product of an age-old fear than of the desire to dominate. Take the example of Saraghina in *8 ½*, with her femininity bordering on the "monstrous," which provokes in the boys a sense of terror and freedom. Fellini's women may not be situated historically but his men—Italian men—are relegated to a perpetual infantilism. This is Fellini's frozen, unchangeable, blocked world turned in on itself, a world in which progressive politics and its claims can emerge only as a threat and in disguise.

"It isn't true that the culture of women is a gold mine to be drawn on to enrich a civilization that until now has ignored it," wrote Rossana Rossanda, "feminist culture is truly critical and therefore unilateral, antagonistic, the negation of other cultures. It doesn't complete it, it accuses it."[71] Fellini is aware of this and, as a radical decadent, is dismayed by it. In *La città delle donne,* as he himself admitted, women refuse male projections: "they have no use for them and throw them back in men's faces… It's like the two halves of an apple growing apart, no longer staying together, it is the end of gravity, of attraction. Can you imagine a world in which men and women no longer have anything to project onto each other?"

The end of the force of gravity, the end of the world. The revolution cannot be carried out—he seems to be saying—least of all in Italy.

In this connection there is a memorable image in the film. Toward the end, the feminists march forward holding up a placard which says *"progressence."* Asked about the meaning of this word, Fellini said: *"Progressence* is progress with decadence, and it is a word that ought to be in the dictionary; in Italy aren't they intrinsically linked, inextricable?"[72]

Notes

1. E. Scalfari, "Con il maestro parlando di donne" [Talking about Women with the Maestro], *la Repubblica,* 17 July 1979.

2. Kezich, *Federico Fellini,* 339.

3. Ibid.

4. As Paolo Fabbri has observed, "The excess in the women characters, the huge Saraghinas, filtered through the paintings of Picasso, disproportional Venuses and proportional Priapuses, underline the comic aspects of sexuality. We should not forget that, speaking of dreams, sexuality can be comic, not always tragic, not invariably associated with tragedy, but also with comedy. For Freud, for example, the products of the unconscious, with their metaphors and metonyms, were involuntarily comic." P. Fabbri, "Prima donna, La Saraghina tra Picasso e Kafka" [Primadonna, Saraghinas in Picasso and Kafka], *Amarcord. Rivista di studi felliniani* no. 3–4 (Dec. 2001), now also at http://www.paolofabbri.it/articoli/sarghina.html.

5. F. Fellini, *Fare un film,* 83.

6. "Io e lei" [Me and Her], *Panorama,* 3 January 1974 (Fellini interviewed by Emilia Granzotto), 114–115.

7. Ibid., 115.

8. C. Paglia, "Sembra Ottoemezzo" [Seems like *8 ½*], *Corriere della Sera,* 3 February 2007.

9. "Manuela Arcuri inaugura la sua statua" [Manuela Arcuri Inaugurates Her Statue], *Corriere della Sera,* 20 July 2002.

10. L. Melandri, "Leadership femminile sì, ma quante contraddizioni" [Female Leadership Sure, but What Contradictions!], *Gli Altri* 3, no. 41 (14 October 2011), 19.

11. Bondanella, *The Cinema of Federico Fellini,* 326

12. According to Giovanni Grazini's review in *Corriere della Sera.*

13. G. Scirè, *Il divorzio in Italia. Partiti, Chiesa, società civile dalla legge al referendum* [Divorce in Italy: Parties, the Church, Secular Society, from the Law to the Referendum] (Milan: Mondadori, 2009), 25–26.

14. A. Ardvisson, "Consumi, media e identità nel lungo dopoguerra. Spunti per una prospettiva d'analisi" [Consumption, Media and Identity in the Lengthy Postwar Period: Suggestions for a Framework of Analysis], in *Genere, generazione e consumi*, ed. P. Capuzzo, 41.

15. It was the subject of a recent Milanese Exhibition, *Lei e le altre. Moda e stili nelle riviste RCS dal 1930 ad oggi* [Lei and the Others: Fashion and Style in RCS magazines from 1930 to the Present Day]—Palazzo della Permanente, 15 September–14 October 2011. See the catalogue edited by M.I. Frisa (Venice: Marsilio, 2011).

16. In *Il Tempo*, 8 December 1965, 55.

17. Ibid., 56.

18. Bondanella, *The Cinema of Federico Fellini*, 307.

19. T. Kezich, "Con Federico mezzo secolo di gloria" [With Federico, Half a Century of Glory], *Corriere della Sera*, 24 March 1994, 35.

20. See "Una moglie da Oscar" [Oscar-Deserving Wife], *Donna*, 22 May 1985.

21. See "Sono Giulietta del tip-tap" [I'm Giulietta, Tap Dancer], *Oggi*, 12 June 1985.

22. Letter from Fellini to Andrea Zanzotto, quoted in L. De Giusti, "Prospezioni di un poeta nel sottosuolo del cinema" [A Poet Prospecting Underground in Film], in A. Zanzotto, *Il cinema brucia e illumina*, 13.

23. Ibid.

24. G.L. Rondi, "Sette domande a Fellini: Tutto deciso Casanova a ferragosto" [Seven Questions to Fellini: Everything for Casanova Is Ready for August Bank Holiday], *Il Tempo*, 13 April 1974, 3.

25. C. Brambilla, "Casanova cioè l'italiano punito" [Casanova or the Punished Italian], *La Notte*, 11 December 1976.

26. J. Costantino, "Danse macabre o quadri d'esposizione. Variazioni sul 'Casanova' di Federico Fellini" [Dance Macabre or Pictures from an Exhibition: Variations on Fellini's Casanova], in *Federico Fellini. Il cinema di Federico Fellini*, Ravenna Conference, 2005 (Ravenna: Culture Series, 2008), 36.

27. See the letter by Giacomo Manzoli in "Italians do it worse. La crisi della mascolinità nella commedia erotica italiana degli anni Settanta" [Italians Do It Worse: The Crisis of Masculinity in Italian Erotic Comedies in the Seventies], *La Valle dell'Eden* 19 (2007), 156–157.

28. B. Grespi, "Cine-femmina: quell'oscuro oggetto del desiderio" [Cine-Female: That Obscure Object of Desire], in *Storia del cinema italiano*, vol. 12, 1970–1876, ed. F. De Bernardinis (Venice: Marsilio, 2009), 116.

29. F. Fellini in L. Betti and G. Angelucci, *Casanova rendez-vous Fellini* (Milan: Bompiani, 1975), 141.

30. J. Costantino, *Danse macabre o quadri d'esposizione. Variazioni sul 'Casanova' di Federico Fellini*, 36.

31. See also A. Zanzotto, "Ipotesi attorno a 'La città delle donne'," in Zanzotto, *Il cinema brucia e illumina*, 41–51.

32. Mulvey's essay was published in *Screen* in 1975 and translated into Italian by the magazine *nuova dwf* in 1978 (no. 8, 26–41). Mulvey subsequently abandoned the radical position of the essay, in light of a broader consideration of the spectator's gaze in film and further analysis of the history of film. For example, see *Afterthoughts on 'Visual Pleasure and Narrative Cinema' Inspired by King Vidor's* Duel in the Sun *(1946)*, published in 1981. For the development of Mulvey's thinking, see V. Pravadelli, "Feminist Film Theory and Gender Studies," in *Metodologie di analisi del film* [Methods of Film Analysis], ed. P. Bertetto (Rome/Bari: Laterza, 2009), 59–102.

33. Susanna Agnelli was an entrepreneur and writer, heir of the Agnelli family, Emma Bonino a leading exponent of the Radical Party, and Biancamaria Frabotta a poet and literary scholar.

34. "Ma la donna utero inghiotte Casanova" [Uterus-woman Swallows Casanova], *la Repubblica*, 28 December 1976. The second quotation is from Biancamaria Frabotta.

35. G. Greer, "Casanova non piace alle donne" [Women Don't Like Casanova], *Il Tempo*, 9 January 1977.

36. A. Zanzotto, "Ipotesi intorno a 'La città delle donne'," 43.

37. For the film script, see *The Journey of G. Mastorna* (Oxford and New York: Berghahn Books, 2013) with a lengthy commentary by Marcus Perryman.

38. B. Grespi, "Cine-femmina: quell'oscuro oggetto del desiderio," 116.

39. A. Zanzotto, *Il cinema brucia e illumina*, 100.

40. Ibid.

41. A. Cambria, "Un antifemminista al mese" [Anti-feminist of the Month], *Effe* no. 2 (1973), 10–11.

42. Ibid., 11.

43. Ibid. According to Pietro Angelini, the criticism missed the mark, the feminists identifying "anti-feminism in what was itself a parody, embodied by the likes of Buzzanca, Samperi, Salce and, of course, Fellini." P. Angelini, "Il cinema e la donna: Federico Fellini" [Cinema and Women: Federico Fellini], *Cinema 60* no. 95 (1974), 43.

44. A. Cambria, *Nove dimissioni e mezzo: le guerre quoditiane di una giornalista ribelle* [Nine and a Half Resignations: The Daily Battles of a Rebellious Woman Journalist] (Rome: Donzelli, 2010), 35–36. Giuliano Ferrara was originally a left-wing intellectual, then a minister under Berlusconi, and is now an influential conservative journalist and opinion leader. He founded the newspaper *Il Foglio*.

45. See R. Monti, *Bottega Fellini: La città delle donne: progetto, lavorazione, film* [Fellini's Workshop: *La città delle donne*: Design, Shooting, the Film] (Rome: De Luca, 1981).

46. For the grotesque in Fellini, see R. De Gaetano, *Il corpo e la maschera. Il grottesco nel cinema italiano* [The Body and the Mask: The Grotesque in Italian Cinema] (Rome: Bulzoni, 1999).

47. E. Guerra, "Una nuova soggettività; femminismo e femminismi nel passaggio degli anni Settanta" [A New Subjectivity: Feminism and Feminist Movements in the Transitional Seventies], in *Il femminismo degli anni Settanta* [Feminism in the Seventies], ed. T. Bertilotti and A. Scattigno (Rome: Viella, 2005), 46. Here,

the historiographic hypotheses of Laura Grasso and Anna Rita Calabrò are being discussed from their book *Dal movimento femminista al femminismo diffuso* [From the Feminist Movement to Widespread Feminism] (Milan: Franco Angeli/Fondazione Badaracco, 2004).

48. A. Rossi-Doria, "Ipotesi per una storia che verrà" [Hypothesis for a Future History], in *Il feminismo negli anni Settanta*, ed. T. Bertilotti and A. Scattigno, 17.

49. A. Todisco, "Un brutto giorno se la donna spara" [A Bad Day When Women Start Shooting], *Corriere della Sera*, 7 February 1979.

50. "Per fare i conti con la violenza armata" [Reckoning with the Use of Arms], *Effe*, 2 March 1979, 15–16.

51. G. Guerrieri, "Fellini: la donna è l'inconscio" [Fellini: Women are the Unconscious], *Il Giorno*, 16 March 1980.

52. T. Kezich, *Federico Fellini*, 332.

53. "Fellini, sulle donne ho gusti orribili" [Fellini: I Have Horrible Tastes in Women], *Il Giorno*, 31 July 1977.

54. "Fellini gira la città delle donne" [Fellini Shoots The City of Women], *Il Giorno*, 11 November 1977.

55. M. Crocella, "L'harem di Fellini" [Fellini's Harem], *Paese Sera*, 24 April 1978.

56. "Le donne servono a Fellini come scimmie ammaestrate" [Fellini Uses Women Like Trained Monkeys], *Quotidiano Donna*, 29 June 1979.

57. Ibid.

58. F. Laudadio, "Per il signor Snaporaz il cinema è donna" [For Mr. Snaporaz the Cinema Is Woman], *l'Unità*, 23 March 1980.

59. L. Tornabuoni, "Fellini: vi spiego perchè gli uomini hanno paura" [Fellini: Let Me Explain Why Men Are Afraid], *La Stampa*, 29 March 1980.

60. Ibid.

61. Apart from the brief affair, the article described a lasting relationship and admiration: "The relationship was self-limiting, because I wasn't always available. Federico made sure I got to see the rough cut of *Casanova* with the studio sound, which was all Federico's voice talking his actors through the characters' streams of consciousness. He showed me storyboards of movies that were never made, and the drawings he made for every sequence of movies that were. I saw how he used actors like props, assembling iconic figures out of elements of different people. I teased him about the way he directed the storm scene in *La Città delle Donne*, flying back and forth on a huge dolly, calling for 'Thunder! Lightning! Rain! More lightning!' like God Himself. Everything was filmed on set at Cinecittà, even the motorway scenes in Fellini's *Roma*. When I asked him why he was building a cornfield blade by blade for *La Voce della Luna*, he said it was not just because an artificial cornfield would be more real on camera than a real one, but because someone had to keep Cinecittà's army of expert craftsmen in work. He only ever talked about work in progress; once a film was made, he lost interest. If the film's inner logic failed to dictate its development and ending, he would panic, which was where I came in."

62. R. Monti, 63.

63. References to phanta-feminism and, in particular, to books such as *Herland* by Charlotte Perkins Gilman (1915) and *El paraíso de las mujeres* (1922), were made

in an article in *Noi donne,* in order to "highlight aspects which the arguments for and against the film had neglected. Fellini's film is part of a precise literary tradition: that of phanta-feminism, in the same sense as *fantascienza,* science fiction, i.e., visions of a possible future world, generally unpleasant, but imagined to the limits of our imaginations"; "Fantafemminismo tra cinema e letteratura" [Phanta-feminism in Film and Literature], in *Noi donne* no. 22 (May 1980), 51 (the author's name is not given). In a note from Zanzotto to Fellini commenting on the screenplay for *La città delle donne,* he says: "The first part of the screenplay talks of a very sci-fi kind of Stock Farm for women, destroyed by the feminist police. This is a new and very intriguing topic not dealt with in science fiction. It reminds me of *Pulsatilla sexuata* by Della Corte. Here, however, there is the program of sexual refinement, the invention/creation of a new eroticism or at least of erogenous zones"; in A. Zanzotto, *Il cinema brucia e illumina,* 195.

64. A. Cambria, "No caro Federico, la donna non è concime dei tuoi vizi" [No, Dear Federico, Women Are Not Fertilizer for Your Vices], *Il Giorno,* 30 March 1980.

65. Ibid.

66. P. Carrano, "Il gigante e la bambina" [The Giant and the Girl], *Noi donne,* 18 April 1980. See also *Città delle donne o paese degli uomini?* [City of Women or Country of Men?], 49–51.

67. B. Zapponi in G. Catalano, "Ē duro a morire il mito katzone" [Hard to Demolish the Big-Dick Myth], *Epoca,* 22 April 1980, 71.

68. *Ebbene sì, Katzone sono io* [I Admit It, Big-Dick C'est Moi], 74.

69. Ibid., 72.

70. Ibid., 73.

71. R. Rossanda, *Le altre. Conversazioni sulle parole della politica* [Other Women: Conversations on the Language of Politics] (Milan: Feltrinelli, 1979), 211.

72. L. Tornabuoni, "Fellini: vi spiego perchè gli uomoni hanno paura."

Chapter 6

A Public Dream
Italy and *Prova d'orchestra*

> *How can you explain that a sacred text is the stone on which freedom and conscience was founded?*
> —Elémire Zolla

> *Not everyone understands and not everyone wants to understand. The Moro Affair is above all a religious book.*
> —Leonardo Sciascia

> *Beauty certainly does not make revolutions. But there comes a time when revolutions need beauty.*
> —Albert Camus

Fellini, the Seventies and Political Cinema in Italy

While *Amarcord* had divided the critics—some thinking Fellini had entered the political realm, others that is was essentially an autobiographical film—the verdict on *Prova d'orchestra* was unanimous: it was Fellini's first out-and-out political film. It was made for the state broadcaster, RAI, and hence for a mass audience, as part of a project begun in the previous decade to bring together cinema and television. The project received a new lease of life after the reform of the state broadcaster in 1975, and included *Padre Padrone* by the Taviani brothers in 1977 and Olmi's *L'albero degli zoccoli* in 1978.

Prova d'orchestra resumes and broadens the political discourse of *Amarcord*. According to Bondanella, both films "portray individuals mesmerized by collective myths—fascism in Italy's recent past and revolutionary Marxism in its confused present."[1] This put Fellini outside the mainstream of Italian political cinema, which tended to take a Marxist point of view: "While Fellini's cinema does not ignore the many social and political problems that have arisen since he first began making films, the approach Fellini takes to such themes and the cinematic style with which he treats such questions differ radically from that typical of the so-called political film…"[2]

Like neorealism, "Italian political cinema" is not something that can be pinned down easily or once and for all. Indeed, in a recent essay, Ortoleva says that the "the reason for its unexpected vitality" lies precisely in the "vagueness of the definition."[3]

In the seventies, Italian cinema reflected and investigated the ongoing changes in society, given impetus by the events of 1968 which, in Italy, had unearthed deep roots: the chronic weakness of Italian democracy and the atavistic lack of confidence and widespread distrust of the state and its institutions, reinforced and encouraged by the series of bombings and outrages from 1969 to 1980. According to Ortoleva, this created "not only in members of left-wing parties or supporters of the extra-parliamentary left (to use the terms current at the time), but also among the right-wing and broadly, across all social classes and within public opinion, a readiness to accept any form of communication involving denunciation, a call for an end to state secrecy and a rallying cry to political action."[4]

In films, such a rallying cry could be launched by mafia stories, thrillers about justice, militant documentaries, filmed investigative journalism, and even comedies after a shift to the left, as well as, more obviously, movies about cops.

And, of course, films dealing with Italian history. Ortoleva continues: "Strange as it may seem, the films about the past were probably the best and longest-lasting political films of the seventies: the least conditioned by often far from disinterested references to current events and the fluctuations of this or that ideology or party line. More than others, these were the films that influenced a generation of intellectuals and teachers."[5]

In part, *Amarcord* was just such a film, where the present could be seen through the prism of the past. Another might have been a film Fellini never in fact made but the idea for which clearly showed the chaos in Italy during the seventies. It was one of Fellini's many unrealized projects, the television adaptation of the book *La valle della farfalla* (Butterfly Valley), an autobiographical novel by a policeman, Nicola Longo.

Poliziotto (the working title) was to have been a program in "six episodes dealing with criminal investigations and police work, with numerous references to Italian terrorism. Probably it was this interest in terror and the reaction of institutions—a dangerous terrain to explore—that led Fellini, after much 'advice' from on high, to resign himself to abandoning the project."[6]

His interest in the film may certainly have come from the desire to tackle a dangerous subject, but was possibly also influenced by the need—after two commercial flops (*Casanova* and *La città delle donne*)—to choose a topic with a certain mass appeal.

That the subject matter would have included violence and terrorism and was to be handled according to Fellini's personal take on the subject is clear from the synopsis in the Bologna Film Library written by Fellini as a presentation of the adaptation:

> The series of stories I intend to show are part of the Detective genre insofar as they will use the narrative form of the genre and be set in the world of criminal investigations. To my mind, at a time like this, this world is the most suited to providing an interpretation, or—more than an interpretation—a description of society, city life, the violence in which we live...The film, urgent, insistent, like reading the headlines of the crime pages of a newspaper with reports of various types of criminal activity, one heading next to another, one story bewilderingly after another, should give the viewer the sense of anguish and dizziness of our times, a dramatic fleeting kaleidoscope of an order that has been overpowered and shot to pieces by the force of a violence that is increasingly blind and commonplace.[7]

According to Kezich, in spring 1978, as the Moro kidnapping was drawing to its fatal end, Fellini jotted down an idea for the beginning of the film that was to become *Prova d'orchestra*. The atmosphere is similar to the detective series he planned to make:

> What if I began with a convulsed, lacerated montage of snippets, excerpts, moments and episodes of extreme violence chosen from the newsreels of recent times? A chaotic, terrifying soundtrack, with shots fired, sprayed bullets, screaming, slogans shouted repeatedly and idiotically, punctuated by the sound of police sirens, the high-pitched shrieking of ambulances, the echoing of loudspeakers, the sound of bombs and Molotovs exploding. A nightmare scene, an "absurd universe" over which the title of the film should appear, *Prova d'orchestra*.[8]

Prova d'orchestra was to enter the arena of the political film, generically embodying a left-wing point of view sympathetic to protest, and remodel the genre. It would not include the customary denunciation of the evil-doing and connivance of politicians and the powers that be, but make a broad appeal, over the entire political spectrum, to end the current madness and rediscover reasons for living peacefully together.

As with *La città delle donne*, current events spurred Fellini's imagination, and, as usual, the film was to deal with universal and timeless issues. Again, it is the poet Andrea Zanzotto who provides the best introduction to the film: "It's almost as if Fellini, after absorbing external reality, takes it off to sediment in dark caverns, from which he then returns… The recent film *Prova d'orchestra*, a rather transparent metaphor for the many ills afflicting society today, particularly in Italy, is at the same time an intricate anthropological document replete with a myriad of timeless symbols, and a particularly good example of the elusive way Fellini's creativity works at different levels at once."[9]

The Sacredness of Art and Collective Hysteria

Prova d'orchestra has a much simpler narrative structure and production setup than most of Fellini's films. It is a genuine film for television, where *I clowns* had been an attempt to oblige the small screen to accommodate the phantasmagoria of his imagination.

"I was particularly concerned with the shots," Fellini said about the production process, "since this was a film for a smaller screen. I wanted to use just one room and a lot of close-ups, ideal for television."[10]

According to the most ancient Aristotelian formula, the three-act story has unity of place, time, and action: an orchestra rehearsal. The film utilizes television language: "it has an atmosphere that is part interview part confession, a characteristic of television, which is immediate, colloquial."[11]

The interviews are carried out off-screen by Fellini himself. Taking their places in the ancient oratory, one by one the musicians are asked about their relationship with the instrument they play. When the rehearsal begins, the conductor becomes irritated by their lack of discipline and threats from the trade unionist; the musicians ignore his instructions. Interviewed for television, the conductor waxes nostalgic: "the time for greatness is past," he says bitterly, going on to complain that there is no longer any respect for authority, no reverence for artistic creation, nothing. Wagner would not have written a note if the trade unions had had anything to do with it. He doesn't trouble himself to hide his contempt for the musicians with their ugly mugs; tired, bored, without the least devotion to art… but then he stops himself and asks the interviewer to cut this reply, otherwise, he says, the musicians will "shoot him in the legs."

After the interview, returning to the rehearsal, he finds the orchestra in revolt. One elderly musician takes out a gun and fires, others begin to make love, some come to blows, and the walls of the oratory are covered with 1968-type slogans. An infernal scene from Hieronymus Bosch.

At the height of the disorder, a huge wrecking ball smashes the walls of the oratory and the harpist is crushed under the rubble. The musicians are dismayed, silence falls. The conductor picks up his baton and in a friendly manner invites them to resume the rehearsal. In a surreal atmosphere, amid piles of rubble, they start playing again. Order has been restored, harmony reigns, but as the film comes to an end and the screen darkens, the voice of the conductor can be heard once more barking out his orders.

In *Prova d'orchestra,* conflict, writes Giorgio De Vincenti, "is everywhere. Inside and out: at the beginning of the film in the noise of congested street traffic and the sound of a siren; then in the stories told by the musicians as they take their places in front of the music stands, bringing into the oratory the outside world with its steam baths and squabbles over the right of way at a traffic light..."[12]

In this way, the final catastrophe is hinted at from the start, and runs like a strange echo throughout the film, culminating in the wrecking ball that breaks down the walls and brings the outside world rushing in.

Conflict is also expressed in the language used in the film, the heavy, deliberately caricatured German accent of the conductor and the numerous dialects of the musicians. The Sardinian chosen for the trade unionist proved problematic. After the first test showings Fellini was asked to change the dialect in order to avoid an explicit reference to the head of the Italian Communist Party, Enrico Berlinguer, a Sardinian. Rather ashamed of himself for bowing to the request, as he subsequently confessed, Fellini dubbed the actor into a vaguely Roman accent. However, in the final version of the film, one sentence slips through and the trade unionist suddenly breaks into Sardinian dialect. A mistake? A refusal to utterly toe the line? An act of revenge on the absurdity of censorship? Whatever the answer, Fellini ruled out any intention to allude to this or that person in his choice of dialects: "A purely Italian accent doesn't exist, and after dubbing all the actors into all the dialects I could think of, I got to the trade unionist and practically only Sardinian was left. I asked the actor where he was from and he said Sardinia."[13]

The choice of the location, reconstructed in Cinecittà by Danilo Donati, is reminiscent of an archaeological space, sacred and mysterious, suggesting a symbol of Italy and its thousand-year history scorned by the vulgarity of the present day.

Light-years away from the classic political film of the seventies, *Prova d'orchestra* is nonetheless a film about the Italy of the time, wielding the full-scale symbolism typical of Fellini. He said he got the idea from watching the musicians recording the soundtrack of his films: "I watched them come in, embittered, thinking about their lunch, some now ugly, everyone with his mind on other things. I saw the saloon cars they drove up in, the black berets they were wearing on their heads."[14]

How could such people produce harmony, Fellini seems to have wondered?

A similar question arises watching a film like *Intervista*. It seems utterly impossible that such a motley troop of extras, bored stagehands, and technicians can produce anything worthwhile; they seem only to be looking forward to the lunch break, yet what emerges is a work of great beauty. Fellini was interested in this aspect of his art, the relationship between the individual and collectivity, which is particularly important, given the many members of a film crew, in cinematic production.

Kezich took violent exception to one of the most common interpretations of *Prova d'orchestra*: "The public's biggest misunderstanding was to think [of the film] as Fellini's first admission of political commitment, a ridiculous conception resulting from the factionalizing that had plagued the industry and distorted the understanding of Fellini's work in the 1950s. Yet Fellini has always talked about everyone when talking about himself, including society—both as it was and as it should be."[15]

"As it should be" is pure hyperbole, since (thankfully) not a trace of such an intention can be found in Fellini's films.

Prova d'orchestra gave Fellini the opportunity to set the record straight, as he saw it. In spring 1978, the personal could not but be political:

> Do you really imagine that up to now I have been having fun making up fairy tales and unburdening onto others my complexes and emotions? *La strada, Le notti di Cabiria*, were they just pathetic stories of frightened souls, or could they perhaps be seen as films portraying the exploitation of poverty? And the bootlickers, panders and pimps everywhere in those films, did they not show us the way society continues to produce such riffraff? *Il bidone*, with all its swindling, did that say nothing about the moral mafia that holds sway in Italy, in public and private life? Didn't *La dolce vita* and *Amarcord* denounce arrogance in the political, economic and religious spheres, then as now: the disgraced fate of an impoverished society that forces people to burn their instincts in the candle of pure illusions, never actually to grow, never to abandon their pipedreams and overcome their fears?[16]

The Press Reaction

The reaction of the press and the subsequent debate about the film took place in fits and starts because of its numerous "premieres" and subsequent appearances. The first private showing was to the president of Italy, Sandro Pertini, at the Quirinale Palace in mid October 1978; the film took part in the Berlin and Cannes Film Festivals in 1979 and there were other showings reserved for critics and journalists, plus one public showing at the Peoples Festival of Florence in November 1978. The official release was in Rome on 22 February 1979.

The time between the first showing at the Quirinale and the official release—five months—meant that the film was being discussed animatedly in the newspapers when it had been seen only by a few politicians and journalists.[17]

One of Fellini's first statements about *Prova d'orchestra* was from summer 1978 in an interview on set by Aldo Tassone, during the two-week shooting of the film. Fellini says: "The orchestra is Italy, us. The rehearsal is what we do every day, as ever." Defending himself from the accusation of being an artist closed in on himself, detached, without political engagement, he answered with a question: "Showing what can be seen, is that not political?"[18]

The title of the interview, *L'Italia è stonata* (Italy is off-key), rammed home the relevance of the film to current events. And when the film was previewed at the Quirinale, rumors were already flying about in relation to its frame of reference. Fellini did nothing to prevent them.

But when the discussion spun out of control into acrimonious debate, he distanced himself from this version, whether it was used to praise or disparage the film, warning against facile parallels with the Italy of the day.

On 19 October 1978, *Prova d'orchestra* was shown at the Quirinale in the presence of President Pertini, Prime Minister Giulio Andreotti, President of the Chamber of Deputies Pietro Ingrao and state television boss Paolo Grassi. The following day, in *la Repubblica*, Corrado Augius wrote: "With *Prova d'orchestra*, Fellini has made his first political film, in the form of allegorical invective and the pamphlet. It confirms the rumors that the musicians and their ugly faces are us, and the ancient oratory, classically composed, gradually filled with indecent slogans daubed on the walls and finally broken into pieces, is Italy."[19]

He went on to say: "... like all apologues, it explains itself. The metaphors are transparent, the references undisguised. As the newspapers have for some time been reporting, Fellini has had the courage to make a film that makes a strong plea. He has put a face, albeit a caricatured face, to the anxieties of the times, which, for example, a few months ago sent shivers down the spine of the Trade Union Assembly in the EUR district of Rome: 'I didn't want to make a political film, but an ethical apologue,' says Fellini."[20]

The newspapers reported the reactions of the politicians. Pertini and Andreotti praised the film's morality. The president who "started the applause" spoke of the universal value of a film that, in his opinion, did not address only the situation in Italy. Pertini declared: "It gave me much food for thought; it isn't the conductor who restores harmony but the terror of an imminent disaster that brings people to their senses. After the collapse, the conductor does not return to the podium, but stands at the same level as the musicians. Not by chance, wouldn't you say?"[21]

Andreotti quickly adopted the film, in which, in his view, Fellini "is saying that all this rumpus has served no useful purpose, everything starts over, only in conditions that are worse than before; that is the moral of the film. And he is also saying that it was necessary to go through a catastrophe before everyone took up their instruments again and resumed work."[22]

Another article had different wording: "I liked it, it is very subtle, very true: without a certain harmony everything collapses, making an uproar serves no purpose, to stage a concert everyone has to play their own instrument, that is to say, accept their role."[23]

Ingrao, the first Communist to preside over the Chamber of Deputies, immediately distanced himself from Andreotti's conservative interpretation of the film: "I don't think the Italy of recent years is just ill, I don't believe in illnesses or, as a consequence, in regeneration. The apologue fails not because it is too simplistic but because it doesn't grasp the essential nature of the problem. Reality is more complicated and diverse: from disorder and excess something has been created, a transformation has been carried out in recent years. And I ask: who is the conductor today? And finally: wouldn't the music change? Really, Fellini!"[24]

In another declaration, he said: "I don't accept it. Things are less dark and more complex than in the film. I don't see degeneration, collapse, and then the restoration of authoritarianism. Italy has changed, people have matured, become democratic, disorder is not an illness but a necessary period of transition, fertile for change."[25]

Initially, the newspapers saw the film as a metaphor for the authoritarian urges historically present in Italian society, an allegory of its fragile democracy, endemically predisposed to violent solutions, and a representation of the historical background to the current violence of terrorism.

But soon the references became more and more honed. The slogans daubed on the walls of the oratory were traced back to the student movement of 1968 and its short-lived rerun in 1977; the Sardinian accent of the trade unionist was turned into an evident reference to Enrico Berlinguer, the elderly musician who fires a gun during the disorders, saying that he has a license to carry firearms, became a "clear allusion" to the so-called deviated services of the state (secret services acting on their own initiative, often unlawfully).

And, of course, there was the problem of solving the enigma of the identity of the orchestra conductor: "Who is he? Dictator, savior, creator? Many people who have seen the film have wondered. Although understandable, perhaps it is a pointless question. Maybe those who choose dictator do so out of a troubled conscience or fear. The three possibilities are all present, and it isn't necessary to choose."[26]

Gradually the name of Edgardo Sogno came to the fore. Four years earlier, he had been accused of a subversive plan to force the president to appoint a new government able to carry out constitutional reform and prevent the victory of the Communist Party. Nothing came of the planned coup. Also mentioned was the owner of Fiat, Gianni Agnelli, perhaps because of a vague similarity with the actor in the role of the conductor, Balduin Baas. This was certainly the opinion of Giorgio Benvenuto, Secretary General of the UIL Trade Union. When invited to the TV program Tam Tam he declared:

> It isn't an attack on the trade union movement, absolutely not. Actually, I don't think Fellini is being a pessimist in this film. What is there in all of Fellini's films? A deep melancholy in relation to the past... *Prova d'orchestra* is not a plea for the restoration... no, it condemns the return to authoritarianism. The conductor not only speaks German, but I would say—and this is a rather malicious personal interpretation—he bears a certain resemblance to one of Italy's leading industrialists; we can recognize in him *someone very like Gianni Agnelli*... this conductor has a fair dose of cynicism, as we see when he says: the times have changed, previously certain things were possible, but now if I criticize the workers they shoot me in the legs.[27]

Like a kaleidoscope reflecting a huge variety of "coincidences" between the film and the recent history of Italy, the hysteria put on screen in *Prova d'orchestra* became a sort of hysteria off-screen, with everyone chipping in, and no one bothering to address the aesthetic specificity of the film. Fellini's attempts to reshape the debate in terms of the film as apologue or fable came to nothing, and the fact that the film was first shown at the Quirinale to the president of Italy made his disclaimers seem somewhat lame. As Guidotti remarked in *Il Giorno*: "Even if Fellini talks of a political or ethical apologue, rest assured *Prova d'orchestra* will make its mark on the conscience of Italians... admittedly a work of art, undoubtedly an aesthetic product of the highest quality, it will be seen as a film of social engagement, perhaps beyond the intentions of the filmmaker, at a time such as this, one of disorientation and confusion."[28]

Allegory, Parable, Apologue

Invariably referred to as conservative, anti-union, and a film against the extreme left, the politicized workers movement outside the unions (*autonomia operaia*) and *Lotta Continua*, *Prova d'orchestra* became the pretext for a heated political debate entirely beyond Fellini's control.

In a letter dated 20 December 1978, Fellini wrote to his friend Georges Simenon:

> In addition to the musicians there is a conductor who, in the difficult dialectics of this type of relationship, sees that the common aim—playing music together—is mortified, misinterpreted, displaced, ignored. In this small film naturally other things happen too; but what I didn't think I had put into the film and had no intention of putting into it are the meanings, promptings, symbolism, that are causing such a fuss these days among politicians, ministers, journalists, sociologists, trade unionists, even the Confederation of Industry, and who knows soon perhaps the EMS. A turmoil I am not able to deal with, that disorients me, intimidates me.[29]

However, as Antonio Costa noted, "in relation to the political interpretations of the film, it is difficult today to credit Fellini's declarations of astonishment."[30] The tactic was one Fellini had used before, particularly in relation to *La città delle donne*. In this case, the amazement was partly justified, given the way journalists appeared to be hunting down precise references in the film as if it were some kind of *roman à clef*, coming up with the names of people supposedly represented on screen. In the face of such exaggerated interpretations, Fellini could only stand on the sidelines and look on in puzzlement.

In a letter sent to the newspaper *Il resto del Carlino* shortly after the film's release, Fellini defended himself:

> I know, at this point you might say: So now, dear Fellini, you complain—but weren't the first showings of the film reserved for politicians? Quite, what can I say in replay to the accusation I have incautiously made against myself? Should I close myself up in an obstinate, dignified silence? Or say that, naively, I thought the politicians would be able to see the film and perhaps reassure me? "Well done, Fellini, you're right, now we'll get to work and put things to rights!" Because we Italians, at least Italians of my generation, cling to a childish and contradictory attitude, a superstitious faith made up entirely of distrust—resigned, full of bluster, wise, and ironic—according to which politics is essentially something that has nothing to do with us, and really concerns only politicians.[31]

The idea of the apologue was always unlikely to replace the clamor about Fellini's "(first) political film," as Moravia seems to have grasped in his review of the film in *L'espresso* (one of the few to point to the ambiguity and not the "evident nature" of the social content of the film): "it is an apologue in the classic or mock classic mode, along the line of Menenius Agrippa, and hence almost automatically takes on a conservative point of view."[32]

In relation to this, the slogans put into the mouths of the musicians and scrawled on the walls of the oratory, even in the conductor's grotesque German accent, are quite explicit:

> Fellini's political allegory is openly political, although the filmmaker, not without caution, calls it an *ethical apologue*. The obvious target is the disorder and ruin of Italy, exemplified in the revolt, one summer afternoon, of some musicians against the orchestra conductor. It is hard to believe the story has only an ethical dimension since the musicians chant slogans reminiscent of the student uprising of 1968, *Orchestra-terror-whoever plays-is a traitor*, and deliver themselves of fatuous statements such as *music is an unalienable right of the people, and the people should control it*, they stoop to violence, support demagogy and the power of an irresponsible trade union. The villainy is punished metaphysically and improbably...after indicating the punishment and the solution to our ills, Fellini hedges his bets toward the end; the actor playing the conductor (one Baas) is dubbed into Italian with caricatured Teutonic fervor, appearing as a farcical SS officer issuing threats. The cure is more dangerous than the disease?[33]

It was even rumored that Gaumont, the producers, and RAI state television didn't see eye to eye politically and that this had delayed the release of the film: "There are whispers about the left and particularly the trade unions exercising pressure against the film, the former because of the film's criticism of the defects of party politics and Marxist demagogy, and the latter because of Fellini's supposedly evident barbed attitude toward the unions."[34]

Fellini was disconsolate when the state broadcaster failed to release the film: "The board meeting debated a two-faced moralistic position: face one, TV mustn't make money out of its products; it is immoral to ask license payers to pay the price of a cinema ticket to see a product made for television. Face two: the crisis of film, television shouldn't take the place of the cinema, and so on... *Prova d'orchestra* has set off a lot of small orchestra rehearsals."[35]

Between the end of 1978 and February 1979, the newspaper *Il Tempo* ran regular features about the film, including articles by the writer Giovanni Testori, the painter Renato Guttuso, and the politician Ugo La Malfa, a supporter of the so-called "historical compromise" between the ruling Christian Democrat Party and the Communist Party.

Testori praised the film but criticized Fellini for making the conductor an all too evident caricature of Hitler and for failing to use a "hybrid" language in which "German is mixed, say, with the Russian of Stalin. I wonder whether a conductor able to express a mixture of all the languages of all the world's present-day dictators wouldn't have achieved, not only as a sum of all experiences of the kind, and as a fitting alarm, but by virtue of this linguistic magma, the density and breadth the rest of the film is able to find."[36]

For Renato Guttuso, the film was Fellini's true masterpiece, playing down the importance of images and delivering an entirely intelligible message. He, too, thought long and hard about the ambiguity of the film's ending:

> After sacrificing their professionalism, the desecrators, the lighters of fire crackers and protagonists of the challenge to the system, the rebellion against the powers-that-be, are finally brought back to order and work by a few simple statements that touch what is best in each of them. It is a moment of great beauty. Would the film have been reactionary if it had ended there? I don't think so. But Fellini obviously didn't want to end the film with a generic mutual slap on the back. So he decided to plunge the ending into the Nazi crescendo of the conductor who, after regaining the obedience of the musicians, cannot resist crushing them. Fellini's motivation is understandable. He is an idealist and he wants to leave things hanging, undecided.[37]

For La Malfa, Fellini had understood "the essential features of the crisis afflicting Italy in recent years." He was reminded of an earlier film: "...not because the circumstances are similar, but because of the identical ability to penetrate reality: *La dolce vita*... Fellini's film thus acquires great ethical value. It embodies and expresses, symbolically and artistically, an extreme plea to democratic conscience. Italians cannot be insensitive to such an appeal, since freedom and democracy in this country were obtained only after a hard-fought struggle and immense sacrifice."[38]

With great acumen, La Malfa recognizes in two very different films, *La dolce vita* and *Prova d'orchestra,* an identical symbolic power and ability to show the decisive historical transitions taking place in Italy. The sea monster dragged along the beach at the end of *La dolce vita* and the wrecking ball that breaks down the walls of the oratory in *Prova d'orchestra* are among Fellini's most disturbing symbols, suggesting some obscure yet familiar fate hanging over the spectator.

In this regard, Fellini said:

The monster at the end of *La dolce vita* was perhaps objectively more well-defined, with an evident single meaning; the collapse and rubble of *Prova d'orchestra* are interior disasters with different resonances for each individual. The idea that each filmgoer has of such things, and the conclusions to which he or she legitimately comes, are part of the film, its ambiguity, the fact that so-called artistic expression doesn't allow for just one interpretation, it is a sort of collective dream from which everyone wakes with different memories and echoes, due to their personal experience, for which the artist has acted as a sounding board.[39]

This statement sets Fellini apart from other directors of political films in Italy. Instead of asserting a position, denouncing malpractice, offering a different version of the history of Italy, or delving into the mysteries of power, Fellini offers the simplicity (and complexity) of a public dream.

The relations Fellini established with politics through the film appear to have been mediated by what Jung called "synchronicity," significant coincidences rather than the wish to analyze social and political phenomena. Analysis was not part of what today we would call his process.

In his review of the film, Morandini shunned the notion of a political *roman è clef* and spoke about the deeper reasons behind the film. It wasn't about Berlinguer or Gianni Agnelli or Edgardo Sogno or a particular trade union: "It is an ethical and political parable: its morality doesn't concern only Italy, but the disorder, chaos and contradictions of our time. Without harmony, with dissonance, nothing can be achieved. A balance needs to be found between the public and private spheres, between individual and collective rights, between taking an active role in decision-making and democracy. It is a political allegory on the way Italy has become a society that is unlivable, corrupted by aberrant ideology, lacerated by revolutionary ravings."[40]

Gramsci's Orchestra and *The Moro Affair*

With some significant exceptions, the left criticized the film for being regressive and conservative. Some spoke of Fellini's "shift to pessimism" (almost the equivalent of a reactionary stance). The *Quotidiano dei lavoratori* [Worker's Daily] stigmatized Fellini's "fascination with ancient harmony": "With *Prova d'orchestra*, Fellini has orchestrated a full-scale repression of the political while, in fact and through its concrete linguistic signs, *Prova d'orchestra* is Fellini's most ideological and regressive film, however much he would like us to think he was addressing the spectator's unconscious. Actually, precisely for this reason. In a certain sense, *Prova d'orchestra* is a confession, the confession of an artist unable to keep pace with the times, incapable of interpreting them."[41]

For *il manifesto* the film fudged every issue, calling it "an armchair for anyone's butt,"[42] while others seized on the private showing at the Quirinale and Andreotti's praise to accuse Fellini of political opportunism, and sucking up to power by issuing a call to order: "Whatever the intentions of the author, never has a message (clearly benefiting those who see in it the current situation in Italy) been clearer or reached its audience more effectively. As we well know, artists of Fellini's stature believe they have no messages to give, but the fact is the film is being shown in cinemas at the taxpayers' expense, has been distributed privately, and advertised the length and breadth of the land. Nobody thought it ill-advised to arrange a private showing at the Quirinale."[43]

Il Secolo XIX also said it was a film that would please the powers that be: "The weakness of the film is the fact that it has been so readily adopted by the Italian political class. That it is a film that appeals to the people who hold the levers of power; a film that flatters the powerful. It is extremely worrying that government officials do not believe that demonstrations and ferment have anything positive to offer but simply look around for a good conductor with a German accent."[44]

Lotta Continua published a review that is worth quoting at length. It shows the left-wing movement seeing itself in Fellini's film rather as Montanelli had feared seeing himself in the vacuity of Steiner's intellectual circle in *La dolce vita*:

> It is a film that captures the attention, you watch with bated breath, almost as if you were one of the spectators of an ancient Greek tragedy, who took such a strong part in the spectacle because they knew precisely how and when the story would end… So you watch and then leave the cinema disconcerted by the apparent inevitability of the finale; you get angry with yourself and the world denying, for a moment, that it could be reality. You wander about unable to stop thinking, *is that really me? Is that actually who we are* with these nod-nod wink-wink references to "movement practices" (slogans on the walls, squabbling, fever-pitch discussions, ecstatic gazes, the appeal to pleasure rather than to work)? We couldn't help wondering whether the film was something Fellini had shot during the occupation of a factory or a trade union assembly some time after 1968. But it was actually like looking at ourselves in masks, the movement seen from the point of the view of the *commedia dell'arte*, exaggerated, colored by caricature, stripped of dignity, made to look ridiculous. It is normal to see yourself in a film, but it is also normal to be scandalized by the images of a filmmaker—his and his alone—dressed up as something other than his

dreams... *Prova d'orchestra* is the game of *homo ludens*, a shrewd and penetrating game, with traces of naïveté and the love of a man who, attached to a balloon, looks down on us and films us with a magic camera, whose lens distorts reality into the forms of a dreamscape.[45]

Few others were able to see the influence of the *commedia dell'arte* on the film and the treatment of the left-wing movement and its street demonstrations. Today, however, this view represents an intriguing interpretation of one of the fundamental aspects of Fellini's films: their profound, subterranean linkage with the *commedia dell'arte* (not to be confused with the tradition of Italian comedy), a rich cultural heritage Fellini made his own, mining its resources and bringing to it the instruments of the dreamwork and Jungian archetypes.

Of course, Fellini also drew on the Italian comic tradition, its sociological content and criticism of customs, turning the dynamics of mirroring into films that spoke of both the past and the present. *Prova d'orchestra* is filmed political philosophy in images. And the philosophy, according to Toni Negri, is reminiscent of Plato's *The Republic*: "Fellini expresses metaphorically an ancient truth which has come back to enlighten our confused civil life. That truth was given to us by Plato (REPVII 565) in the Babel of democratic-seeming (i.e., anti-democratic) claims and counter-claims, a social and political situation that leads those who had caused it to call for, or recall, a *peristàtes*, a leader, guide, Duce, Führer, embodied here in a figure that lends itself precisely to this metaphor, the maestro of the orchestra, a man who restores order among the ranks of the musicians."[46]

Another possible reference, which seems to have been mentioned only by Negri, was to Gramsci's orchestra:

> This image is set out in one entry for 1933 of Gramsci's *Quaderni del carcere* [Prison Notebooks]. The page is about democratic or organic centralism, to be carried out, it should be noted, without excluding "the direct and active consent" and hence the involvement of individuals, even if this provokes an appearance of disintegration and tumult. Gramsci writes: "A collective consciousness, i.e., a living being, cannot be formed until after multiplicity has been worn away by the friction between individuals: and it cannot be said that silence isn't multiplicity. An orchestra rehearsing, each instrument on its own, gives the impression of a terrible noise; but these rehearsals are necessary for the orchestra to become a single (instrument)." Fellini's metaphor is not directed at the people for whom Gramsci created this image. The designated recipients of Gramsci's message were used to hiding behind the shield of "democratic centralism" and pretended not to understand that Hitler spoke like Stalin. They exhibit a freedom that is subsequently curtailed in the order imposed by a

peristàtes, not in the guise of a conductor raising his baton but as a party official in the most bourgeois of double-breasted jackets. But who are the designated recipients of Fellini's metaphor? I fear they may be—or in fact are—the secular political parties who are unable to get their orchestras to play as a sole instrument. It is sad for the secular and democratic conscience that the individualistically managed use of freedom, by fostering continuous friction and conflicting opinions, may lead to the wish for an orchestra conductor speaking the German of Hitler; or, simply the Sardinian dialect of Berlinguer. Or is it not the case that inside these parties there is more noise than harmony? It is time for the Liberal, Republican, and Socialist orchestras to stop rehearsing and play some genuine political music.[47]

Antonello Trombadori, who had criticized *La strada* many years earlier, launched a strenuous defense of the film on the basis of the idea that a true work of art, by its very nature, cannot be reactionary.

At the same time, a new cultural debate was taking form, following the publication of Leonardo Sciascia's *L'affaire Moro*, an inexorable and lucid pamphlet about the spectacular kidnapping and murder of Aldo Moro, elsewhere—rightly—called an Italian morality play.[48] Sciascia suggested that Moro had been used as sacrificial lamb in the name of the age-old principle that "everything must change so nothing changes" which, says Sciascia, "Lampedusa considers a constant feature of Sicilian history and, today, can be seen as a constant feature of Italian history."[49]

Sciascia too was fiercely attacked, for dressing up politics as literature. He criticized the persistent myth of the impossibility of capturing the Red Brigades with the farce of the so-called party of "intransigence" that refused to negotiate with terrorists to obtain Moro's release. The symbolic proclamation of the death of the statesman, long before his body was actually found in Via Caetani, and the refusal to consider the letters written by Moro from the "People's Prison" as authentic, all of this—analyzed by Sciascia with his customary lucidity only weeks after the events—was bound to cause heated debate.

Before the book came out, Sciascia said: "I can hear them now. They'll say I'm on Craxi's side, that I've entered politics. The truth is I'm not on Craxi's side, I'm on Moro's side, the Moro who, for me, has always been a political adversary, but whom today I wish to defend. Bernanos said there comes a time when a writer has to decide whether to retain the trust of his readers or lose it, and I have decided to lose it rather than deceive them. I, too, have taken that decision."[50]

An article in *Il Borghese* explicitly compared the ways Sciascia and Fellini were being treated:

On the same day that the newspaper *la Repubblica* insults Fellini with the "right-wing" epithet, Leonardo Sciascia is attacked for *l'Affaire Moro*... Anyone who rebels has breakwaters erected around him and triggers the censors and castrators of unacceptable ideas; anyone who rebels condemns himself to the sidelines, is labeled right-wing and denied freedom of expression. But it is no easy matter to gag Sciascia and Fellini; even getting them to toe the line is arduous. The attempts to silence them have not finished, maybe in the future using something a little harsher than a breakwater, like the Red Brigades or a P38.[51]

One Communist Party, at least, found the film impeccable. Screened in October for a delegation of Chinese journalists headed by the deputy director of the "New China" News Agency, Mu Quing, *Prova d'orchestra* was praised unreservedly in an article in *Rassegna* (by Wenhui Bao) for its opposition to "unbridled freedom and anarchy."

Fellini's Republic

Asked about the meaning of the death of the harpist, the only victim of the wrecking ball, Fellini replied: "It represents the sacrifice of the spirit."[52]

Prova d'orchestra was interpreted not only politically, but also spiritually, again from various points of view. Indeed it would have been hard to imagine the Catholic newspaper *Avvenire* sharing the opinion of *Alfabeta*, a left-wing intellectual journal that denied that the film had any political value, but saw it as part of a religious discourse.[53]

For the Italian Episcopal Conference, the ritualism of the film evoked a higher order:

> The references to the trade union movement, or rather to today's unionism *tout court*, immediately recognizable to the filmgoer, have fostered recourse to a term that I, personally, find too simplistic by far... *Prova d'orchestra* is in fact a representation of the sacred, or rather, a tragedy in the ancient sense of the word... A film that utilizes ritual and the sacred as in Greek tragedy by means of eliminating the distance between the spectator and the spectacle... One question remains open, however: how can the stasis implicit in a society based on the sacred be reconciled with the dynamism and movement of today's society? Fellini doesn't answer this question, he goes no further than dropping hints; but great artist that he is, he forces us to face the question.[54]

The philosopher Emilio Garroni also cited the tragic, in its metaphysical dimension, albeit indicating the film's debt to forms of comedy: "The film is 'pessimistic,' but of the kind of pessimism that arises when the existing is left to itself and retold. So the film is pessimistic but not grave or grotesque. It rebounds between apologue, tragic perforce, and the circumstantially comic, based on neorealist quips and caricatures... perhaps the beauty of the film comes precisely from its scallywag air of metaphysics, confined to representation and never investigated extensively or deeply. Behind it, there is nothing. A disquieting nothing. A metaphysics of nothing played in a comic theater."[55]

These interpretations that moved the film away from strictly political commentary suggest an affinity with Sciascia's *L'Affaire Moro*, which the author never tired of calling a "religious book."

Similarly, Fellini never tired of insisting on the archetypal as the key to interpreting the film:

> The filmgoer or viewer becomes involved in the film in a strange way, very private, which strikes me as quite different from the usual experience of seeing a film, even a particularly enthralling one. It is as if unconsciously the viewer recognized that something ideal and real and belonging to everyone is being touched upon, the film speaks about all of us, our lives, our problems, throwing light involuntarily on the nature of, and fundamental conflict between, "the individual" and "society," which politics has always tried to resolve, denying one or other of the terms.[56]

As stated above, *Prova d'orchestra* the apologue draws on Plato's Republic, where questions of the difficult relations between ethics and politics, the individual and society, are dealt with. Despite Fellini's lifelong interest in the archetypes of the collective unconscious, in this film Fellini seems to have been more influenced by Plato than by Jung, and more by the questions Plato sought to answer than by the specificity of the political struggles in Italy at the end of the seventies.

Plato describes the fundamental logic of the tyrannical regime as insinuating in the people the desire for the tyrant, the need for a leader, hence paving the way for the transition from "the height of liberty" to "the fiercest extreme of servitude." In *The Republic*, the insatiable thirst for freedom is shown as leading, inevitably, to the downfall of democracy. The plea at the end of *Prova d'orchestra* that everyone "play well their instrument" is reminiscent of Plato's discussion of the "principle of specialization" or the possession of different skills as the only way to save the *polis*.

The film shows the orchestra producing harmony when everyone is playing their own instrument well, society as a sum of individuals not as the annihilation of individuality. According to Petrucciani, Plato's reasoning about justice "is based on the analogy between a political community and that small community *in interiore homine* that is the individual soul."[57] The irrationalism of violence, of firebrand protest, is a Platonic degeneration, the emergence of arrogance and anarchy following the overthrow of the rational in the individual.

This is Fellini the idealist rather than the reactionary or the nostalgic longing for a return to an order and suspect harmonies. What has been said of *The Republic*, that "it should be understood as an ideal model and ethical paradigm rather than a political system, and certainly not the basis for any kind of political program,"[58] could also be said of *Prova d'orchestra*.

Some light is shed on aspects of the sacred in the film, picked up immediately in the most perceptive reviews, by Elémire Zolla's essay, "Che cos'è la tradizione?" (What Is Tradition?). It caused fierce arguments at the time of its publication in 1971 but today, together with Raymond Aron's *La revolution introuvable*, it is perhaps the most lucid "instant book" about the dynamics involved in the student uprising of 1968.

A complex text in Zolla's characteristic magmatic style, borrowing from mysticism and spiritualism, soteriology and oriental philosophies, the essay was—one would be tempted to say starting from the title—an accusation against the progressive *habitus* that the irrational aims and violence of protest movements hid behind. Zolla, like Fellini, was immediately called an anti-historical thinker and a "man of the right" (according to the Italian tradition of considering anyone on the right a poor thinker).

Zolla traced the etiological framework of the revolution of 1968 in the opposition between a "civilization of criticism" and a "civilization of comment." He redefined the relationship between the concepts of "authority" and "tradition," at the time subject to vehement and confused criticism. His radical dissent from the ongoing political movement looks to the sacred for a possibility of salvation, not unlike the role assigned to art by Fellini in *Prova d'orchestra*.

On the one hand, in the so-called civilization of comment, he sees the canons of ascesis, order, and morality that a sacred text offers to a civilization for discussion. On the other, in the civilization of criticism, the text is oppressive and obstructs freedom. As such, it is subject to radical criticism. But what has the appearance of a dichotomy is in fact an essential and irresolvable tension in man:

> The sum of joys and sufferings seems the same in one and the other. Peace and order are ephemeral flowers under the empire of a text, freedom and pleasures are imaginary in the bombardment of criticism… The civilization of criticism leads to suffering because men need certainties, the apodictical, deductions, end causes, and a center around which to rotate like a planet around the sun… The civilization of comment, on the other hand, will never satisfy the whole of man, create an earthly life on the model of the heavenly, because it is bound to take on a fragile body of authority.[59]

The obscure ending of the film, the ambiguity of a rediscovered harmony that immediately takes on the contours of authoritarianism, suggesting some kind of infinite cycle, with a new rebellion in the future, expresses the perennial nature of this dialectic without offering Zolla's solution. In the eternal tension between the search for harmony and the pleasure of freedom: "The civilization of comment is a tension toward something impossible and, in fact, can be realized only on the other side of death. But equally the civilization of criticism tends toward the impossible, an Eden of equals, since it has an envious hatred of hierarchy."[60]

In both Fellini's film and Zolla's essay, the preference is for the civilization and hence the permanence of a sacred text. Why? Zolla says it is because the civilization of comment proclaims and openly praises its text, whereas the civilization of criticism hides it and pretends to have no text, offering an illusory promise of freedom. According to Zolla, this is the "great secret" running through the student rebellion of 1968: "The civilization of criticism is based on a hidden text, which it reveres and imposes with force. It does so secretly, writing it fraudulently into hearts and minds, masquerading as openness and criticism. It survives only because it prevents its hidden sacred nature from being revealed. All of critical culture comes down to rhetorical variations on the hidden sacred text; it is iron-clad and asphyxiating like no sacred culture."[61]

Certainly, Fellini is less explicit than Zolla on this point. But the musicians who are protesting, the slogans against Beethoven and Verdi, the grotesque attempt to replace the conductor with a giant metronome, merely return us to the asphyxiating cul-de-sac of a freedom imposed with the violence of dogma.

The search for order, with the risks and dangers involved in the plea for the tyrant, is countered by another inversion with "the stereotypes of an irrationality destined to leave in its wake only signs of death," as Fellini said.[62]

Watching *Prova d'orchestra* Today

In the recent unstable history of Italian democracy, the discovery of Aldo Moro's body, left by the Red Brigades halfway between the headquarters of the Christian Democrat Party and the Communist Party, acted as a collective catharsis. Shortly before being kidnapped, in one of his last speeches as a free man, addressed to Christian Democrat parliamentarians, he wondered out loud: "What would happen in Italy, right now, at this precise moment in history, if the logic of opposition were carried out to its bitter end, whoever were to carry it out, by us or others, if this country of uninterrupted passion and fragile structures, were put to the test, day in day out, by an opposition taken as far as it will go?"[63]

Uninterrupted passion and fragile structures. As Fabio Vander has said, Moro was here famously espousing an interpretation of the election result of June 1976 "as having two victors, the DC and the PCI, each able to paralyze the other: hence the need to cooperate, in order to maintain the democratic framework of the country and manage the permanent economic crisis."[64] During his imprisonment the democratic framework of the country was under intense pressure.

His murder, his "inevitable" sacrifice, as it was called even at the time, was the summation of ten years of radical conflict beginning in 1968. In *L'Affaire Moro*, Sciascia writes: "the truth—harsh, tragic, as it appeared in the headlines of the newspapers, a truth that could not be ignored or twisted out of true—seemed to come from literature."[65]

In the same way, a few years later (on 2 August 1980), the devastation of Bologna Station by a terrifying explosion seemed to come from film. Precisely, from the wrecking ball in *Prova d'orchestra* and the death of the harpist, crushed under the rubble.

The resonance, or Jungian synchronicity, linking that obscure ending to the reality of Italy is one of the most disquieting aspects of *Prova d'orchestra* (and disquieting, at the very least, was another famous instance of the cinema foreshadowing events: Elio Petri's 1976 film *Todo Modo* from the novel by Sciascia).

Today, the most sophisticated criticism of the film takes quite a different view of its meaning. With specific reference to the spiritual reading by *Alfabeta* at the time, Antonio Costa writes: "Over time the interpretations that are radically opposed to a political reading of the film—for example the nonsense about the supposed usurpers of power—are the ones that have survived, i.e., the religious and symbolic readings, the sense of ritual and of the dissolution (only to begin again) of the orchestra."[66]

Or, as De Vincenti believes, the film has emerged as a reflection about making art, which, typically for Fellini, excluded "what is happening around him":

> Fellini thinks of art as a process of approaching a mysterious sense, given as hypostatized, existing somewhere, some kind of a religious world of ideas, a place of perfection, a golden age, precisely. For him, making art means looking for this lost world and this places him at a distance from what is happening around him. A profound distance, the mark of a fundamental difference between life as he conceives it, which is irreducibly Catholic, and certain cultural movements of the time, specifically those that rejected the metaphysical, thinking of sense as something immanent and part of a process and not as a somehow divine hypostasis.[67]

However, in my opinion, in removing the political content of *Prova d'orchestra* today, critics run the risk of making the opposite mistake of their colleagues many years before, when they tended to overread the politics of the film.

Fellini's symbolic language shows us a country that is tired of demonstrations and protests in the streets, of violence, the annulment of the individual in schematic ideologies; all recurrent features of Italian history, no less than the call for a strong leader, the conductor with an iron fist. The production of harmony, starting by making individuals responsible for their actions, was and is the thorny issue the film grasps, and its final message. The seventies were a time of immense upheaval and transformation, but at the same time they were a decade that set out culturally and institutionally to consolidate some of the dogmas of 1968, which in later years were to show themselves to be severely limited ideologically and in terms of concrete life.[68] Against these limits, the appeal to the sacred nature of art seems inseparable from the appeal to the sacred nature of the individual. The need for harmony and the victory of the rational over the irrational can be seen not metaphorically but in the specific history of Italy and its chronic structural weaknesses, the logic of a head-on collision that produces, and is intended to produce, only stasis, an immobile transformation, what Fellini called, with reference to *La città delle donne*, "progressence." And, here, above all, what can be seen is the everlasting cathartic role of national tragedies, the single event, from which the only real call for unity emerges in a country divided on everything, worn down by continuous daily squabbling, and that comes to its senses only among the rubble and debris it has produced, finding momentarily some kind of collective cohesion.

In an interview by Giovanni Grazzini, replying to a question on the years of terrorism in Italy, Fellini placed the faces of the common people who attended the funerals in opposition to revolutionary hysteria and its cowardly intellectual apologists:

> Perhaps more than the atrocious facts, the ferocity, the eighteen-year-old carabinieri machine-gunned in bars as they drank their cappuccino, at dawn, on the outskirts of the city, beyond all the horror and the slaughter-house pictures revoltingly paraded by the television of elderly people cut down like animals by butchers, what was most frightful were the abject, cowardly justifications of the intellectuals... The only comfort was in the face of the people at the funerals, their silence, their compact opposition to the madness that sought to overthrow and contaminate everything.[69]

One reading of *Prova d'orchestra*, which proved prescient, was that the film was a biting catalogue of the future vulgarity of television. The idea of a sort of "reality show" of musicians and phony documentary of the life of an orchestra, parodied by Fellini, was seen by some as a broader investigation of the new forms of "direct appeal" on television and the fake intimacy of television talk shows, foreshadowing the radical shift in the collective imagination of the subsequent decades.

This is how we should see the supposed confessions of the musicians, their posing in front of the camera, as Fellini gives us pitiless close-ups of them as they answer his questions. If it is part of the so-called "cinema of reflux" (or reaction), *Prova d'orchestra* investigates the fundamental implications and breaking point of the shift of the collective imagination away from cinema toward television:

> The examples of humanity we are given in *Prova d'orchestra* are more suited to television these days than to the filmgoers of the time. First and foremost because of the guarantees collectively enjoyed by the musicians, which are far from the conditions of the new social and political subjects emerging at the time, which Fellini seems not to notice. And in the vulgarity that Fellini clearly understood way ahead of the times to be a characteristic of television, as became obvious only with Craxi and Berlusconi and the general degradation into wretchedness of the political and cultural life of the nation.[70]

In this sense, Paolo Valmarana, the man behind the production of the film for RAI state television in 1979, recalls that Fellini presented *Prova d'orchestra* as a film about television and the ambitions and frustrations it is able to unleash.

1978, the year of the kidnapping and death of Aldo Moro, was a turning point in the history of Italy. On 7 September of that year, Silvio Berlusconi officially inaugurated his first TV station, "TeleMilano58," with headquarters in Milano Due.

Notes

1. Bondanella, *The Cinema of Federico Fellini*, 291.
2. Ibid., 264.
3. P. Ortoleva, "Cinema politica e uso politico del cinema" [Political Cinema and the Political use of Film], in F. De Bernardinis, *Storia del cinema italiano*, 152.
4. Ibid., 153.
5. Ibid., 164.
6. A. Casanova, *Scritti e immaginati. I film mai realizzati di Federico Fellini* [Written and Imagined: Fellini's Unmade Films] (Rimini: Guaraldi, 2005), 105.
7. F. Fellini, *Poliziotti. Storie vere di Nicola Longo raccolte da Gianfranco Angelucci* [Policemen: True Stories of Nicola Longo Collected by Gianfranco Angelucci],

Introduction to Film Adaptation, Creec Foundation (0041) in the Bologna Film Library.

8. T. Kezich, *Federico Fellini*, 318. Translation by M. Proctor.

9. A. Zanzotto, *Il cinema brucia e illumina*, 100.

10. F. Fellini, *Prova d'orchestra*, ed. O. del Buono (Milan: Garzanti, 1980), 138.

11. Ibid.

12. G. De Vincenti, "Prova d'orchestra di F. Fellini. Sonorità senza sacralità" [Fellini's *Prova d'orchestra*: Sound without the Sacred], in *Il cinema del riflusso. Film e cineaste italiani degli anni Settanta* [The Cinema of Reflux: Italian Films and Filmmakers of the Seventies], ed. L. Miccciché (Venice: Marsilio, 1997), 415.

13. F. Fellini, *Prova d'orchestra*, 14.

14. Ibid., 14.

15. T. Kezich, *Federico Fellini*, 336.

16. F. Fellini, *Prova d'orchestra*, 140.

17. For the reconstruction of the debate in the newspapers and magazines of the time, I consulted the Dario Zanelli collection at the Federico Fellini Foundation. I also consulted a file with excerpts of the press coverage of films, compiled specifically for Andreotti by employees of the Press and Publications Department and the Center for Reproduction and Duplication of the Chamber of Deputies, following the television broadcast of the film (26 December 1979). This file is in the Historical Archives of the Luigi Sturzi Institute, specifically in the Andreotti Archives, under "Fellini Federico," folder B 1484. The volume *Prova d'orchestra* includes the complete screenplay and various interviews with Fellini that were published in the press.

18. A. Tassone, "L'Italia è stonata" [Italy is Off-key], *Euro*, 1 June 1978.

19. C. Augius, ".... ma chi è il direttore d'Orchestra?" [... Who is the Conductor?], *la Repubblica*, 20 October 1978.

20. In the so-called "about face" in the EUR district of Rome, in February 1978 the trade union decided to support the government and its wage control policy in order to tackle the emergency caused by the economic crisis and by terrorism.

21. L. Tornabuoni, "Prova d'orchestra al Quirinale," *La Stampa*, 20 October 1978.

22. C. Augius, "...ma chi è il direttore d'orchestra?."

23. L. Tornabuoni, "Prova d'orchestra al Quirinale."

24. C. Augius, "...ma chi è il direttore d'orchestra?."

25. L. Tornabuoni, "Prova d'orchestra al Quirinale."

26. M. Guidotti, "Ma questa orchestra è l'Italia" [This Orchestra Is Italy], *Il Giorno*, 22 October 1978.

27. The statements were quoted in an article in *Corriere della Sera*, "Giorgio Benvenuto: il direttore ricorda Agnelli" [Giorgio Benvenuto: The Conductor is Like Agnelli], 24 February 1979.

28. M. Guidotti, "Ma questa orchestra è l'Italia."

29. *Carissimo Simenon, Mon cher Fellini, Carteggio di Federico Fellini e Georges Simenon* [Correspondence between Fellini and Simenon] (Milan: Adelphi, 1998), 66–67.

30. A. Costa, "Le immagini superstiti, Fellini e Antonioni" [Surviving Images, Fellini and Antonioni], in *Storia del cinema italiano, vol. 12, 1977-1985*, ed. V. Zagarrio (Venice/Rome: Marsilio, 2005), 107.

31. "Una lettera di Fellini 'A-po-lo-go po-li-tic-co'" [A Letter by Fellini, "Po-li-ti-cal A-po-lo-gue"], *il Resto del Carlino*, 27 February 1979. I was able to see the original letter in the papers of Dario Zanelli (Folder 306), which includes a correction—the word *infantile* added by hand—not published in the newspaper.

32. A. Moravia, "Sul podio c'è Menino Agrippa" [Menenius Agrippa on the Podium], *L'espresso*, 26 November 1978.

33. C. Laurenzi, "Piccola rivoluzione in musica" [Small Musical Revolution], *Il Giornale*, 25 October 1978.

34. D. Zanelli, "Perchè non si può ancora vedere Prova d'orchestra di Fellini?" [Why Can We Still Not See Fellini's *Prova d'orchestra*?], *il Resto del Carlino*, 14 January 1979.

35. An article in *Corriere della Sera* on 27 January 1979 (*Fellini tra tante piccole prove d'orchestra* [Fellini and a Host of Small Orchestra Rehearsals]) described the problems preventing the screening of the film.

36. G. Testori, "Un'insubordinazione di natura metafisica" [Metaphysical Insubordination], *Il Tempo*, 14 January 1979.

37. R. Guttuso, *Prova d'orchestra*—folder ("Federico Fellini" B.1484 A.A.), 29.

38. U. La Malfa, 30.

39. F. Fellini interviewed by Gian Luigi Rondi in *Il Tempo*, 5 November 1978, now in *Prova d'orchestra*, 134.

40. M. Morandini, "Macché Rebus, è solo un film di Fellini" [No Enigma, Just a Fellini Film], *Corriere della Sera*, 25 February 1979.

41. R. Alemanno, "Oh, il fascino dell'antica armonia" [Oh, the Fascination of Ancient Harmony], *Quotidiano dei lavoratori*, 24 February 1979.

42. Fellini, "il tintinnio dell'arte" [Fellini, the Rattle of Art], *il manifesto*, 24 February 1979.

43. C. Vallauri, "Fellini e l'orchestra di Menenio Agrippa" [Fellini and the Orchestra of Menenius Agrippa], *La Sinistra*, 25–26 February 1979.

44. M. Manciotti, "Il film che piace al palazzo" [The Film the Establishment Likes], *Il Secolo XIX*, 23 February 1979.

45. R. Antonella, "Il direttore, l'orchestra, lo stupore e la rabbia" [The Conductor, the Orchestra, Astonishment, and Rage], *Lotta Continua*, 23 February 1979.

46. A. Negri, "L'orchestra di Fellini e quella di Gramsci" [The Orchestras of Fellini and Gramsci], *Il Settimanale*, 2 May 1979.

47. Ibid.

48. See R. Wagner-Pacifici, *The Moro Morality Play: Terrorism as Social Drama* (Chicago: University of Chicago Press, 1986).

49. L. Sciascia, *L'Affaire Moro* [The Moro Affair] (Milan: Adelphi, 2003 [1978]), 138.

50. Now in G. Giacovazzo, *Moro, 25 anni di misteri* [Moro, 25 Years of Mysteries] (Bari: Palomar, 2003), 41–42.

51. I. Koba, "I pinzocheri contro Fellini" [Bigots against Fellini], *Il Borghese*, 29 October 1978.

52. F. Fellini, *Prova d'orchestra*, 153.

53. See P. Crovetto, "Fellini, l'orchestra sacra" [Fellini, the Sacred Orchestra], *Alfabeta* no. 3–4, (July–August 1979), 17–19.

54. A. Sani, "L'orchestra metafisica di Fellini" [Fellini's Metaphysical Orchestra], *Avvenire*, 6 March 1979.

55. E. Garroni, "La morte e il nulla nel film di Fellini" [Death and Nothingness in Fellini's Film], *Paese Sera*, 9 March 1979.

56. Interview with Federico Fellini in *la Repubblica*, 23 February 1979, now in *Prova d'orchestra*, 143.

57. S. Petrucciani, *Modelli di filosofia politica* [Models of Political Philosophy] (Turin: Einaudi, 2003), 41.

58. M. Isnardi Parente, *Il pensiero politico di Platone* [Plato's Political Thought] (Rome/Bari: Laterza, 1996), 35.

59. E. Zolla, *Che cos'è la tradizione* [What Tradition Is] (Milan: Bompiani, 1971), 21–22.

60. Ibid., 22.

61. Ibid, 23.

62. F. Fellini, *Prova d'orchestra*, 133.

63. A. Moro, "Garanzia e limiti di una politica" [Guarantee and Limits of a Policy], 28 February 1978, cited in F. Vander, *Aldo Moro. La cultura politica cattolica e la crisi della democrazia italiana* [Catholic Political Culture and the Crisis of Democracy in Italy] (Genova: Marietti, 1999), 184.

64. Ibid., 183.

65. L. Sciascia, *L'Affaire Moro*, 29.

66. A. Costa, "Le immagini superstiti. Fellini e Antonioni," 108.

67. See G. De Vincenti, "Prova d'orchestra di F. Fellini. Sonorità senza sacralità," 414–415.

68. See G. Cazzola, S. Mattone, F. Mazzotti, and D. Sugamele, *Anni Settanta. I peggiori anni della nostra vita* [The Seventies: The Worst Years of Our Lives] (Venice: Marsilio, 2011).

69. F. Fellini, *Intervista sul cinema*, 141–142.

70. G. De Vincenti, "Prova d'orchestra di F. Fellini. Sonorità senza sacralità," 417.

Chapter 7

You Don't Interrupt an Emotion

I think the cinema has lost authority, prestige, mystery, magic...now there is a tyrannical filmgoer, an absolute despot, who does what he likes and thinks he is the director or at least the editor of the film he is watching. How can the cinema try to seduce such a person?
—Federico Fellini

Television is not just a formidable moment of family communion, it is an instrument that has gradually improved the quality of life. Wherever you go in Italy there is entertainment, escapism, so that our leisure hours (just think of people at home alone or in a hospital bed) can be passed pleasantly.
—Silvio Berlusconi

Cacao cacao cacao...sponserao of the transmissao.
—The TV show, *Indietro tutta*, 1987

After Cinema, the Eighties

"You don't interrupt an emotion." With this slogan, Fellini became one of the most vociferous opponents of commercial breaks in films shown on television, a battle that raged from 1985 to 1995, the year of the referendum on TV advertising.

The PCI adopted the slogan as its own. Walter Veltroni, then the head of the propaganda and information commission of the party, was particularly enthusiastic. In 1989, at the height of the battle, Veltroni described what was at stake: "This is an important struggle. We have the support of two hundred important names and, above all, 80 percent of the Italian population: the country is going through a massive change in television taste."[1]

Berlusconi's Fininvest channels adopted the slogan "Forbidden to forbid," as used during a memorable sit-in on the *Maurizio Costanzo [Talk] Show* and in a campaign that was a dress rehearsal for the coming inversion of roles between politics and television in the "Second Republic."

A slogan invoking freedom, borrowed from the rhetoric of the student uprising of 1968, pressed into service in order to defend the rights of a private television station to finance itself through advertising, is, in itself, an indication of how much things had changed. The 80 percent of Italians Veltroni spoke of was, at the very least, a fluctuating majority and in 1995 Italians castigated the state broadcaster and political parties with their traditional view of television, in the referendum, voting in favor of commercial advertising.

With its differing ideological standpoints and frequent examples of shortsightedness, the battle over commercial TV was a measure of the anthropological changes taking place in Italy. This chapter describes these changes and how they were reflected in Fellini's cinema.

From *E la nave va* to *La voce della luna*, Fellini's films in the eighties are radically idiosyncratic in their understanding of Italian society, in the loss of a sense of belonging and of any lower common denominator. Up to then, these had nurtured and inspired his creativity. Fellini's nostalgia, so perfectly captured in *Amarcord*, becomes darker, bordering on invective, as he adopted the tones of the polemicist, closer to the pungency of Pasolini than to the poetic disenchantment of his previous years.

In his later years, Fellini was convinced that cinema, so lucid in its reading of the world for people of his generation, was becoming a blunt instrument, no longer unique, no longer an extraordinary ritual experience in a movie theater, now served up daily at home on a small screen. This was part and parcel of the growing pessimism of an artist who had never been a champion of civil rights but nonetheless possessed an acute understanding of society, often before others and frequently pointing to how society would develop.

In the eighties, universally venerated, Fellini found work hard to come by in a country that seemed to have a new collective imagination, new needs and wants. His films, his use of film sets as powerful reinventions of the world, required enormous investments and the returns were uncertain, particularly when people seemed to be abandoning movie theaters. Long past was the time in which he and society were in perfect step with *La dolce vita*, Fellini's undying myth.

A decade of radical reconfiguration for politics and ideology, culture and consumerism, the eighties inevitably produced apocalyptic visions of vacuity, embodied in television subculture. And many intellectuals have not seen any reason to change their minds.

Most of these interpretations are based on reasons and prejudices of a political nature rather than on historical analysis (the eighties are quite recent and their effects are still being felt). They also suffer from the nostalgic celebration of the previous decade, the seventies, seen as an era of social conquest subsequently suffocated in the individualism of the next decade. Only recently have less ideological analyses of the period started to emerge.

According to the historian Marco Gervasoni, for example, the eighties and not the sixties were the true decade of Italy's modernity, the real culmination of the years of the economic boom:

> We need to rethink the commonly held view that Italy entered the era of mass consumption during the sixties. While the boom touched mainly urban areas, with a marked difference between the provinces and large cities and between the north and south, consumption in the eighties reached all levels of society and all geographical regions, from the most affluent to the most depressed. The expansion of consumption during the years of the economic miracle filled the gap between us and advanced countries, while the eighties was a decade in which the developments in Italy were along the same lines as in the United States, Japan, and the rest of Western Europe. In other words, in the eighties, Italy was in every way a modern country, which it had not been in the sixties.[2]

In the political and cultural fields, the comparison between the two decades reveals much the same:

> The transformation of the sixties took place in a context that confirmed the prevailing interpretations of society provided by the leading political cultures. Granted, the economic miracle had caused a crisis among the most orthodox and mummified Marxists, but at the same time it inspired factory-based neo-Marxism, and revisionist tendencies in social democratic parties, which not accidentally were governing almost all Western European nations... The explosion of consumption in the eighties, on the other hand—in the philosophical language of the time—challenged the *dominant narratives* of the era. The economic boom was the beginning of the end of twentieth-century mass society but the eighties were the beginning of something entirely new and utterly different.[3]

In relation to this interpretation, Fellini's position was paradoxical: in the eighties the precociously postmodern artist of *La dolce vita* gave way to apocalyptic stances as the postmodern changes in society began to bite.

Until that moment, within hyper-politicized Italian society, Fellini had been fleet-footed, looking on with the ironic gaze of a visitor from another planet. He was disenchanted with the "political" and with the collective ideologies of the day; in a commonly accepted view these were characteristics of the postmodern individual, i.e., an individual "in daily contact with a universe of symbols, images and goods" and who "lends the greatest weight to fun, leisure and the pleasure of the senses."[4]

In the eighties, this attitude—for so long Fellini's—became the norm, causing Fellini to react by entering into collision with the present. In this political battle, added to the allegories in his films, he openly took positions. For him, the hegemony of television profits was the sign of the degradation of contemporary life. Commercial television was: "the principal theater of the world of consumerism; without it, the new consumer would not have been born, at least not in such a strong form. And, vice versa, without the dizziness of consumption, private television would not have taken on the central role in society that it now has."[5]

Hence, "for Italians in the eighties, commercial TV was an instructional handbook on how to take part in modernity."[6]

Although the cinema, Italian cinema in particular, was an archaeological relic, Fellini's position on commercial television was not one of radical rejection, as many intellectual moralists at the time hoped. In the latter part of his career, "entrenched behind the friendly walls and protected by the placenta of Cinecittà,"[7] he seemed to embody the image of cinema under siege. A siege Fellini was to show explicitly at the end of *Intervista*, with native Americans armed with television antennae circling around Cinecittà, ready to launch their final attack on the circled wagons, as in a Western by John Ford.

The unstoppable advance of private television stations resulted from and expressed needs from below. The left and the world of cinema, by and large anchored to an old idea of the passive spectator and the top-down hegemony of a subculture,[8] was no match: "Perhaps the most relevant feature of the development of private TV, that attracted the greatest number of viewers, was the direction it took against the nanny state and the party system, its irritation with institutional paralysis and its distance from politics, and this gradually entered civil and social life: in this, first the 'war of the airwaves' and then the battle over commercials, represented broader social issues, as has been rightly observed."[9]

Technique and Magic

The idea of cinema buried under television trash and vulgarity has the persuasive force of Manichaeism, but doesn't explain the profound reasons behind such a change of era.

The prophetic finale of *Intervista* and the invective of *Ginger e Fred* are inseparable from a nostalgia for cinema that Fellini realized could no longer exist.

Although auteurial cinema had tried to adapt to television, it found itself unable to cope with the new public taste provoked by private television stations. Spectators had become more mobile and impatient, less inclined to accept "time passing" as in Antonioni or the static shots of the Taviani brothers:

> In the sixties and seventies many young directors, scriptwriters, and professionals in the Italian film industry worked in television as external consultants or through small companies. Under close political control, they created new productions, drama, experimental programs; between the two forms of expression there were subterranean but far from sporadic exchanges. For example Italian comic films increasingly imitated TV conversations. Now, all this came to an abrupt end. Private television stations broadcast mainly American films or domestic product for a mass audience with the small sexual transgressions of Italy after the divorce law: as far from auteurial cinema as you could get.[10]

Private television didn't help, but Italian cinema was in decline for other reasons,[11] mistakes, the lack of long-term planning, the passing during the eighties of the craftsmanship that had previously nurtured the film industry: "Following these decisions, the technicians in Cinecittà, toolmakers, cameramen, makeup artists, hoards of extras, character actors, costume designers, scriptwriters, entire families of craftsmen who had been working there for generations, were used less and less and gradually let go."[12]

Fellini's *Intervista* is a final, epic homage to the disappearing Italian film industry of Cinecittà.

But the *cupio dissolvi* of the cinema, which some critics see as already present in *Prova d'orchestra,* is expressed in all its gloom by the metaphor of *E la nave va.* The reference to the world of opera is a homage to art *tout court,* to its ritual and mysterious nature that society and ideology in the eighties seem perfectly able to do without. The end of the film—revealing the wings of Studio 5 of Cinecittà with the platform of the ship—is less a metalinguistic *coup de théâtre* than a nostalgic tribute to the workers in the industry.

Zanzotto reviewed the film in *Corriere della Sera* with his customary refinement. He spoke of an anamnesis in Fellini, of an *Amarcord* of the film industry associated less with a *fin de siècle* pessimism than the inevitable obsolescence of its materials:

> Fellini shows us the memories of cinema, frozen embryos become ectoplasms, and he piles them up on the horizon of a shipwreck (but is it

really a shipwreck?) which undoubtedly is connected with the rapid obsolescence typical both of technologies and their/our time, characterized to the nth degree by the presence of audiovisuals. Naturally, this obsolescence and these shipwrecked people will also become food to be devoured by the audiovisuals. Now the gladiators of Tron are lying in wait, computers are what matters in filmmaking, for every moment of the film, which may perhaps become a single moment; it is the dominion of High Definition, the small and giant screens have united, soon film and silk will disappear. And in this way it will be possible to ramp up to the freest empyrean of the visual, without any reference to reality or simulated reality: in the not unlikely prospect that everything will become a "special effect" obtained electronically.[13]

This farsighted vision, with its ancestral foreboding, is also true of the symbolic nucleus of *E la nave va*. With rather more linguistic verve than was customary, Zanzotto was expressing a fairly common sentiment at the time, the sense of an imminent catastrophe, the fear of the new that automatically accompanies radical change. The metalinguistic version of the film would nonetheless not have been out of place among other auteurial films of the seventies and eighties, in which evoking the history of cinema was, as Brunetta has said, "the most appropriate and least compromising level of auteurial skill," a far from playful postmodernism characterized by a sense of mourning, loss, and the disappearance of a world.

The provinces reconstructed in Fellini's last film, *La voce della luna*, exemplified the archaic and consumerism, the "synthesis and symbol of Italian anarchy." Wandering about the set during shooting, Lietta Tornabuoni observed: "The exemplary small Italian town is twinned with Tucson, Arizona, includes writing in Arabic, features fast food restaurants and cathedrals, thousands of TV antennae and a monument to the fallen, porticoes and videogames. In the square you can see all the architectural styles of Italy, as the architect Dante Ferretti explains, 'a medieval church, a renaissance fortress, a bourgeois building from the era of Umberto I, a rationalist fascist construction and a postmodern Church in transparent fiberglass. The square is the country.'"[14]

In response to the disappearance of the world replaced by an "enormous special effect," and the loss of the sacred nature of auteurial cinema, Fellini turns himself into a living work of art. According to Kezich, "During the time he was developing, filming and showing *E la nave va*, Fellini had become a charismatic figure with the media, ubiquitous in the papers and on TV, almost to the point of obsession."[15] He goes on to say: "We could discuss at length the disconnect between the widespread interest in Fellini the character and the indifference over Fellini's art. It may be evidence that society is more interested in appearance… Or maybe it's a symptom of the fact that Italy in the 1980s was nurturing a gap between artists and common people..."[16]

In reality, Fellini had always cultivated the myth of the set and of the directorial role, confining—if that is the right word—the ritual of cinema to the space between *technique* and *magic*. He was the first to nurture the myth of Fellini the artist, "witchdoctor," "magician," "enchanter," as the press called him, and the set as ritual location, shooting as the "actions" of an informal artist, and these defined a cultural value (to use Benjamin's famous expression) which was not objectified in a work of art, but in Fellini himself.

Begun as far back as *La dolce vita*, the process culminates in Fellini's late career. After the institutional premieres and the festival circuit, his films were immediately forgotten. Praising Fellini, but not going to see his films, giving him awards but not allowing him to work, was, as Pierre Bordieu has shown, part and parcel of the mechanisms of social distinction that define the essential motivations of the ideology of art in a society.

The reaction of the paying public, reported by the newspapers after the Rome premiere of the film at the Barberini cinema (Friday, 7 October 1983) was in striking contrast to the ritual homage of critics and socialites. Vignettes portrayed the boredom and excessive length of the film. Interviewed at the exit of the cinema, one spectator said: "If everything in Fellini is a dream, why not fall asleep?"[17]

From Campari to La Malfa: TV, Commercials

After his first experiences in television (the NBC documentary *A Director's Notebook* and *I clowns* for RAI), Fellini quickly concluded it wasn't for him. During the preparations for *Amarcord*, he confessed: "The experiment of *I clowns* was enough for me to realize that television is not a medium I am suited to. It's a question of lighting, of rhythm, which forces you to adopt a repetitive language in order to keep the spectator at home in his seat, watching on the divan, maybe in his underwear, as his wife talks, grandma chips in, a kid gets slapped and starts to cry."[18]

Above all, television was not a medium in which the director was the absolute creator, as he had always seen himself:

> While the radio has had radio authors, i.e., authors that used that particular medium and were able to create works interpreting reality, and therefore were artists, for television I do not know who might be able to do the same... perhaps, without knowing it, the only real television author is Mike Bongiorno, since he reproduces, through his own person, such a

distorted image, such a weird version of the country, or of the human condition—I mean, his shows bring out the ferocity, ignorance, competition, superficial erudition, which is itself a reflection of our country and its provincialism—so much so that I am forced to say he is an author because he interprets reality.[19]

These words are worth examining closely. Here, Fellini is joining in with Umberto Eco and his famous "phenomenological" investigation of the TV quiz-show host Mike Bongiorno, and wonders under what conditions television can produce art and therefore whether a writer or producer for television can be considered an artist. As Fellini knew only too well, this blind alley was an impossible attempt to defend a pyramid structure for culture within television, which, by its very nature, erodes distinctions between communications and entertainment, art and popular culture, information and spectacle.

To Fellini, television was the negation of the ineffable mystery of art, which could still be expressed in film:

> First and foremost the fact that television enters people's homes deprives it of its—*let me call it—religious character*...In the theater or cinema this ritual, to varying degrees and not excluding a certain shabbiness, can take place; in other words the *location of the experience* becomes a *church*, a place suited to receiving communications, a message. This is not the case with television... you have to engage the interest of TV viewers immediately, to entertain them. Because this public, this master who has bought you, switches off or changes channel as soon as you fail to keep him entertained and goes to have his dinner... there is none of the ritual required and instead there is an upside down abuse by the viewer. Viewers rule television and, if they want to, they can throw the TV set out the window.[20]

Reread today, this declaration shows how aware Fellini was of the changes in society and how an intellectual reacted to the dawn of a new world. The use of liturgical terms serves to draw a distinction between the "sacred" and "profane" and to maintain a distance between art and communication, according to canons that were soon to appear obsolete.

Fellini also seems to have understood something about viewers whom web 2.0 called "prosumers," a mixture of producer and consumer, redefined horizontally and proactively. Even back then Umberto Eco was criticizing those who wished to maintain the strict division of art and mass media: "Once upon a time there were mass media, bad, of course, guilty. And there were the virtuous who accused them of committing crimes. And Art (thankfully), which provided an alternative to those who were prisoners of the mass media. Well, that's all over and done with. We need to rethink the entire situation."[21]

Interestingly, the broadcast of *8 ½* by RAI on 16 October 1972, advertised as the canonization of Fellini and his masterpiece,[22] turned out to be a fiasco. With great disappointment, Angelo Solmi observed: "We have learned more than a month after the event that the television presentation of *8 ½* was not appreciated by the 14.5 million viewers who saw the film, the result of the questionnaire, 43, being in the lower range of scores. The first thing that comes to mind is this: how does RAI know that 14.5 million watched the film without liking it? These questionnaires are a mystery it is time to learn something about."[23]

More ironically, Fellini told the story of a taxi driver who complained to him during a fare that he didn't understand anything about the film, which he'd seen on television with his wife. ("That film of yours, the other night, on the box, what's it called? Ah *yes, Eight Thirty*! I argued with my wife over it....I'm sorry, but I just didn't get it.")

The film, with its contrasting black and white, proved unsuited to television. Yet Fellini was to find a use for television, after all—in advertising, which he had, to some extent, "invented" in his films and their short self-contained scenes. Indeed, after the tribute to Fellini organized at the Lincoln Center in June 1985, the *New York Times* film critic, Vincent Canby, wrote:

> When you think of Federico Fellini, what are the images that first come to your mind?
>
> The initial sequence of *La Dolce Vita* when a statue of Jesus, the arms outstretched, suspended from a helicopter, is seen sailing above the rooftops of Rome, as if heading for very cold storage? The wonder on the face of Cabiria, who has just suffered yet another unkind but not entirely unfunny knock by fate, as she comes upon a laughing band of traveling players on a country road?
>
> The twilight scene that concludes *8 ½*, as Guido, the egomaniacal film director, leads all of the warring characters, real and imagined, alive and dead, who have shared his life, in a dance of celebratory reconciliation around the base of the scaffold of a giant movie set? That moment in *Amarcord* when the great liner *Rex,* all lights ablaze, suddenly looms up out of the darkness on a cellophane sea?
>
> It is one of the identifying idiosyncrasies of Fellini films that all of us tend to remember such individual moments as vividly as—and sometimes even better than—the films that contain them. They are visual phrases that, by their ever-surprising, mysterious perfection, rather than by their specific meaning, have become a part of our own memories, as if created by our own imaginations.[24]

Fellini's work for Campari, Barilla, and the Bank of Italy shows him at his imaginative best, putting to use his ability to think in images whatever the language used, and his instinct for communicative force.²⁵ One example was the Barilla pasta commercial, where Fellini highlighted the sexual connotation of the word *rigatoni,* pronounced with a sort of verbal wink, which was repeated the length and breadth of the land with the same savvy air.

In February 1992, Fellini also made a less well-known commercial for the Republican Party, in the name of his lifelong friendship with Ugo La Malfa, the historic leader of the party. It is a sort of video clip filmed in Cinecittà, at the entrance to Studio 5 in which Fellini launches into praise of the party secretary, Giorgio La Malfa, reeling off eleven adjectives one after another: polite, honest, civil, discreet, elegant, likeable, kind, reliable, different, calm, well-mannered.²⁶

Ginger e Fred and *Indietro tutta*

Orwell's famous date, 1984, was a year of fundamental change for television broadcasting in Italy: "With the acquisition of Rete 4, Fininvest now had the same number of channels as RAI; the malicious said it had one more, given the poor ratings of RAI 3 dedicated to education and localization. Also in 1984, the Fininvest Group advertising concessionaire, Pubblitalia '80, overtook the turnover of Sipra, the RAI equivalent. 1984 can be considered the end of the state television monopoly in Italy; for ten years, until at least 1994, the RAI-Fininvest duopoly was essentially stable."²⁷

A year earlier, Umberto Eco had coined the famous expression "neo-television," meaning the rapid Americanization of the small screen in Italy, with multiple channels, private stations, a frenetic rhythm, and frequent call-ins to involve viewers directly. This was completely different from the archaeological television of the state broadcaster, funded by the TV license and not advertising revenues, which provided its viewers with cultural programs and historical/literary TV plays, rather than American soap operas, zany comedy, and Brazilian *telenovelas*. The role of television was no longer, as it was in the sixties, to educate and inform, but to capture viewers and keep hold of them with their remote control devices.

The duopoly was seen, at first, as the contrast between a solid cultural tradition and the assault of the ephemeral myths of consumerism. One ideological account (which omits the more pragmatic needs of private TV) put it like this: "The Americanized choices of Canale 5 (not so different from the other channels) is not based on ideology: accused of wanting to bastardize Italian culture, Berlusconi said he had looked for series and serials elsewhere in Europe, but they were 'slow-moving, no good at all for our advertising and competitive needs.' Keeping bums on seats in front of the TV was more important than for the state broadcaster, because the revenue of private channels came solely from commercials, and its programs were therefore designed as platforms for the commercials."[28]

The result was a huge increase in commercials on television (with a record of over half a million in 1985) and a self-referential TV ("neo-television talks about itself and the contact it establishes with the general public," as Eco wrote). These were the topics hotly debated (on television) at the time.

For intellectuals and the Communist left, with their built-in anti-Americanism, and ingrained suspicions of state TV, neo-television was the embodiment of a cultural and political enemy, the epitome of the consumer society. During the seventies, however, the PCI gradually overcame its aversion to new forms of communication, and "intellectuals on the left repositioned themselves in relation to television,"[29] so much so, indeed, that in the eighties the state broadcaster found itself copying the competition rather than seeking to distinguish itself from private channels.

As the politicians bemoaned private channels, *Portobello, Pronto Raffaella, Dallas, Drive In,* and Japanese cartoons were at the top of the ratings. Explaining the Communist position, Walter Veltroni felt the need to say that "watching television is not a crime." This was the TV parodied artfully by Fellini in *Ginger e Fred* and by Renzo Arbore in his famous RAI program *Indietro tutta* (1987). Nonetheless, where Arbore's program was exquisitely postmodern, Fellini's film had a pervasive melancholy and sense of defeat.

Preceded by a lengthy press campaign in which the film was spoken of as an attack on television, *Ginger e Fred* was shown at the Quirinale on 15 November 1985. Andreotti reviewed it on the front page of *Corriere della Sera* but this time the political significance of the event was read differently from *Prova d'orchestra*, with the institutions defending the state broadcaster—the "good"—against the upstart tycoon Silvio Berlusconi and his private channels—"evil"—mocked by Fellini. Fellini himself declared: "Competition, at least here in Italy, is based on who can be most mediocre, vulgar, stupid... I am not aware of any attempts by private television channels to build up an audience through emotionally satisfying cultural programs."[30]

After the screening of the film at the Quirinale, the cultural spokesman for the Socialist Party (PSI), Paolo Pillitteri (at the time involved in the battle over the reform of broadcasting), declared: "Fellini's film is a masterpiece, with which one can agree wholeheartedly. It shows how intrusive advertising is, the degeneration and anxiety produced by television."

As we know, Craxi's Socialist Party was the most eminent political resource of Berlusconi and these words summed up the situation perfectly by paying hollow lip service to the state broadcaster while it was known by everyone in the industry and politics that private television was here to stay, and no consensus could be obtained to regulate it.

The television shown by Fellini in *Ginger e Fred* is a sort of monstrous and star-spangled exaggeration of the Barafonda theater in *Roma*, but now with a political message of its own, a television that would soon change the way politics was carried out and thought about.

The romance between Amelia Bonetti (Giulietta Masina) and Pippo Botticella (Marcello Mastroianni), former famous vaudeville tap dancers with the stage name of Ginger and Fred, brought back together one more time for a television show, has a pathos that is utterly lacking in cynical television, as shown behind the scenes: a Dantescan circle of Hell with freaks to be served up to the public and bored technicians uninterested in what goes onto the screen.

Fellini's view is entrusted to the stupor of Amelia and the indignation of Pippo, alias Fred. His parody of television is shown by this oscillation between incredulity and invective, the inability to understand a world without magic and poetry and the wish not to withdraw into the past. Fellini said: "Television is itself a sort of elephantine parody of reality, and you cannot make a parody of a parody... Television Center is today, in 1985, the place where anything and everything can happen."[31]

In other words, television—in Fellini's opinion—was the postmodern instrument *par excellence*. Discussing the film, the historian Aldo Schiavone observed: "If I may be allowed to make a suggestion to our politicians, whose duty is to understand where the country is going—and particularly to those Socialist senior party officials and intellectuals whose minds and hearts are full of the "postmodern"—I'd recommend that they go and see Fellini's latest film. Yes, because *Ginger e Fred* is an extraordinary contemporary document which shines an analytical light on some features of today's society, lucidly, describing and anticipating an entire world."[32]

During the shooting of *Ginger e Fred*, the press greedily reported the use of doubles, asked by Fellini to come to the set. Doubles of Reagan, Proust, Kafka, Clark Gable. For Fellini they represented television as a copy and imitation of reality, and a spectacle that sought "to resemble the cinema." Advertising and television commercials rule this world: hoardings in city streets strewn with rubbish, an uninterrupted series of commercials on giant screens erected everywhere. Fellini made a number of parody commercials, only some of which made it into the film: delicious sauces poured onto pasta, slender models inviting women to diet (one of the actresses used was the porn star Moana Pozzi).[33] The film was viewed as an attack on television and intellectuals were quick to roll out moralistic theories of society in support of it. Fellini probably didn't share these views and may have felt they expressed a conservative position. As the auteur of *La dolce vita* he was well aware that the new isn't welcomed with open arms and that declaring war on television was a way of refusing to understand modernity: "Destroy television screens? It's absurd even to think of such a thing, like wanting to destroy the combustion engine, the electric light bulb, computers. What sense would there be in that? What is the point in continuing to criticize television, which is merely the mirror and reflection, for disrupting the whole cultural system, and hence the system of communication, on which society, as we know it, is based? I don't think I'm a nostalgic, I've never felt too much sympathy for praise *temporis acti*, belly-aching, complaining, bitterness, the discontented grimace."[34]

For example, he said he was a fan of video clips: "I'm looking forward to making video clips because they can be the purest form of cinema. Why not make one on Milan Cathedral? Or a beautiful woman? Or the Leaning Tower of Pisa? Anyway, I've made some. The parade of priests in *Roma* was a video clip, and the traffic jam on the Orbital Road, and the *Rex*. You could make some extraordinary clips in Italy about out customs, our national identity."[35]

Despite this, the doom and gloom of *Ginger e Fred* remains, as well as Fellini's melancholy and nostalgia for a world that is no more, now invaded by vulgarity, commercials, trash on the streets. Fellini has Pippo Botticella raise a metaphorical middle finger to the public in a television studio, as once he had had Alberto Sordi blow a metaphorical raspberry at the workers in *I vitelloni*.

What is lacking is the lightness, the ironic disenchantment of his best cinema. And this was probably due to Fellini's sense of outrage at the commercials that cut into his films on TV, a practice he considered a profanation, and felt as a laceration and offense to his person.

In contrast, Arbore's *Indietro tutta* denounced the lack of culture of the times by staging the lucid disenchantment of television nonsense. It poked fun at and ridiculed vulgarity, but kept away from righteous indignation. It accepted the challenge by producing a television show of intelligence, irony, and gentle mockery, accepting the television of the day as indeed a mirror of society.

While Fellini fiercely mocked commercials, Arbore invented *cacao meraviglao*, an imaginary Brazilian coffee maker and the sponsor of his show, demonstrating—more effectively than a dozen sociological papers—the persuasive force of repeated television jingles. The program, genuinely postmodern, joined "high" with "low" culture, provocatively and intelligently displaying the superficiality and hollowness of entertainment. Unlike Fellini's film, *Indietro tutta* (Full Steam Astern) invited numerous levels of interpretation.

Fellini against Berlusconi

RAI and Fininvest have often been described as two opposites fighting an eternal duel. The "duel" is one of the many self-referential stories the television has told about itself, a sort of fictional series itself in which culture is supposed to face off against entertainment, good taste against vulgarity, politicized television against private enterprise, Rome against Milan, the state against the free market. A good story for the people to follow, fluctuating between the ideal Italy of legality and Italy as it really is, with elements of truth but essentially a lavish piece of showmanship designed to confer sense solely on television itself.[36]

Ginger e Fred attacked television in general, but it should not be forgotten that the film opens and closes with a gigantic stuffed pig's trotter inside Termini Station in Rome, produced by one Cavalier Lombardoni, an explicit reference to Berlusconi that Fellini tried to soften by changing the name from the original Lambrusconi ("That was the name I originally thought of, to make it similar to Berlusconi,"[37] he told journalists).

Less explicit but no less interesting is an episode in the film in which a woman is invited onto the stage during the TV show *Ed ecco a voi* (presented by Franco Fabrizi). She has just undergone an experiment in which she has been deprived of television for a month. Angrily, sobbing, she says that no one should be made to suffer such a horrific fate; it is "terrible" to be without television.

The reference is to an episode during October 1984, when in Turin, Rome, and Pescara the legal authorities ordered a black-out of Fininvest channels, based on the interpretation of almost nonexistent laws governing private TV stations, and almost certainly influenced by the fact that Berlusconi's private channels had just overtaken RAI in the ratings. The magistrates did not outlaw broadcasting itself, but stopped simultaneous broadcasts simulating a national network. In the cities blacked out, the broadcaster informed its viewers: "By order of the Magistrate, Fininvest programs currently being broadcast as usual in the rest of Italy cannot appear on your screens."[38]

The reaction was like that of the woman on the TV show in Fellini's film: outrage. The prime minister's office, Magistrates Courts, and the offices of RAI were bombarded with phone calls from mothers and fathers demanding that their children by allowed to see *I Puffi* (The Smurfs): "An elderly woman explained to me 'in this country that ignores the weak,' private television 'has become a public service, free of charge, providing emotions, smiles, even some tears... There is something inhuman in this ban that penalizes the poor and weak where they are most fragile, in the miniscule things that give their lives some balance.'"[39]

Fellini's all-out attack on Berlusconi was launched before the release of the film, on 7 December 1985, in an article in *L'Europeo*:

> I'm not in television. It doesn't attract me or arouse my curiosity... I don't believe television is a means of expression; it is only a means of distribution, using films, for example, as vehicles, but cutting them, changing them, deforming them, reducing them to picture postcards, and reaching into homes to give viewers some kind of a feeling, a little dirty, smug, voyeuristic, cheap... the continuous interruptions of films on private television is an arbitrary abuse, not only for the author of the film or against the film, but in relation to viewers as well. They get used to the rhythm of hiccups, of stammering, in which the brain is asked to switch off momentarily, like a series of small strokes, turning them into impatient cretins, unable to concentrate, to reflect, to make mental connections, to anticipate, to appreciate the music and harmony, the eurythmy that always accompanies the telling of a story... Private television says it needs to advertise to survive. Why should we be worried about the fate of television stations that for twenty-four hours a day clutter up our homes with demented programs featuring comics that would not have been given the stage even in the worst type of vaudeville, in the days of Cacini, and old films are continuously interrupted by sizzling frozen foods, dripping sauces, and sprayed armpits? Burying viewers in commercials is dishonest, intrusive, violent, in a society based on mutual respect, and where freedom requires the acknowledgment of the freedom of others, including the freedom not to smear everything—the floor, the walls—with filth. I don't like the fact that private television seeks to justify the way it treats works to which others have dedicated thought, attention, and hard work. Even criminals, delinquents, can claim they need to commit crimes, to run amok.[40]

This is Fellini without his characteristic levity. The tone is angry, the position adopted at least open to question, not least because of the message summarized in the title of the article, *These unworthy TV channels do not deserve to survive.* The defense of the integrity of films spills over into a condemnation of popular culture *tout court,* joining him to the ranks of the intellectuals he had always opposed in their inability to understand changes in society and in forms of communication.

In an interview on RAI television, Fellini mocked the "Cavaliere" by suggesting that he take out advertising during religious ceremonies and interrupt the mass with a commercial break (again the comparison between cinema and religious rituals).

The reactions came thick and fast. During the RAI TV show *Fantastico* the comic Beppe Grillo[41] accused Fellini of railing against commercials while making a pretty penny from making them. The comic's words, further evidence of populism in society, were off the mark, however, as Fellini explained: "I object only to commercials that interrupt films. I have nothing against advertising in itself, that would be ridiculous... my indignation, which will continue for as long as this situation persists, is about the utter failure to respect an author's work, the way it is hijacked and taken possession of, massacred in order to make money, stuffing it with commercial breaks in the most abject manner."[42]

Then, speaking directly to the interviewer, he declared: "Do me the favor of explaining two things. First: I don't accept the justification of private television; they say they have to live, but this would justify any action, even crime, because the person committing it has to live, is that not so? Second: I've never said that the actors working in private TV are lousy comics."[43]

The second statement—a little hard to agree with in light of his article—shows Fellini partially climbing down from a position he must have found uncomfortable, that of the critic of popular culture intolerant of new forms of comedy and pushing his criticism of private television beyond the realm of intrusive advertising into rage against the machine.

Abandoned to empty movie theaters, *Ginger e Fred* was adopted by France as the symbol of ostracism in relation to La Cinq, Berlusconi's attempt to enter the French market. The political support provided by Mitterand was withdrawn after the 1986 elections, won by Chirac. A harsh public campaign was organized against Berlusconi, referred to as the head of télépizzeria or of "canaille 5" with a hint of racism against the self-made Italian who dared to pollute French culture. Fellini's film was seen in France at just the right time, with the world premiere at the Palais de Chaillot in Paris, before its Italian release.

Instead of criticizing French journalists for thinking Berlusconi would bring the plague, the Italian press aligned itself with their fears. Barbara Spinelli, the Paris correspondent of *La Stampa*, wrote:

> [The film] mocks Berlusconi, a mockery the French know by heart because the first private TV station to be authorized by the French president will be his. He will arrive and it will all be very Felliniesque... We will see how Berlusconi will be outdone by reality. How television has become so important in our lives and how it has radically changed language, ambitions, the relationship between power and society... *Ginger e Fred* describes an unconfined kitsch beautifying and deforming the world. "It isn't about television but about something fundamental and much more serious: the loss of sense in Western Europe today." So says the philosopher Jean-Paul Aron.[44]

Jean-Paul Aron—not a philosopher but a writer of historical essays—put into a nutshell the iconoclastic fury and shortsightedness of the intellectuals of the day.

You Don't Interrupt an Emotion, or Do You?

In May 1985, after Berlusconi had bought from Rizzoli the rights to some of Fellini's greatest films including *Lo sceicco bianco*, *I vitelloni*, *La dolce vita*, and *8 ½*, the films were broadcast on television with repeated commercial breaks.

That same month, Fellini lodged a complaint with the Magistrates Court of Rome against Canale 5.[45] His lawyers said he was acting in defense of the rights of authors against abuses by private television stations, in relation to the "serious detrimental effect on the artistic quality of the film and the professional reputation of the filmmaker" of the continuous interruption of films by commercials. The complaint aimed to force lawmakers to take a position in a legislative void.

After the failure of the lawyers on the two sides to come to any sort of agreement, the Magistrates Court delivered the following response, summarized by a number of different newspapers:

> The artistic level of Fellini's films is beyond question and it is understandable that a complaint has been made about the modification of the narrative rhythm of works universally recognized to be masterpieces, but it is also true that in recent years the viewing public has gotten used to commercial breaks. And given that "the damage to the moral rights of the author from the repeated use of commercial breaks depends on a series of elements that need to be assessed on a case by case basis and which exclude preventive safeguards," the only criterion the Court could apply is that of the law on private TV stations, which sets a limit for advertising of 16 percent of the total number of hours broadcast in a week, and 20 percent in any given hour, without making any reference to the quality of the programs in which the commercial breaks are broadcast. Hence the Court was unable to uphold the complaint but invited Parliament to find "an immediate and satisfactory" solution to the problem.[46]

Despite the request by the Court for new legislation, the reference to viewers who have "gotten used to commercials breaks" suggests the irreversibility of the practice. Without explicitly saying so, the Court appears to be acknowledging a new use of cinematic products and the lack of applicability of measures to ensure the inviolable nature of artistic works. Beyond question was the artistic level of Fellini's films, and equally beyond question was the fact that private television broadcast films and dictated the culture of the medium used as a vehicle for the films. And legislation wasn't going to change that.

After approval of new regulations governing radio and television broadcasts, the so-called "Mammi" Law (6 August 1990), which substantially gave legislative approval to—photographed, some said—the state of things on the ground, the Association of Cinema Authors (ANAC) made a video letter in which numerous authors appeared. It opened with Fellini, who spoke of a fight against invasiveness, bullying, and arrogance: "... violence, a form of hooliganism against a person... because a work has a life of its own, has become a person, with a certain character, a personality... Interrupting a film, altering it, mortifying it, altering its narrative structure, its rhythm, sense and meaning with commercial breaks is a Criminal Act."

Commenting on the video letter, Kezich spoke of Fellini's intolerance for the increasing stupidity surrounding him and his "complete understanding of the difficult period that Italy was passing through."[47]

But the question was more complex. Certainly, commercials had begun to interrupt films on private television in the absence of a specific legal framework regulating television advertising, or delays in bringing in this legislation. As Enzo Biagi said of Berlusconi in 1984: "He has done his job legitimately... before him there was a no-man's land and maybe some didn't want the terrain to be occupied at all; well, he occupied it, what's wrong with that?"[48]

The logic of profits, the raison d'être of commercial television, was part of a more general change. The bills put forward by the PCI, with prison sentences for over-advertising, were reminiscent, in the cultural field, of Khomeini's Iran,[49] an accusation not restricted to Craxi's Socialist Party and other friends of Berlusconi. Even the left-wing *il manifesto* wondered: "Does the Bill put forward by the PCI represent one of the key battles in the telecommunications field? I don't think so... Taking sides with the old corporations in the broadcasting industry, with 'authors' who have come out in defense of the integrity of art, has brought no new strategies for the future... it's a rearguard action, good for a facile consensus... the PCI is on the side of production (the Author) and against consumption (the viewer, the collective author)."[50]

The term "collective author" is a perfect description of the situation today, an era in which the integrity of the work of art appears as a hollow concept, legally and culturally. The battle against commercial breaks was a lost cause, a rearguard action, from a world that was coming to an end and, in the name of the author, tried to turn back the tide.

The romantic idea of the artist, the individualist and creative genius, is what the monument built to Fellini represents and is the reason the PCI adopted him in his (and its) battle against Berlusconi. Previously, in his neorealist days, the party had slighted and snubbed him precisely for the breath of fresh air he introduced into his films.

In the fight over television and the ostracism of commercial television, the role assigned to the cinema was one of conservatism, the function of a museum, a romantic backwater opposed to the new and more dynamic forms of popular culture: "Strangely, but significantly, the trajectory of the cultural policy of the Communist Party in Italy in the postwar period ran from the fight for a free and national film industry to the defense—under the hammer blows of the new media—of film art as a cultural value to be protected, renewing the pact with everyone who worked in or around the cinema."[51]

A conservative pact, as most voters judged it to be, defeating the attempt by referendum in 1995 to curtail television advertising during films and soccer matches.

Evidently, in certain quarters, old prejudices were very much alive, age-old positions were maintained and the phenomenon was largely misunderstood. As television was later to do in relation to new media and the internet.

Fellini's long journey through the depths of the Italian unconscious ended with the gloomy prophecies of *Ginger e Fred*, *Intervista*, and *La voce della luna* and with a sincere confession of dismay. Although he would not have wanted to give in to the fear of the new, the declaration below (made on the set of *Ginger e Fred*), which has the tone of an epigraph, denotes a prescient, bitter understanding:

> This cultural shift should not be viewed with suspicion or fear. Even if I am dismayed to see certain values overthrown, including emotions with which I have always identified myself and which gave me a point of view on the world, I am tempted to look on these new phenomena with respect. I only wonder how it happened, when, where I was when it took place. There is a new human creature, apparently very much like us—despite the stereo headphones and skateboard—*who is able, quite extraordinarily, to do without the things we were brought up to cherish.*[52]

Notes

1. "Veltroni: 'Non siamo contro la pubblicità ma è davvero troppa'" [Veltroni: We're Not against Commercials, but There Are Just Too Many], *la Repubblica*, February 1989.
2. M. Gervasoni, *Storia d'Italia degli anni Ottanta. Quando eravamo moderni* [History of Italy in the Eighties: When We Were Modern] (Venice: Marsilio, 2010), 65.
3. Ibid., 66.
4. Ibid., 17.
5. Ibid., 82.
6. Ibid.
7. G.P. Brunetta, *Storia del cinema italiano*, 337.
8. As it has recently been called by Massimiliano Panarari in *L'egemonia sotto culturale. L'Italia da Gramsci al gossip* [Sub-cultural Hegemony: Italy from Gramsci

to Gossip] (Turin: Einaudi, 2010), a book open to criticism from various points of view that espouses the position against television taken up in the eighties.

9. G. Crapis, *Il frigorifero del cervello. Il Pci e la televisione da 'Lascia o raddoppia' alla battaglia contro gli spot* [The Brain Fridge: The PCI and Television from Quiz Shows to the Battle against Commercials] (Rome: Editori Riuniti, 2002), 160. The words in quotation marks are from M. Morcellini, "La guerra dell'etere nel sistema misto" [War on the Airwaves in the Dual Broadcasting System], in *Lo spettacolo del consumo* [The Spectacle of Consumption] (Milan: Franco Angeli, 1986).

10. E. Menduni, *Televisione e società italiana, 1975-2000* [Television and Italian Society, 1975-2000] (Milan: Bompiani, 2002), 82.

11. The chronic lack of any long-term planning in the seventies became evident at this time, with fewer and fewer ideas, the dismantling of a homegrown, independent system of filmmaking (able through its profits to finance films by auteurs), and the failure to keep pace with the times by insisting on self-referential films for the select few. In other words, the "system" was no longer able—as it had been in the sixties and even later—to compete with American films and their universal appeal. See for example V. Zagarrio, *Storia del cinema italiano*.

12. G.P. Brunetta, *Storia del cinema italiano*, 538.

13. A. Zanzotto, "Stramba crociera per inseguire la 'Voce' del nostro mondo quazzabuglio," [Bizarre Cruise Following the "Voice" of Our Jumbled-Up World], *Corriere della sera*, 26 February 1983; now in A. Zanzotto, *Il cinema brucia e illumina*, 60–61.

14. L. Tornabuoni, "Fellini: 'Il mondo che non c'è'" [Fellini: "The Imaginary World"], *La Stampa*, 14 April 1989.

15. T. Kezich, *Federico Fellini*, 357.

16. Ibid., 358.

17. F. Fellini, "E la nava va" [The Ship Sails On], *Paese Sera*, 8 October 1983. See "L'uomo è invaso annuncia Fellini" [Fellini Announces: Man Is Possessed], *Il Tempo*, 16 December 1972.

18. See "L'uomo è invaso annuncia Fellini," *Il Tempo*, 16 December 1972; F. Fellini, *Fare un film*, 141.

19. F. Fellini, *Fare un film*, 141, see also 138–139.

20. Ibid., 138–139; U. Eco, "La moltiplicazione dei media" [The Multiplication of the Media], *L'espresso*, 22 May 1983.

21. U. Eco, "La moltiplicazione dei media."

22. "25 milioni di teleabbonati vedranno 8 ½. Canonizzazione di Federico Fellini" [25 million License Payers Will Watch 8 ½: Canonization of Federico Fellini], *Cronache degli spettacoli*, 16 October 1972; A. Solmi in *Oggi*, 7 December 1972.

23. A. Solmi in *Oggi*, 7 December 1972, quoted in E. Franceschini, "Gran festa a New York per Federico Fellini."

24. Quoted less extensively in E. Franceschini, "Gran festa a New York per Federico Fellini."

25. For an analysis of Fellini's commercials, see F. Burke, "Fellini's Commercials: Biting the Hand that Feeds," *The Italianist* no. 31 (2011), 205–242.

26. "E nello studio di Casanova girò il sogno di La Malfa" [In Casanova's Studio, Shooting La Malfa's Dream], *Corriere della Sera*, 3 November 1993.

27. E. Menduni, *Televisione e società italiana*, 80.
28. M. Gervasoni, *Storia d'Italia degli anni Ottanta*, 86.
29. G. Crapis, *Il frigorifero del cervello*, 159.
30. R. Cirio, "1997 Fuga dalla TV" [Escape from Television], *L'espresso*, 16 June 1985.
31. M. Guerrini, "Fellini sedici e mezzo" [Fellini Sixteen and a Half], *Grazia*, 5 May 1985.
32. A. Schiavone, "Il postmoderno di Ginger e Fred," *la Repubblica*, 4 February 1986.
33. The commercials shot by Fellini and not included in the film were collected by Tatti Sanguineti in *La tivù di Fellini* [Fellini's TV], part of Mario Sesti's documentary *L'ultima sequenza* [The Last Scene], a DVD released by the Istituto Luce.
34. G.L. Rondi, "Sette domande a Fellini: 'Ginger e Fred'," *Il Tempo*, 5 May 1985.
35. R. Cirio, "1997 Fuga dalla TV."
36. E. Menduni, *Televisione e società italiana*, 128.
37. B. Palombelli, "Spegnetela prima che ci spenga" [Switch Off before It Switches Us Off], *L'Europeo*, 7 December 1985.
38. E. Menduni, *Televisione e società italiana*, 86–89.
39. M. Gervasoni, *Storia d'Italia degli anni Ottanta*, 90.
40. F. Fellini, "Italiani ribellatevi a queste TV" [Italians, Reject These TV Stations], *L'Europeo*, 7 December 1985.
41. Grillo was later to become leader of the Five Star political movement.
42. F. Fellini, quoted in "Ci ammazza a colpi di spot. Fellini si sfoga contro la TV e ci parla di 'Ginger e Fred'" [Killing Us with Commercials: Fellini Lets off Steam about Television and Talks to Us about *Ginger e Fred*], *il Resto del Carlino*, 11 December 1985.
43. Ibid.
44. B. Spinelli, "La Francia elettorale fa tip tap" [France Tap Dances to the Elections], *La Stampa*, 18 January 1986.
45. "Fellini denuncia canale 5 per gli spot pubblicitari" [Fellini Lodges Complaint against Canale 5 for Its Commercials], *la Repubblica*, 21 May 1985.
46. "Fellini non ferma Berlusconi ma sugli spot serve una legge" [Fellini Fails to Stop Berlusconi but a Law is Needed for Commercials], in *la Repubblica*, 1 August 1985.
47. T. Kezich, *Federico Fellini*, 386
48. Quoted by Gervasoni, *Storia d'Italia degli anni Ottanta*, 91.
49. G. Crapis, *Il frigorifero del cervello*, 168.
50. Article signed by Mariuccia Ciotta in *il manifesto*, 15 February 1989, quoted in G. Crapis, *Il frigorifero del cervello*, 169.
51. G. Crapis, *Il frigorifero del cervello*, 170.
52. D. Gabutti, "Gli anni Ottanta sulla passerella" [The Eighties on the Catwalk], *Giornale Nuovo*, 26 March 1985. My italics.

Appendix
The Divo and the Maestro
Fellini in the Andreotti Archives

Two Quintessential Italians

There is something fateful about the relationship between the "Divo" and the "Maestro," born almost on the same day, one in 1919, the other in 1920. Their formidable careers in politics and art came to represent aspects of the Italian identity so strongly that each became a sort of living monument to that identity. Somehow, both embodied a metaphysical quality, something enigmatic, mysterious, ambiguous.

Commentators have wondered which of them, Andreotti or Fellini, really invented the *dolce vita*. Without the law promoted by Andreotti in 1949 encouraging American film crews to move to Rome, Hollywood on the Tiber would not have existed and there would have been no film stars in Via Veneto.[1]

Fellini had a number of friends in the top flight of politics, including President of the Republic Giovanni Leone and the leader of the Republican Party, Ugo la Malfa. He said he voted Republican, "then for the Socialists of Pietro Nenni, once for the Christian Democrats (in 1976, when the Communists were threatening to overtake them as the largest party in the country), and never for the PCI."[2] He confessed, "all I can say about politics comes from personal relations and this ambiguous feeling I nonetheless trust: likeability."[3]

There were likeable people across the full political spectrum, of course. In 1984, Fellini was part of the guard of honor, standing petrified before the coffin of Enrico Berlinguer. In 1985, he signed a petition in favor of Socialist politicians and journalists found guilty of defamation for their criticism of the public prosecutor, Armando Spataro, in the Tobagi murder trial.[4]

In the nineties, after the commercial he made for the Republican Giorgio La Malfa out of friendship and respect for his father Ugo,[5] he was photographed at an electoral gathering for Franco Evangelisti, a Christian Democrat in the Andreotti camp.[6] At that moment the newspapers were beginning to pick up the story of the arrest of Mario Chiesa, which was about to bring the whole house of cards of the First Republic tumbling down.

Fellini may have admired La Malfa for his politics but he was undoubtedly fascinated by Andreotti. A sort of literary fascination, as if Andreotti had been invented by a great novelist: "I'd love to spend a whole evening in conversation with him, through the small hours, until the morning. He is like a Shakespeare character, Othello say."[7] When Fellini was presented with a career Golden Lion, Andreotti remarked with acumen on the filmmaker's pictorial, as well as poetical sense, and reviewed his entire experience of Fellini's films, confessing an initial perplexity:

> Personally I found it difficult at the beginning to understand Fellini. I didn't see why everyone applauded *Lo sceicco bianco,* for example; it didn't strike me as a masterpiece. But then *La strada* came along and I changed my mind; I've never grown tired of watching it again, with the same emotions as the first time, but finding something new in it each time, in the story… The *dolce vita* phenomenon was part of an era and page upon page has been written about whether Federico was part of that consumer world or was mocking it… I don't think a poet is in favor or against the customs of the day, attacks or defends a pleasure-seeking way of life… I use the word poetry because that is certainly the best way to think of Fellini's films. But I'd also say that he is a painter, and paints perfectly in the two films I've mentioned [*Prova d'orchestra* and *E la nave va*] for both film and television.[8]

Interviewed a few days after Fellini's death, Andreotti was asked if he was a friend:

> Very much so. I have some beautiful letters of his. The last is recent and is extraordinary. In relation to my, let's call them, judicial problems, he phoned often, and the most comforting words, the words of greatest friendship, on this matter, have come from him. Sadly, Giulietta is also very ill…

Asked by the journalist to see the letter, he replied;

> No, better not. They'd say I'm a fanatic, that I want to turn it to my advantage…Come and see me again and I'll show it to you.[9]

Appendix

Most of those letters are now in the Andreotti Archive donated in 2007 by Andreotti himself to the Luigi Sturzo Institute in Rome.[10]

"Dear Giulio, I Am Very Happy to Be Able to Address You in This Manner"

The correspondence between Fellini and Andreotti covers the period from 1974 to 1993. It is warm, intensifying in the eighties, and at the same time is formal, with a form of address—"lei" rather than "tu"—that maintained a respectful distance.

In a letter dated 7 October 1974, Andreotti wrote:

> Dear Fellini, I have read with great joy of your American success. It is a success for Italy too, which the American press usually doesn't mention unless it is to say that things are going badly.

On 14 October Fellini replied:

> Dear Andreotti, we are so unused to courteousness that a gesture of kindness finds us unprepared and leaves us astonished, perplexed, as if before something we no longer recognize.

After the release of *Prova d'orchestra,* as the newspapers debated the film, Fellini thanked Andreotti for his remarks in *L'Europeo,* where he was quoted as saying:

> It's a matter of choosing the executives well, according to their skills, moral rectitude, objectivity. And it's a question of adequate controls ensuring respect for everyone, eliminating abuse at the root, that devil that shows his head sometimes where you least expect.[11]

Fellini replied:

> Dear Prime Minister,
> In *L'Europeo* I read your precise, intelligent and perfectly balanced analysis of my film and if, on the one hand, I am embarrassed and sorry that journalists continually ask you for your opinion, on the other, I must confess that it is a great satisfaction for me... I hope we can meet soon so I can say to you personally how much I appreciated your friendly gesture.[12]

Years later, when *Corriere della Sera* published Andreotti's review of *Ginger e Fred,* Fellini wrote to thank him again, this time with a confidential tone:

Dear Giulio,

I am very happy to be able to address you in this manner, contingently by name, as I was once again overcome to receive further proof of your esteem for my work, reading your comments on my film.[13]

When it was decided to give Fellini a career Golden Lion, Gian Luigi Rondi wrote to Andreotti on the letterhead of the Venice Biennale:

A dew days ago, at the Quirinale, I reminded you that on 6 September the Venice Film Festival will give him a Golden Lion for his work in films, as decided last October, on my recommendation, by the Executive Committee of the Biennale. He assured me he would be there to receive the award (not so common these days) but would accept it *only from your hands*.[14]

Fellini continued to use a confidential tone, not without a certain reverential bashfulness, as shown by a letter dated 8 February 1986:

Dear Giulio,
So, are we on first name terms?
I have received a letter from the Fiuggi Foundation that carries your greetings and signature at the bottom. They want me to become a member of the General Council of the Foundation for Art and Entertainment. Could you let me know, through our friend Evangelisti, if this request has your full support or if it is just one of those things they have asked you to do but that doesn't much interest you either way?[15]

The Fiuggi Foundation later attracted the attention of investigators when a scandal blew up over the wiretapping of Judge Corrado Carnevale, in which he is heard insulting the frontline anti-mafia magistrates Giovanni Falcone and Paolo Borsellino (until 1986, Carnevale was a director of the Fiuggi Foundation and was always at Andreotti's side at meetings and lunches).

Andreotti also asked Fellini to join the executive team of the *Casa di Dante* (Andreotti became its president in 2010). Fellini turned him down: "In all honesty, if I look at myself objectively, I realize I do not have the literary understanding or authority to discuss with students topics that would inevitably involve religion, philosophy, poetry."[16]

As the debate raged over television advertising, Fellini mentions his archenemy Berlusconi in another letter, although the tone is far from acrimonious:

Dear Giulio,
Your kind call yesterday evening surprised and touched me. You are a very likeable chap! I admire your generosity and solidarity with friends… I'll try to reach Berlusconi and thank him for his very friendly homage.[17]

During the making of his last film, Fellini invited Andreotti onto the set[18] and in 1991, for Andreotti's seventy-second birthday, Fellini gave him a color sketch showing him in papal garb dispensing blessings with his unmistakably mocking smile. An affectionate caricature with the caption: "Although the job is not yet vacant, I willingly accept your blessing."[19]

Andreotti and Fellini Disagree

Not long before, Andreotti and Fellini had clashed heavily on television advertising. The Mammi Law had just been passed—a victory for Berlusconi—with the support of Craxi. By a shrewd move, Andreotti had prevented a government crisis which would have kicked the broadcasting bill into the long grass.

In his column in *L'Europeo, Bloc Notes*,[20] Andreotti asked Fellini to reconsider his position on television advertising. "It is right not to interrupt a film, but if as a result no more films were made, it would be a Pyrrhic victory." Given the crisis of the cinema, he considered the help of television for co-production and for rentals "indispensable." He drove his point home with a reference to the Gospels:

> My friend Fellini reminds me of Mary of Bethany where, of the two sisters, Mary is praised because she had chosen "what is better," conversation and philosophy. But if Martha had not been humbly active, the Lord would have found the home untidy and the oven in the kitchen dirty.[21]

Fellini was not won over. From the pages of *La Repubblica* he hinted that his friend Andreotti was trying to rid himself of a sense of guilt "from the old and tormented affair of the legislation on broadcasting." Fellini said "the whole episode smacks of a moral, even more than a palpably political, loss of direction."[22]

In his review of *Ginger e Fred*, Andreotti had shown that he understood Fellini's position, identifying the psychological arrogance of television as the leitmotif of the film, but, he said, Fellini showed that television was something "we cannot do without."[23]

Fellini may have been aware of Andreotti's defense of *La dolce vita* many years earlier. In the Fellini file, a letter to Andreotti dated 18 February 1960 from Franz Turchi shows the founder and director of the right-wing newspaper *Il Secolo d'Italia* seeking the politician's support for a full-scale attack on Fellini's film:

> My dear Friend,
> You will no doubt have followed in the columns of the *Secolo* the attack we have launched on Fellini's latest film, *La dolce vita*, anticipating and de-

fusing the violent reactions of the most noble part of the press and broad sections of public opinion. You will also have seen that the comments continue every day, with new and valid reasons to be added to ours, on the moral, religious and social plane, in defense of our country and particularly of Rome... To lend authority to the position we have taken through a number of contributions from people of great value—confident that you will not wish to deny us, on this occasion, the support you have unfailingly provided—we would appreciate receiving your opinion of the film, to be published with due prominence. We are sure you will want to join with us in this sacred crusade for our nation, for our morals and our politics, and look forward to hearing from you. Please accept our sincerest and warmest regards.[24]

The sacred crusade against *La dolce vita* did not receive the support of the then minister of defense and president of the Rome Olympic Committee.

Back in the days of neorealism, Andreotti had dreamt of "a Christian cinema to counterbalance the preponderant cultural weight of the Communists."[25] Over *La dolce vita,* he overcame the anxieties of conservatives and the Church through his natural inclination to deal with matters concretely and his long-term view of the future of the country. Perhaps he saw in the film not just a description of phenomena that were unavoidable and unstoppable, but—like Pasolini—a profoundly Catholic and modern film, able to "stimulate Christian consciousness through the cinema." This was the culmination of the battle Andreotti had waged throughout the fifties to shift the orthodoxy of the Church and win over the diffidence of the priests in relation to film.

Notes

1. See A. Magistà, *Dolce vita gossip. Star, amori e mondanità negli anni d'oro di Cinecittà* [Dolce Vita Gossip: Stars, Love Affairs, and the Jet Set in the Golden Years of Cinecittà] (Milan: Mondadori, 2007).

2. P. Guzzanti, "Intervista a Fellini," *Panorama,* 6 April 1992, 57.

3. Ibid.

4. Signatories included leading politicians, writers, intellectuals, and, in addition to Fellini from the world of film, Francesco Rosi. See "Caso Tobagi. Solidarietà ai socialisti condannati" [The Tobagi Case: Solidarity with the Convicted Socialists], *la Repubblica,* 1 December 1985.

5. B. Palombelli, "Fellini gira il sogno di Giorgio" [Fellini Shoots Giorgio's Dream], *la Repubblica,* 22 February 1992, 6.

6. See "Con DC e PRI Federico Fellini sponsor di due nemici" [With the DC and PRI, Federico Fellini Sponsors Two Enemies], *Corriere della Sera,* 18 March 1992.

Appendix

7. V. Spiga, "Re Federico senza trucchi. Fellini fa gli auguri e tira le orecchie all'Italia" [King Federico with No Tricks: Fellini Wishes Italy a Happy New Year with a Wag of the Finger], *il Resto del Carlino*, 31 December 1986.

8. G. Andreotti, "Omaggio al regista poeta e pittore" [Homage to the Filmmaker, Poet, and Painter], *Il Giorno*, 7 September 1985.

9. F. Merlo, "Andreotti, 'Io i complotti, Fellini, Evangelisti e la Verità'" [Andreotti, "Me, Plots, Fellini, Evangelisti, and the Truth"], *Corriere della Sera*, 6 November 1993.

10. The Luigi Sturzo Institute Historical Archive, Giulio Andreotti Archive, Federico Fellini folder B. 1484. It includes press cuttings and documents on censorship. The letters between Andreotti and Fellini are in a separate envelope.

11. C. Lazzaro, "Andreotti guidica Fellini" [Andreotti Judges Fellini], *L'Europeo*, 7 December 1978.

12. Letter by F. Fellini, 14 December 1978.

13. Letter by F. Fellini, 22 November 1985.

14. G.L. Rondi, letterhead paper (Prot. No. 308/85), 30 August 1985. My italics.

15. Letter by F. Fellini, 8 February 1986.

16. Letter by F. Fellini, 16 April 1993.

17. Letter by F. Fellini, 4 June 1988.

18. Letter by F. Fellini, 15 March 1989.

19. Letter by F. Fellini, 14 January 1991.

20. G. Andreotti, "Caro Fellini lo spot è tuo alleato" [Dear Fellini, Commercials Are Your Allies], *L'Europeo*, 11 August 1990.

21. Ibid. The reference is to Luke 10: 39–42.

22. F. Fellini, "Caro Giulio ti senti in colpa" [Dear Giulio, You Feel Guilty], *la Repubblica*, 15 August 1990.

23. G. Andreotti, "Il film di Fellini visto da Andreotti" [Fellini's Film Seen by Andreotti], *Corriere della Sera*, 17 November 1985.

24. F. Turchi, on letterhead, *Il secolo d'Italia*, 18 February 1960. A note at the end of the letter asks Andreotti to reply with a photo of himself.

25. M. Franco, "Andreotti. La vita di un uomo politico, la storia di un'epoca" [Andreotti: The Life of a Politician, the History of an Era] (Milan: Mondadori, 2010), 51.

Selected Bibliography

Archival Collections Consulted

The Giulio Andreotti Archive, Federico Fellini folder, B. 1484, in the Luigi Sturzo Institute Historical Archive.
The Giovanni Calendoli Collection, Padua University, in the Bologna Film Library.
The Rizzoli Fund in the Luigi Chiarini Library of the National Film School in Rome.
The Dario Zanelli Collection of the Federico Fellini Foundation in Rimini.

Other Sources

Ajello, Nello. *Intellettuali e Pci 1944-1958*. Rome/Bari: Laterza, 1997 (1979).
Alvaro, Corrado. *Il nostro tempo e la speranza. Saggi di vita contemporanea.* Milan: Bompiani, 1952.
Amendola, Giorgio. *Intervista sull'antifascismo,* ed. Piero Melograni, Rome/Bari: Laterza, 2009 (1976).
Angelini, Pietro. *Controfellini. Il fellinismo tra restaurazione e magia bianca.* Milan: Ottaviano, 1974.
Arpa, Angelo. *L'Arpa di Fellini.* Rome: Edizioni dell'Oleandro, 2001.
———. *Federico Fellini: La dolce vita. Cronaca di una passione.* Cantalupo in Sabina: Edizioni Sabinae, 2010.
Asor Rosa, Alberto. *La cultura* in *Storia d'Italia dall'Unità a oggi*. Turin: Einaudi, 1975, vol. 4, t. ii.
———. *Genus Italicum. Saggi sull'identità letteraria italiana nel corso del tempo.* Turin: Einaudi, 1997.
Battista, Pierluigi. *I conformisti. L'estinzione degli intellettuali d'Italia.* Milan: Rizzoli, 2009.
Belpoliti, Marco. *Senza vergogna.* Rome: Guanda, 2010.
Ben-Ghiat, R. *Fascist Modernities: Italy, 1922-1945.* Oakland: University of California Press, 2001.
Bernardi, Sandro, ed. *Storia del cinema italiano, vol. 9. 1954-1959.* Venice: Marsilio, 2004.
Bertelli, Giovanna. *Divi e paparazzi: La dolce vita di Fellini.* Genoa: Le Mani, 2009.
Bertetto, Paolo, ed. *Metodologie di analisi del film.* Rome/Bari: Laterza, 2009.
———., ed. *Storia del cinema italiano. Uno sguardo d'insieme.* Venice: Marsilio, 2011.
Bertilotti, Teresa, and Anna Scattigno, eds. *Il femminismo degli anni Settanta.* Rome: Viella, 2005.
Bizzocchi, Roberto. *Cicisbei. Morale privata e identità nazionale in Italia.* Rome/Bari: Laterza, 2008.
Boarini, Vittorio, and Tullio Kezich, eds. *Fellini. Mezzo secolo di dolce vita.* Rimini/Bologna: The Fellini Foundation, Cineteca di Bologna, 2010.
Bobbio, Norberto. *Politica e cultura.* Turin: Einaudi, 1955.
———. *Etica e politica. Scritti di impegno civile.* Milan: Mondadori, 2009.

Selected Bibliography

Bollati, Giulio. *L'italiano. Il carattere nazionale come storia e invenzione.* Turin: Einaudi, 1983.
Bondanella, Peter. *The Cinema of Federico Fellini.* Princeton: Princeton University Press, 1992.
Boorstin, Daniel J. *The Image: A Guide to Pseudo-vents in America.* New York: Vintage Books, 1987 (1962).
Bordieu, Pierre. *Les règles de l'art. Genèse et structure du champ littéraire.* Paris: Seuil, 1992. Italian translation: A. Boschetti and E. Bottaro. *Le regole dell'arte. Genesi e struttura del campo letterario.* Milan: il Saggiatore, 2005.
Brannigan, John. *New Historicism and Cultural Materialism.* Houndmills: Macmillan, 1998.
Brunetta, Gian Piero. *Storia del cinema italiano,* 4 vols. Rome: Editori Riuniti, 1993.
———. *Gli intellettuali italiani e il cinema.* Milan: Mondadori, 2004.
———. *Il cinema neorealista italiano. Storia economica, politica e culturale.* Rome/Bari: Laterza, 2009.
Capuzzo, Paolo, ed. *Genere, generazione e consumi. L'Italia degli anni Sessanta.* Foundation of the Gramsci Institute, Annuals, 12. Rome: Carocci, 2003.
Casetti, Francesco. *L'occhio del novecento. Cinema, esperienza, modernità.* Milan: Bompiani, 2005.
Cassirer, Ernst. *Sprache und Mythos.* Teubner: Lipsia, 1925. Italian translation: V.E. Alfieri. *Linguaggio e mito: contributo al problema dei nome degli dei.* Milan: il Saggiatore, 1975.
Cazzola, Giuliano, Simonetta Matone, Filippo Mazzotti, and Domenico Sugamiele. *Anni Settanta. I peggiori anni della nostra vita.* Venice: Marsilio 2011.
Chiarotto, Francesca. *Operazione Gramsci.* Milan: Mondadori, 2011.
Contri, Giulia. *L'individualismo neorealistico di Fellini.* Milan: cucmi, 1964.
Costa, Antonio. *Il cinema e le arti visive.* Turin: Einaudi 2002.
———. *La dolce vita.* Turin: Lindau, 2010.
Cosulich, Callisto. *Storia del cinema italiano, vol. 7. 1945/1948.* Venice: Marsilio, 2003.
Crainz, Guido. *Storia del miracolo economico.* Rome: Donzelli, 2003 (1997).
Crapis, Giandomenico. *Il frigorifero del cervello. Il Pci e la televisione da "Lascia o raddoppia?" alla battaglia contro gli spot.* Rome: Editori Riuniti, 2002.
Debenedetti, Franco, and Antonio Pilati. *La guerra dei trent'anni. Politica e televisione in Italia 1975-2008.* Turin: Einaudi 2009.
De Bernardinis, Flavio. *Storia del cinema italiano, vol. 7. 1970-1976.* Venice: Marsilio, 2009.
De Berti, Raffaele, ed. *Federico Fellini. Analisi di film: possibili letture.* Milan: McGraw-Hill, 2006.
De Berti, Raffaele, Elisabetta Gaggetti, and Fabrizio Slavazzi. *Fellini-Satyricon. L'immaginario dell'antico.* Milan: Cisalpino, 2009.
de Certeau, Michel, and Jean-Marie Domenach. *Le Christianisme éclaté.* Paris: Seuil, 1974. Italian translation: S. Morra, *Il cristianesimo in frantumi.* Cantalupa: Effatà, 2010.
De Felice, Renzo. *Intervista sul fascismo,* ed. Michael A. Ledeen. Rome/Bari: Laterza, 2008 (1975).
De Gaetano, Roberto. *Il corpo e la maschera. Il grottesco nel cinema italiano.* Rome: Bulzoni, 1999.
———. *Teorie del cinema in Italia.* Soveria Mannelli: Rubbettino, 2005.
De Martino, Ernesto. *Il mondo magico. Prolegomeni a una storia del magismo.* Turin: Einaudi, 1948.
———. *Sud e magia.* Milan: Feltrinelli, 1959.
De Santi, Pier Marco. *La dolce vita. Scandalo a Rome, Palma d'oro a Cannes.* Pisa: Ets, 2004.
Del Noce, Augusto. *Il cattolico comunista.* Milan: Rusconi, 1981.
———. *Secolarizzazione e crisi della modernità.* Naples: Esi, 1982.
Eugeni, Ruggero, and Dario Viganò, eds. *Attraverso lo schermo. Cinema e cultura cattolica in Italia.* Rome: Eds, 2006, vol. 2.
Faeta, Francesco. *Le ragioni dello sguardo. Pratiche dell'osservazione, della rappresentazione e della memoria.* Turin: Bollati Boringhieri, 2011.
Falasca-Zamponi, Simonetta. *Fascist Spectacle: The Aesthetics of Power in Mussolini's Italy.* Oakland: University of California Press, 1997.

Selected Bibliography

Fellini. Da Rimini a Roma 1937-1947, Atti del convegno di studi e testimonianze [Conference Papers] (Rimini 31 October 1997). Rimini: Federico Fellini Foundation, 1997.
Fortunati, Vita, and Giovanna Franci, eds. *Il neostoricismo.* Modena: Mucchi, 1995.
Galli, Giorgio. *Il bipartitismo imperfetto. Comunisti e democristiani in Italia.* Bologna: il Mulino, 1966.
Galli della Loggia, Ernesto. *L'identità italiana.* Bologna: Il Mulino, 2011 (1998).
Gentile, Emilio. *Il culto del littorio. La sacralizzazione della politica nell'Italia fascista.* Rome/Bari: Laterza, 2009.
———. *Fascismo di pietra.* Rome/Bari: Laterza, 2007.
———. *La grande Italia. Il mito della nazione nel xx secolo.* Rome/Bari: Laterza, 2009.
Gervasoni, Marco. *Storia d'Italia degli anni ottanta. Quando eravamo moderni.* Venice: Marsilio, 2010.
Gramsci, Antonio. *Il materialismo storico.* Rome: Editori Riuniti, 1971.
———. *Il lettore in catene. La critica letteraria nei "Quaderni",* ed. Andrea Menetti. Rome: Carocci, 2004.
Grande, Maurizio. *La commedia all'italiana.* Rome: Bulzoni, 2003.
Grasso, Aldo, ed. *L'Italia alla Tv. La critica televisiva nelle pagine del Corriere della sera.* Milan: Rizzoli 2010.
Gundle, Stephen. *Death and the Dolce Vita: The Dark Side of Rome in the 1950s.* Edinburgh: Canongate, 2011.
Jameson, Fredric. *The Political Unconscious: Narrative as a Socially Symbolic Act.* New York: Cornell University Press, 1981.
Kezich, Tullio. *Federico. Fellini, la vita i film.* Milan: Feltrinelli 2007. English translation: Minna Proctor and Viviana Mazza, *Federico Felini: His Life and Work.* London: Tauris, 2007.
Lizzani, Carlo. *Il mio lungo viaggio nel secolo breve.* Turin: Einaudi, 2007.
Luzzatto, Sergio. *Padre Pio. Miracoli e politica nell'Italia del Novecento.* Turin: Einaudi, 2007.
Mariuzzo, Andrea. *Divergenze parallele. Comunismo e anticomunismo alle origini del linguaggio politico dell'Italia repubblicana.* Soveria Mannelli: Rubbettino, 2010.
Marramao, Giacomo. *Potere e secolarizzazione.* Turin: Bollati Boringhieri, 2005 (1983).
Matteucci, Nicola. *Sul Sessantotto. Crisi del riformismo e "insorgenza populistica" nell'Italia degli anni Sessanta.* Soveria Mannelli: Rubbettino, 2008.
Menduni, Enrico. *Televisione e società italiana.* Milan: Bompiani 2002.
Miccichè, Lino. *Patrie visioni. Saggi sul cinema italiano 1930-1980,* ed. Giorgio Tinazzi and Bruno Torri. Venice: Marsilio 2010.
Misler, Nicoletta. *La via italiana al realismo. La politica culturale del Pci dal 1944 al 1956.* Milan: Mazzotta, 1976 (1973).
Moravia, Alberto. *Cinema italiano. Recensioni e interventi 1933-1990,* ed. Alberto Pezzotta and Anna Girardelli. Milan: Bompiani, 2010.
Nicoloso, Paolo. *Mussolini architetto. Propaganda e paesaggio urbano nell'Italia fascista.* Turin: Einaudi, 2008.
Olivieri, Angelo. *Fellini Satyricon Politikon. Le vignette tra guerra e partiti.* Rome: Unmondoaparte, 2005.
Ortoleva, Peppino. *Un ventennio a colori. Televisione privata e società in Italia (1975-1995).* Florence: Giunti, 1995.
Painter, Borden W. *Mussolini's Rome: Rebuilding the Eternal City.* Houndmills: Palgrave Macmillan, 2007.
Patriarca, Silvana. *Italianità. La costruzione del carattere nazionale.* Rome/Bari: Laterza, 2010.
Rancière, Jacques. *Le destin des images.* Paris: La fabrique editions, 2003.
Ricciardi, A. *After* La Dolce Vita: *A Cultural Prehistory of Berlusconi's Italy.* Redwood City: Stanford University Press, 2011.

Selected Bibliography

Risset, Jacqueline. *L'incantatore. Scritti su Fellini*. Milan: Schweiller, 1994.
Rondi, Brunello. *Il cinema di Fellini*. Rome: Bianco e Nero, 1965.
Schellenberg, John. *Lo scetticismo come inizio della religione*. Pisa: Ets, 2010.
Schnapp, Jeffrey. *Anno x. La Mostra della rivoluzione fascista del 1932: genesi—sviluppo—contesto culturale-storico—ricezione*. Rome/Pisa: Istituti editoriali e poligrafici internazionali, 2003.
Spackman, Barbara. *Fascist Virilities: Rhetoric, Ideology, and Social Fantasy in Italy*. Minneapolis: University of Minnesota Press, 1996.
Stewart-Steinberg, Suzanne. *The Pinocchio-Effect: On Making Italians, 1860-1920*. Chicago/London: Chicago University Press, 2007.
Vander, Fabio. *Aldo Moro. La cultura politica cattolica e la crisi della democrazia italiana*. Genoa: Marietti, 1999.
Venzi Luca, ed. *Incontro al neorealismo. Luoghi e visioni di un cinema pensato al presente*. Rome: Eds, 2007.
Zagarrio, Vito. *Storia del cinema italiano, vol. 12. 1977-1985*. Venice: Marsilio, 2005.
———. *L'immagine del fascismo. La re-visione del cinema e dei media nel regime*. Rome: Bulzoni, 2009.
Zanzotto, Andrea. *Il cinema brucia e illumina. Intorno a Fellini e altri rari*, ed. Luciano De Giusti. Venice: Marsilio, 2011.
Zinni, Maurizio. *Fascisti di celluloide. La memoria del ventennio nel cinema italiano (1945-2001)*. Venice: Marsilio, 2010.
Zolla, Elémire. *Che cos'è la tradizione*. Milan: Bompiani, 1971.

Index

A
Agnelli, Giovanni, 144, 148, 159n
Agnelli, Susanna, 119, 133n
Ajello, Nello, 12, 28n, 29n
Andreotti, Giulio, ix, 65, 83, 142, 149, 172, 183–188
Angelini, Pietro, 3, 7, 28n, 100n, 133n
Antonioni, Michelangelo, xiv, 38, 99n, 159n, 161n, 166
Arbasino, Alberto, 26, 27, 32n
Arbore, Renzo, 172, 174
Arena, Maurizio, 129
Aristarco, Guido, 10, 26, 38, 54n, 127
Arpa, Father Angelo, 18, 19, 30n, 34, 53n

B
Baas, Balduin, 144, 146
Barzini, Luigi Jr, 41, 55n
Bataille, Georges, 87, 98n
Bazin, André, 10, 13
Benjamin, Walter, 49, 168
Berlinguer, Enrico, xv, xvi, 140, 143, 148, 151, 183
Berlusconi, Silvio, xvi, 3, 53n, 73, 113, 133n, 158, 162, 163, 171, 172, 175–177, 178, 179, 182n, 186, 187
Bernhard, Ernst, xiv, 34, 53n
Bertolucci, Bernardo, xv, 45, 100
Bollati, Giulio, 4, 48, 49, 50, 57n, 94
Bondanella, Peter, 3, 39, 41, 56n, 114, 116, 137
Buzzati, Dino, xv, 16, 30n, 70
Byron, Gordon George, 88

C
Calvino, Italo, 8, 25, 26, 47, 56n
Cambria Adele, 121, 128, 129
Carducci, Giosuè, 44, 49, 85
Casanova, Giacomo, 38, 40

Cavazzoni, Ermanno, 50, 72
Chiarini, Luigi, 13
Christian Democrat Party (DC), xii, xiii, xvi, xvii, 18, 28n, 35, 53n, 84, 95, 146, 155, 183, 184
Cinecittà, xii, xvii, 9, 17, 48, 65, 66, 75n, 79, 89, 90, 95, 124, 125, 134n, 140, 165, 166, 171, 188n
commedia dell'arte, 38, 39, 149, 150
Cossiga, Francesco, 34, 53n
Costa, Antonio, 56n, 145, 156
Craxi, Bettino, xvi, xvii, 151, 158, 172, 179, 187
Croce, Benedetto, 11, 46, 47, 49, 51, 114

D
D'Agostino, Roberto, 61
D'Annunzio, Gabriele, ix, xii, 49
Dante Alighieri, 3, 42, 48, 120
De Amicis, Edmondo, 85, 86
de Certeau, Michel, 19, 20, 22, 31n
De Martino, Ernesto, xiii, 14–18, 29n, 30n, 71
De Santis, Giuseppe, 8
De Sica, Vittorio, xiii, 8

E
Eco, Umberto, 25, 169, 171
Ekberg, Anita, 8, 59, 67, 68, 75n, 81, 82, 91
effeminacy, 39–41

F
Fanfani, Amintore, xiv, 121
Fellini, Federico,
 8 ½, xiv, xv, 9, 16, 19, 20, 25, 26, 31n, 32n, 42, 44, 51, 54n, 112, 113, 114, 115, 121, 124, 125, 126, 127, 130, 131n, 170, 181n
 A Director's Notebook, xv, 90, 92, 93, 168

– 194 –

Index

Amarcord, vi, xv, 1, 2, 3, 7, 19, 25, 33, 34, 44, 45, 46, 47, 48–50, 56n, 89, 104, 105, 121, 136, 137, 141, 163, 166, 168, 170

E la nave va, xvi, 2, 163, 166, 167, 184

Fellini Roma, xv, 11, 16, 19, 44, 45, 78, 89, 90, 91, 93, 95, 96n, 134, 173, 174

Ginger e Fred, xvii, 3, 79, 80, 110, 116, 166, 171–175, 177, 180, 182n, 185, 187

Giulietta degli spiriti, xv, 8, 16, 30, 44, 107, 110, 111, 114, 115, 116

I clowns, xv, 3, 11, 45, 80, 139, 168

Il bidone, xiv, 37, 38, 92, 141

Il Casanova, xvi, 40, 111, 117–120, 126, 132n, 133n, 134n, 138

Intervista, xvii, 11, 141, 165, 166, 180

I vitelloni, xiv, 10, 26, 33, 34, 36, 37, 38, 39, 40, 41, 52, 53, 54n, 102, 174, 178

La città delle donne, xvi, 3, 51, 57n, 80, 107, 109, 111, 113, 120–124, 125, 126, 130, 131, 132n, 133n, 134n, 135n, 138, 139, 145, 157

La dolce vita, vi, viii, ix, xiv, xv, 2, 3, 8, 12, 17, 18, 19, 20, 21, 22, 23, 24, 25, 26, 27, 30n, 31n, 38, 42, 43, 44, 50, 54n, 55n, 58–74, 74n, 75n, 76n, 81, 82, 83, 84, 89, 90, 91, 92, 93, 95, 96n, 97n, 99n, 101, 102, 103, 104, 117, 129, 141, 147, 148, 149, 163, 164, 168, 170, 174, 178, 184, 187, 188, 188n

La strada, xiv, 3, 11–14, 15, 16, 17, 29n, 38, 51, 56n, 111, 122, 141, 151, 184

La voce della luna, xvii, 50, 72, 134n, 163, 167, 180

Le notti di Cabiria, xiv, 16, 17, 18, 19, 70, 92, 111, 112, 141, 170

Le tentazioni del dottor Antonio, xiv, 82, 91

Prova d'orchestra, xvi, 1, 2, 3, 11, 35, 108, 109, 136–154, 159n, 160n, 166, 172, 184, 185

Satyricon, xv, 44, 84, 88, 89, 92, 98n, 99n, 100n, 127

and Catholicism, 7, 16, 17, 18–24, 26, 30n, 31n, 36, 38, 69, 79, 97n, 115, 116, 117, 156, 188

and fascism, xii, 1–7, 14, 23, 31n, 34, 42, 43, 44–48, 50, 56n, 79, 80, 81, 84, 86, 87, 88, 89–91, 92, 98n, 99n, 103, 104, 117–120, 128, 130, 137, 167

autobiography, 8, 33–35, 38, 45, 53n, 136

biographer of a nation, 1–2, 4, 7, 8, 12, 14, 17, 33–53, 55n, 57n, 62, 63, 65, 66, 67–72, 75n, 79–96, 96n, 99n, 120–124, 139, 148–152, 155–158

commercials by, 168–171, 172, 173

death of, xvii, 72–74

Flaiano, Ennio, xiii, xv, 26, 47, 54n, 69, 98n, 127

Freud, Sigmund, 92, 100n, 131n

Foucault, Michel, 14

G

Gentile, Emilio, 4, 47, 84, 91, 98n, 99n

Gentile, Giovanni, 49

Gherardi, Piero, 66, 90

Ginzburg, Natalia, 33, 129

Goya, Francisco, 25

Gramsci, Antonio, vi, xi, xii, xiii, 6, 10, 15, 26, 148, 150, 160n, 180n

Greer, Germaine, 120, 126, 128, 134n

I

immaturity, as national characteristic, 2, 34, 95, 113, 130, 160n

Irigary, Luce, 122

Italian Communist Party (PCI), xii, xiii, xiv, xv, xvi, xvii, 11–14, 28n, 29n, 122, 156, 162, 172, 179, 181n, 183

Italian national identity, viii, ix, 1, 4, 5, 6, 18, 19, 23, 34, 36, 37, 38, 40, 48, 50, 52, 55n, 58, 79, 81, 84, 85, 86, 95, 97n, 112, 117, 132n, 174, 183

J

Jung, Carl Gustav, 15, 148, 153

K

Kafka, Franz, 50, 173

Kezich, Tullio, 3, 7, 15, 25, 179

Kracauer, Siegfried, 49

L

La Malfa, Giorgio, 170, 172, 181n, 184

La Malfa, Ugo, 146, 147, 172, 183

Leopardi, Giacomo, 1, 19, 49, 58
Levi, Carlo, 15

M

masculinity, 42–44, 55n, 99, 118, 126, 129, 130, 132n, 135n
Masina, Giulietta, xii, xiii, xvii, 9, 74, 106, 116, 173
Mastroianni, Marcello, 42, 43, 55n, 59, 74, 80, 97n, 113, 124, 125, 126, 128, 129, 130, 173
modernity, 1, 2, 4, 5–7, 10, 20, 21–24, 43, 48–52, 57n, 64–68, 79, 82, 86, 87, 89–91, 92, 94, 95, 99n, 123, 164, 165, 174
Mollica, Vincenzo, 95
Montanelli, Indro, vi, 25, 26, 27, 149
Montesi, Wilma (and the Montesi case), 68, 69, 76n
Montini, Giovanni Battista (Pope Paul VI), 22, 75n
Morandi, Giorgio, 12
Moravia, Alberto, 19, 25, 33, 41, 45, 62, 64, 68, 95, 145
Morlion, Father Felix, 18, 19
Moro Affair, the, 136, 148–152
Moro, Aldo, xvi, 123, 124, 138
Mulvey, Laura, 119, 133n
Mussolini, Benito, xi, xii, xiii, 4, 23, 38, 46, 78–91, 95, 96, 98n, 100n

N

neorealism, 3, 6, 8–11, 13,14,15, 27n, 28n, 29n, 30n, 39, 60, 70, 72, 80, 137, 153, 179, 188

P

Paglia, Camille, 113, 131n
Parise, Goffredo, 78, 79
Pasolini, Pier Paolo, xiv, xv, 1, 22, 23, 24, 27n, 31n, 32n, 99n, 121, 163, 188
Patriarca, Silvana, 4, 40
Pavese Cesare, 15,
Pertini, Sandro, xvi, 5, 142, 143
Pinelli, Tullio, 15, 16, 26, 41, 51, 127
Pinocchio, 38, 50–53, 57n, 96n, 118, 119, 130
Pirandello, Luigi, 9
Pizzi, Umberto, viii, 61–64

Plato, 118, 150, 153
Proust, Marcel, 24, 25, 173

R

Rampi, Alfredo ('Alfredino'), 71
Reich, Jacqueline, 42
Renzi, Renzo, 13, 53, 56n
Rondi, Brunello, 10, 21
Rondi, Gian Luigi, 13, 56n, 186
Rossellini, Roberto, xiii, 9, 10, 11, 13, 18, 28n, 29n, 80, 121
Rota, Nino, xvi, 25, 97n
Rushdie, Salman, 42

S

Scalfaro, Oscar Luigi, 82, 97n
Sciascia, Leonardo, 58, 72, 136, 151–154
Scola, Ettore, 1
Simenon, Georges, 145, 159n
Sordi, Alberto, xvi, 36, 38, 40, 41, 95, 174
Sorrentino, Paolo, viii, ix, 60, 61, 75n
    La grande bellezza, viii, ix, 101
    Il divo, ix
Staël, Madame de, 41
Stewart-Steinberg, Suzanne, 4, 51, 52, 96n
Sutherland, Donald, 118

T

Taviani, Paolo and Vittorio, 115, 136, 166
Togliatti, Palmiro, xi, xiv, xv, 10, 12, 27
Tornabuoni, Lietta, 98n, 167

V

Veltroni, Walter, 95, 162, 163, 172, 180
Vidal, Gore, 96
Visconti, Lucchino, xiii, 8, 10
Vittorini, Elio, 12

W

Warhol, Andy, 63, 68, 72, 75n

Z

Zanzotto, Andrea, 28n, 117, 120, 121, 132n, 135n, 139, 166, 167, 181n
Zapponi, Bernardino, 92, 94, 96n, 100n, 127, 129, 130, 135n
Zavattini, Cesare, xii, 8, 9, 28n

www.ingramcontent.com/pod-product-compliance
Lightning Source LLC
Chambersburg PA
CBHW072153100526
44589CB00015B/2216